The Man Who Lives In Paradise

A. C. Gilbert with his best-known invention, Erector

The Man Who Lives In Paradise

the autobiography of A. C. GILBERT

with MARSHALL McCLINTOCK

RINEHART & COMPANY, INCORPORATED

new york   toronto

Published simultaneously in Canada by
Clarke, Irwin & Company, Ltd., Toronto
Copyright, 1954, by A. C. Gilbert
Printed in the United States of America
All rights reserved
Library of Congress Catalog Card Number: 54–9126

This edition is reprinted by arrangement with Henry Holt and Company, Inc.

Published by Heimburger House Publishing Company, 7236 West Madison Street, Forest Park, Illinois 60130. All rights reserved. Nothing may be reprinted or copied in whole or in part without express written permission from the Publisher. Printed in the United States of America.

ISBN: 0-911581-20-0

Co-Author's Note

This is A.C.'s story, but I have occasionally interrupted it to set the scene or to quote from a newspaper, a friend, or a diary. These interpolations are printed in a different type so the reader can readily distinguish between A.C.'s words and those of others.

M.McC.

Contents

1   *Salem Magic*   3

2   *The Moscow Athletic Club*   22

3   *Indian Pony*   34

4   *Young Love and Tomfoolery*   48

5   *Chinning, Diving, and Other Sports*   56

6   *Cadavers and Competitions*   66

7   *New Heights, New Tricks*   74

8   *Hatchet-Man of the Olympics*   91

9   *Little Acorn in Westville*   102

10   *"Hello Boys! Make Lots of Toys!"*   111

11   *Five Dollar Breeze*   133

CONTENTS

12 *Statesmen at Play* 148

13 *Radio and Circus Car* 165

14 *New Places, Products, and People* 182

15 *Maraldene* 196

16 *Dog's Life* 207

17 *Back to the Outdoors* 225

18 *Paradise Gained* 237

19 *Non-Participating Athlete* 245

20 *Boom but Not Bust* 259

21 *Flares, Mines, and Booby Traps* 272

22 *Fish, Bear, and a Volcano* 283

23 *Mountains and Glaciers* 303

24 *Agent for Santa Claus* 326

25 *Co-workers* 341

26 *Trouble in Paradise* 357

27 *It's Still Exciting* 365

Notable Events in the Life of
A. C. Gilbert 372

The Man Who Lives In Paradise

One

Salem Magic

(*The scene is A. C. Gilbert's room in his home on a high hill north of New Haven. A combination living room, bedroom, and office, it is roughly paneled in knotty pine, and is large enough to be uncrowded by a bed, a desk, a big fireplace, two davenports, and several comfortable chairs. It is a place for relaxing with your feet up on a bench.*)

(*The south wall takes the room outdoors through a huge picture window. A hundred yards down the sloping hill, the open clearing ends in a thick stand of laurel that encircles the whole yard. Behind the laurel bushes are dogwoods, and behind them giant oaks, with one spire-like pine in the southwest dominating them all. Tree-covered hills roll away below several miles to the settled sections of Hamden, with New Haven visible*

3

beyond and—on clear days—the waters of the Sound and occasionally Long Island on the other side.)

(The landscape serves as the perfect background for eighteen white-tail deer gnawing at the ears of corn that are thrown out for them in the months when natural forage is sparse. They are not tame; a sudden movement near the window will send them loping gracefully for the cover of the laurels and dogwoods only to return, a few minutes later, cautiously lifting noses into the wind and fanning ears in all directions.)

(A spike buck puts one foot on an ear of corn to hold it while he rips off the kernels with his teeth. A ten-point local king looks up, decides that ear of corn is better than his own, and moves with a mildly menacing toss of his antlers toward the spike buck, who quickly departs. Two of last year's fawns dispute the ownership of an ear of corn and practice at fighting by rearing on hind legs and pawing the air ferociously with sharp front hooves.)

(A. C. Gilbert knocks the ashes out of his pipe and starts talking.)

I never get tired of looking at the deer. And no matter how much I know about them, after all these years, there's always something new to learn. For instance, there's that old story about every point on a buck's antlers representing a year of his life. Well, I found out that was wrong when I got to know the deer on my place here. The truth is—and I've never seen this printed anywhere although I've read just about everything written on white-tail deer—the truth is that in his second year a male is a spike buck, and in his third year he gets his full growth of antlers. Those antlers are essentially the same all the rest of his life, although he casts them and grows a new set each year. In the spring I've picked up antlers in the woods and known which deer they came from. If they were upright, his new horns would be upright. If they were broad, the new growth would be broad each year, and usually with the identical number of points.

Another thing—the white-tail is the most affectionate member of the deer family, one of the most affectionate animals I've ever seen. During the rutting season the buck is very attentive to the doe and stays with her all the time.

Yes, I'm very attached to them, which makes it difficult for me every fall when the herd must be thinned out. You see, the deer have the run of most of the game preserve, which totals almost six hundred acres, but only about a hundred white-tails can support themselves on such a tract, even with our supplementary feeding in the winter. Since there are thirty-five or forty new fawns each year, that number of older deer must be disposed of every fall. Someone has to do it, and I feel responsible for seeing to it that they are killed cleanly and not wounded.

(It takes a good deal of stalking through the thick woods of six hundred acres for A.C. to do his selective thinning of the herd. He never shoots does with fawns, of course, and there are other exempt favorites. One is a doe that was raised on a bottle when young and is so tame she will not run away. Another is Charlie, a rather

5

homely buck with an underslung jaw that gives him difficulty when he tries to gnaw hard kernels from ears of corn. Any deer with a name is too much like a friend to dispose of. So A.C. hunts, in the main, for older bucks that are wild enough to offer a good challenge to his hunting skill, which is considerable. In a recent year, for instance, he got thirty-nine deer with thirty-nine shots, a remarkable record for efficient and humane shooting. One reason for this success lies in his knowledge of anatomy and his discovery that a white-tail's heart is about six inches farther forward than most hunters think it is. Largely as a result of the necessary annual thinning of his herd, A.C. figures that he has probably shot more white-tail than any man alive—around six hundred forty.)

I've hunted deer all my life. My first hunting trips were made when I was so young that I can't even remember them. My father used to take the family up into the Cascade Mountains from our home in Salem, Oregon—I was born there February 15, 1884—and we would all camp out for a week or two. I must have been only five or six when I saw Dad get his first buck, and I got my own about two years later during a trip to Nye Creek, near Newport, on the Pacific Coast. That was wild country in those days.

I wasn't much older when I first used my father's shotgun—without his knowing it. There were lots of pheasants in the fields around Salem, and one day I just borrowed his gun and went out to bag some. When a cloud of pheasants rose into the air I put my fingers on both triggers and pulled. One barrel alone might have bowled me over, but both barrels knocked me as flat as a pancake and bashed in my nose. Blood was streaming down the front of me, and I was pretty scared. I had enough hunting for that day and was somewhat discouraged about hunting pheasants. But most of all I was worried about what my father and mother would say.

Mother just cleaned me up and made sure my nose wasn't broken, and Dad didn't even spank me. He spoke to me sternly about taking his gun without permission, but he figured that I had learned my lesson the hard way and given myself my own punishment, with the help of the gun.

My father always showed an uncanny understanding of the spirit behind my escapades, adventures, and hobbies, and was never very upset about things I did as a result of curiosity and an excess of energy. Only two things really bothered him—willful shirking of my job and needlessly hurting somebody else. Generally, he let me do just about anything I wanted, and often backed me with co-operation and enthusiasm. Many times I must have taxed his patience and understanding to the breaking point—from my boyhood conversion of our barn into a firehouse to my mature decision to manufacture magic gadgets instead of practicing medicine after I had already earned my M.D.

My mother's attitude and fortitude were even more amazing. My father joined in many of my projects and had almost as much fun out of them as I did, but Mother just had to look on as I repeatedly tried to break my neck and cluttered up the house, yard, and barn

7

with strange pets, athletic paraphernalia, the accessories of various hobbies, and a gang of friends. She took it all with calm good humor, and was always there to wipe up the blood and take care of me when necessary.

My brother Frank Wellington was eight years younger than I, so I never played with him nor knew him particularly well until we were both grown up. My older brother Harold was a good companion, but from the beginning we were interested in different things. My hobbies all involved action and movement. His were quiet, more intellectual. While I was trapping squirrels, he was working with his stamp collection, or taking photographs. He never went in for sports, but was an ardent rooter for me in every contest and sometimes acted as my manager. Later, in college, he was a top student, while I was not overly concerned about my scholastic standing. His chief extra-curricular activities were in Y.M.C.A. and church work, for he carried on the religious tradition of the family.

It was a strong tradition, and my father and mother were deeply religious people. We had morning devotions every day, during which my father read from the Bible and we all recited the Lord's Prayer. Sunday was reserved as a thoroughly sacred day, without work and without play, although on fine days we sometimes took a ride in the hack after church. I found it something of a strain, because I've never been able to sit still very long.

My father was Frank N. Gilbert. He was born on a farm near Kalamazoo, Michigan, but when he was about three, his family moved to a little town across the state line in Indiana, where his father built a sawmill and ran a general store. An uncle had crossed the plains to Oregon in 1844—one of the real pioneers—and my father went out there to join him when he was nineteen years old. That was in 1869, and he made the trip by way of New York, Panama, and San Francisco. When he landed in Portland, it was a town of about 7,500 people.

He worked on his uncle's farm for a while, then as bookkeeper in a store. His brother Andy followed him to Oregon, and in a few years they became partners in a brokerage and insurance business. I liked my Uncle Andy. He was an inventor, and patented a couple of things, though they were never marketed.

My father became interested in his family history later and with the help of others began work on the Gilbert genealogy. Last year I finally had it completed and published.

It is possible that the Gilberts were descended from Sir Humphrey Gilbert, one of the biggest promoters of colonization in America in the sixteenth century, but not enough English records have been studied to verify this. The genealogy really starts with Thomas Gilbert, who was born in England about 1582 and came to Massachusetts to found one big branch of the Gilbert family in America. Other Gilberts came from England, too, one of whom was governor of New Haven Colony.

The first Thomas Gilbert spent most of his life in or near Windsor and Wethersfield, Connecticut, and his sons lived in Hartford, and in Springfield and Brookfield, Massachusetts. In time there were Gilberts in Fairfield, Middletown, Berlin, Stratford, Glastonbury, Lyme,

New Haven, and most of the towns around here. It's strange to think that when I came three thousand miles across the country from where I was born and settled down, I chose, without realizing it, a spot near the original homes of my ancestors of three hundred years before. I found myself in a hotbed of Gilberts.

The genealogy told me some amusing things about my family and revealed some startling parallels with my own activities. There was one early Gilbert, for instance, who built a log cabin near Kent, Connecticut. I built a log cabin near Kent myself in 1930. Several Gilberts were prominent business men in New Haven, where I've built up my business. An early letter speaks of "the Gilbert passion for land," which struck me because one of my greatest delights has been buying and developing land.

The American Revolution was full of Gilberts, mostly on the side of Independence but some of them Tories. In the army Gilberts were colonels, majors, captains, sergeants, corporals, and privates. One Gilbert was a fifer, one a deserter, and one an aide or private secretary to George Washington.

One early Gilbert man married a girl with the unbelievable name of Tamson Triplet, and one early Gilbert girl married Daniel Shays, who led Shays' Rebellion in New England after the Revolution. Most interesting, perhaps, is the fact that my great-great-great-great-great-great-great grandmother—let's see, that should be seven greats—was hanged as a witch. It's funny to think that I, a descendant of a witch, took up magic as a hobby before I was eight years old, helped earn my way through college giving performances as a magician, and started a business which for its first few years manufactured and sold magic tricks. Then, too, I was born in a town called Salem, a name closely associated with witches. Of course, it was a different Salem, and anyway my seven-greats grandmother was convicted in Wethersfield, Connecticut, which started its witch-hunts before Salem did.

I don't know as much about my mother's family, but what I do know convinces me that the Hovendon family tree would reveal as many fascinating products as that of the Gilberts. Her mother emigrated with a sizable group from Tasmania to Hawaii, where some remained to become the first families of Honolulu. But my grandmother traveled on to America, where she married my grandfather, who had come from England and crossed the plains and mountains by way of the Oregon Trail in 1849. He intended to go to California, but the large crowds heading there in the gold rush made him change his mind. At the fork in the trail, he headed north to Oregon, where he established one of the first ranches of the West, at Hubbard.

As a boy I spent a good deal of time at the farm at Hubbard, which was a tremendous place of several thousand acres. My earliest recollections concern our visits at Christmas, when all the Hovendon sons and daughters, with husbands, wives and grandchildren, gathered for talk, laughter, good food and happiness. Not long ago I received a letter from a cousin, Mabel Jones Cannon, which reminded me of those days. It brought back many wonderful memories, and I especially liked her reference to my father, who is the Uncle Frank in her letter:

("*I guess most of my memories center around Grandma Hovendon's household and all the fun she planned. Can you recall when the parlor door was closed and we could only slide down the bannisters and wonder what was going on in there? Any strange noises seemed surely to be Santa Claus preparing to descend the chimney. I can hear Uncle Frank's gay voice, the first one in the morning to call Merry Christmas, and a real thrill would go through my whole body when he would call it with so much of real joy.*)

("*Did you come on the train and get into the carriage and go through several feet of mud and ruts, bundled up with coats and scarfs? Then winter was winter, and no amount of heat out of the huge fireplaces displaced the real cold of midwinter. I can't seem to remember so much of presents but just the excitement and bustle and constant conversation and simple happiness of the group.*)

("*Of course you recall the big gray team that had to live in a log barn alone because they would cause so much trouble with the other horses. I was so afraid of them! The smokehouse was next in line, where they kept all the meat, and the carriage house, and the chicken house, and the doghouse, and the sawdust cellar to keep the ice if any had been made by the weather. Sometimes we drive by the old farm and, since it is off the main highway, some of the quiet and peace of the countryside remain.*")

12

I was not so impressed by the peace and quiet, but by the excitement and work and the innumerable activities of the farm. I spent several summers there when I was a boy and found a hundred things to do. The most profitable was trapping squirrels, which I turned into a regular business one summer when I was seven or eight years old. The state offered a bounty of three cents a skin because squirrels did so much damage, so I set out a lot of traps and tended them regularly. It seemed wonderful to have so much fun and at the same time make money, an idea which must have made a deep impression, because I have never worked at anything to make money unless it was fun, too. As a matter of fact, the fun always came first.

By the end of the summer I had collected between five hundred and six hundred skins, strung on a wire. Back in Salem, I took them to the capitol building to collect my bounty. I tossed them up on a counter, and a man snapped, "How many?" I had thought he would count them, and at that moment I couldn't for the life of me remember how many I had.

"Five hundred and forty-two," I finally blurted out. The man counted out sixteen dollars and twenty-six cents, which I put in my pocket. But on the way home I began to worry. Then I checked my records and found that I actually had only five hundred thirty-eight skins.

I had a hard time getting to sleep that night. Lying in bed, I heard someone come to the door and talk to my father. I felt sure it was a policeman coming after me and that extra twelve cents, but the man went away. I never did take the money back, but it was on my conscience for quite a while.

I was too busy to worry for long, however. Aside from hunting, fishing, trapping, and caring for my pets, there were sports, chores and school. I looked upon school as a sort of mixed blessing. I did well and felt no strong dislike for it, but frequently it interfered with activities I considered more important. Chores I took in my stride most of the time, for I grew up with the idea that every member of a family did his share of the work, according to his ability.

Two regular chores were mine—bringing the cows home and getting firewood into the house. We had two cows that were kept during the day in a pasture about a mile from home. Maybe it wasn't a mile, really. Things seem bigger and distances longer when you're young. Anyway, it took me quite a while to walk to the pasture after school and bring the cows back to our barn.

Getting the wood in was a big job. We had no furnace in our house—nobody out there did in those days—but heated and cooked with wood-burning stoves and fireplaces. Dad used to buy a big load of cordwood from a farmer who dumped it in the back yard near the barn. After it was sawed up in the right lengths, I had to get it into the cellar.

My friends gave me a good deal of help because they liked to play with some of the special apparatus I had rigged up, and I made a rule that all wood had to be in before play could begin.

The most exciting of these inducements was the

14

fire department in our barn. Dad let me cut a hole through the floor of the haymow upstairs so we could set up a pole to slide down. We kids wore blisters on our hands sandpapering the wooden pole so we wouldn't pick up splinters. Then we fixed cots in the haymow and pretended to go to bed there—a few times we really did stay all night. The fireman who was "off duty" went to a vacant lot nearby and set a fire in the brush, then raced back and clanged our alarm bell. We bounded off our cots, scrambled into clothes, and slid down the pole.

The first man down struck a lever that made doors open automatically, and we dashed out with our engine which was a regular boy's wagon with about a hundred feet of lawn hose. We had a bell, too, that made a fearful noise and startled the neighbors out of their wits, I'm sure.

Once we helped form a bucket brigade at a real fire, and the chief gave us special commendation, which brought us a write-up in the Salem newspaper, with our names printed.

One of the most exciting events I remember in Salem was the balloon ascension, though maybe I recall it so vividly because it led to one of the two spankings I ever got. A real balloon and a parachute jump were such rare events that I could not imagine missing them. I thought that I could rush there after school, watch the man leap in his parachute, and get home in time to pick up the cows. But there were delays, and I was too fascinated to leave. I thought my heart would stop beating when the man finally did jump and the parachute blossomed out above him like a great umbrella while he floated gently to earth.

By the time I reached home it was late, and my father had already got the cows! He spanked me. I had shirked my job, and that could not be excused. If I had asked him, he probably would have let me go to the balloon ascension, but it was wrong to leave my chore for somebody else, without permission.

The spanking did not kill an idea that had popped into my head. Whenever I saw someone perform an exciting feat, I wanted to do it myself. If another person could do it, I thought, I could too. Now the urge to jump in a parachute was overpowering. I thought I could make a good parachute from the big canvas that covered our hack in the barn. It was square and had metal-reinforced holes in the corners, to which I could tie ropes securely. I decided to jump from the house roof, but first I tested my equipment carefully. I checked the whole apparatus by sending down a rock first. It dropped like an anchor for ten feet, and then the parachute opened. I was so excited I almost fell off the roof as I watched it slowly fall the rest of the way.

Quite a crowd gathered in our yard the next afternoon to watch me jump. I don't know exactly when my mother realized what was going on, but she sent Harold after my father as fast as he could run. I was on the roof tying the ropes to my belt when Dad arrived. He leaned out of the attic window and told me to come inside. I did. In a calm voice he told me I could not jump—it would be too dangerous and I would almost certainly

16

break my legs if nothing else. I explained how I had tested my parachute with a rock, but he still insisted that I call the whole thing off. He didn't even bawl me out. He knew how disappointed I was.

The other spanking I got? Well, that was just for being mean. For some unfathomable reason, I yanked the pigtail of a Chinese laundryman who used to pass our house. He dropped his basket of clean clothes and let out a piercing howl that brought the neighbors running. I was so scared I hid for several hours. When Dad found me, he spanked me pretty hard.

But I didn't get spanked when I played hookey to see the foot race between two famous runners, probably because my father never found out about it. They staged the race at Willamette University in Salem, and I used to go there to see all the sports events I could. Once I watched a rope-climbing contest, a feature of almost every indoor track meet in those days but rarely seen any more. The boys I watched could not have been very good because not one of them could even reach the top. When I tried it, I was surprised to go clear up without any trouble. The boys exclaimed over me, and I was mighty proud. This was probably the first time I realized that my shoulders and arms were well developed.

I was not a really husky boy, but I was not skinny or a weakling, as has been written about me many times. I don't know where the fable started, but I've read half a dozen times that I was so sickly that my father and mother didn't really expect me to grow up. The truth is that I was very healthy as a boy, with only a few of the

17

usual childhood ailments. I was a bit small for my age, I guess—I'm just five feet seven now. I never carried any extra fat as a boy, but I was wiry and strong.

No sick or weak boy could have done all the things I did. I was busy with sports of some kind as far back as my memory goes, and I worked hard at them. The first competition I recall took place when I was five or six, and I trained for it as if the championship of the world depended upon me. It was just a tricycle race, but winning it was as important then as winning the Olympics seventeen or eighteen years later.

The biggest and most exciting event of my years in Salem was connected not with hunting or sports but with another activity that has been just as important a part of my life—magic. I had a set of simple magic tricks and an instruction book which I won as a premium for selling subscriptions to *Youth's Companion*. When I think of the number of different premiums I won, I realize I must have sold subscriptions to half the children in Salem. The magazine put out a new premium book every year, and I always looked forward to it so I could choose my new prize to work for. The two premiums I remember best were the magic set and a punching bag, because both had a lot to do with crucial events later.

The magic tricks I learned were simple sleight-of-hand stunts, making cards and coins and handkerchiefs disappear and reappear in unexpected places. Even the most elementary tricks look good when they are done well, with ease and confidence. You can gain that ease and confidence in only one way—through long and painstaking practice. I worked at my tricks hour after hour, day after day—a good deal of the time in front of a mirror, so I could see my act as an audience would see it. Of course, it wasn't very good, but in time it was good enough to astound and delight my family and my friends.

Then Hermann the Great came to Salem. People today probably don't remember him, but he was one of the great magicians of his time, on a par with Harry Keller, Thurston, Houdini, and Blackstone. Nobody could beat him as a showman, and his stage presence was electrifying. A pleasant Mephistopheles was the character he assumed, with black pointed beard, arched black eyebrows, flashing eyes, and a dress suit with dashing black cape.

Magicians drew big crowds in those days, before radio and television and other marvels made mysteries commonplace. Tickets for Hermann the Great's show were sold out before he arrived, and I had one of them. But I wanted to do more than watch. I wanted to be one of the persons called up from the audience to help or act as foil for the performer.

The manager of the hotel in which Hermann was staying was a good friend of my father's, and he persuaded Hermann to call on me as one of the volunteers. When the curtain went up, I was almost as scared as I was happy. For the first half hour I was so nervous about my own appearance that I could not concentrate on the performance. I had thought that, being something of a magician myself, I could figure out how Hermann performed his illusions, but I was as baffled as those who thought he possessed supernatural powers. Even when

19

he did a handkerchief trick that I knew, it seemed like a different trick because he did it so deftly.

Every time he went into a new routine and called for someone from the audience, my heart jumped into my throat. Since he called on me last, I was in a state of suspense for quite a while. When he smiled and pointed to that "fine-looking boy on the aisle," I got up and walked to the stage as if in a trance. I hardly heard the applause and whoops of some of my friends. But Hermann was a warm and friendly person who put me at ease quickly. I examined metal rings to make sure they had no gaps and then saw him pass these apparently solid rings through and over each other as if they had secret openings. I myself put an egg in a box and locked it, then thirty seconds later unlocked it to find a live Rhode Island Red sitting on four eggs. I must have looked so startled that the audience enjoyed my bewilderment as much as they did the act itself. They laughed, but I laughed too, for I was having a good time.

Hermann began extracting odd and amazing things from my pockets and sleeves—a huge American flag, a white rabbit, a bunch of bananas, a bouquet of roses, and several silver dollars which I was very sure I did not have before coming to the stage. As the applause died down, Hermann turned to me and asked, "Well, son, don't you wish you could do things like that?"

If he hadn't been such a nice fellow, I would never have had the nerve to answer as I did. I said, "I can." Hermann looked a little startled, but handed me a deck of cards and made a gesture for me to go ahead. I selected a card, held it up for all to see, waved my hand,

and made it disappear. Back-palming a card was one trick I had practiced a long time. The audience howled with delight, and Hermann played his part well, appearing to be astounded and baffled. Of course, he completely won the hearts of his audience this way. I did another card trick or two. He applauded along with the audience, then shook my hand and said, "You're very good, son. You'll be a great success. Come back to my dressing room after the show. I'd like to talk to you."

When I went backstage, the great man talked to me for about fifteen minutes. Then he showed me a few of his best simple tricks, explained how they were done, and sent me home with his best wishes. I was just about the happiest human being in the world at that moment, and vowed I would work hard and become as great a magician as Hermann the Great. I said, "Gilbert the Great" aloud a few times, and it sounded good. Even though I didn't carry out this promise, I came much closer than might have been expected. Hermann's encouragement set me firmly on a magic hobby-horse that would in time carry me to heights I never dreamed of— and I had wonderful dreams!

Two

The Moscow Athletic Club

(In the basement of A. C. Gilbert's home in Hamden, one room is equipped as a small gymnasium. On the floor there is a tumbling mat, and next to it a rowing machine, facing a large mirror. Indian clubs, handgrip exercisers, dumbbells, and weights are arranged in racks along the walls. To the right of the door a punching bag hangs beneath its round wooden rebound board. On most mornings, A.C. comes to the gym a few minutes after six for a half hour's exercise. Occasionally, on fine mornings, he jogs half a mile down his driveway.)

(Stripped to the waist, A.C. stands in front of the punching bag. His shoulders, forearms, and chest are large for a man of his slight build. The muscles are firm and hard, and there is no bulge below the chest—unusual for a man who says that he must push himself away

22

from the table, for a man who likes desserts. He folds his hands into formidable fists, hits the bag with the right, with the left. A slow, rhythmic tap begins as the bag hits the board. Suddenly its tempo doubles, and a syncopated beat suggests tap-dancing. The tempo changes again as A.C. uses right and left elbows, in addition to both fists. Reverting to slow time, he smacks the bag a few final blows that threaten to rip it from the board.)

I used to wind up my act by grabbing the board with my hands and punching at the bag with my knees and feet. It made a spectacular climax, but I can't do it any more. I used to punch the bag blindfolded, too. It takes lots of practice to do such things, and when I was a boy I practiced for hours. I'd go out to the barn and practice all alone for an hour or two a day. That's the way I spent my spare time—practicing magic or bag-punching or something else I was interested in, until I was really expert.

Later, when I went away to school, I used to put on special acts at shows. One was bag-punching, and another was with lighted Indian clubs which looked very pretty when all the lights were turned out. That always got a good hand.

I almost became a professional performer when I was a boy. At least I tried to. I was eleven or twelve years old at the time. I know, because it was when we lived in Moscow, Idaho. We moved there first when I was about eight, stayed a couple of years, and moved back to Salem for a year. Then my father dissolved partnership with his brother Andy and moved to Moscow again, where he was cashier of the First National Bank. It was shortly after that second move that I ran away with the minstrel show.

Someone told the manager about my bag-punching, so he came to our barn and asked me to show him what I could do. After I performed, he offered me a job —fifteen dollars a week and expenses. That was a pretty fair wage in the eighteen-nineties, and for a boy it was a fortune.

I knew what my parents would say, so I didn't ask them. When the minstrel show left town I was with it. I was excited and half scared, but the men in the show were so nice that I felt better right away. I didn't think of myself as "running away from home" because only boys with unhappy homes ran away from them, and I had the happiest home anyone could imagine. No, I was just starting my career, that's all—perhaps a bit younger than most people did. I was as good a performer in my way as most of the people in the show, which was proved by the billing I got. The gaudy posters plastered all over the towns we visited featured "THE CHAMPION BOY BAG-PUNCHER OF THE WORLD!"

My father caught up with me in Lewiston, Idaho, and brought my first career to a sudden end less than a week after it started. I didn't put up much argument about going back home, but I tried to tell Dad that this was too good an opportunity for me to miss. He insisted that in time I would have a far more rewarding career than bag-punching in a minstrel show, and reminded me of hunting and fishing and magic and pole-vaulting

24

and my pets and a dozen other things I loved, pointing out that I wouldn't have much time for them if I made bag-punching my whole career so early in life.

We went back to Moscow and I took up the many things I was busy with when the minstrel-show manager interrupted me. The center of these activities was a wonderful gymnasium I had made on the second floor of the barn, which was considerably larger than the one in Salem. I also kept my guinea pigs there during the time I was in the guinea-pig business. That was my first real business venture and a successful one, too.

The University of Idaho, which was in Moscow, advertised that it would trade guinea pigs for cats. Both animals were used in anatomy and biology classes, but they had apparently run out of cats at a time when they had more than enough guinea pigs.

Moscow was full of half-wild cats, like many frontier towns. People let their cats run loose; they multiplied fast and ran wild, belonging to nobody and taking care of themselves. They were pretty tough and did a good deal of damage, killing birds and chickens.

I'd had many different animals as pets but no guinea pigs, so I decided to get some by the simple method of catching cats. I rigged up a figure-four trap and set it up one evening behind the barn. The next morning it had one very angry cat inside it, which almost clawed my arm off when I tried to get it out. I fought him hard, but he got away.

That afternoon I cut a hole in one end of my box trap, then covered it with a movable door. The next morning I had two cats inside, both waiting to tear me to pieces. But I was ready for them. I slipped a gunny sack over the end of the box, slid the door away from the hole, and dumped my cats into the bag without touching them. I never cared much for cats after that, but I liked them for bringing me the two guinea pigs I got in exchange.

Now, I know that memory plays tricks, but I swear that three months later I had more than twenty guinea pigs. The ones I got were in whelp, and all of them kept on reproducing. I sold guinea pigs to my friends. And in time I sold them to the university, which reached a period when it was long on cats and short on guinea pigs. I sold them to the Washington State Agricultural College in Pullman, not far away. I can't remember how much money I made on these deals, but it was considerable for those days. I bought my horizontal bar for the gym from the earnings, plus a few other things. I had guinea pigs working for me for about a year—outside in cages in good weather, in the barn during cold weather.

The most important thing in the barn was the gymnasium with my punching bag, horizontal bar, an old mattress that served as a tumbling mat, homemade flying rings, a flying trapeze, weights, Indian clubs, a boxing and wrestling ring—just about everything for a well-equipped gym except parallel bars and a gym horse. The walls were decorated in real sporting-club style with posters from all the shows that ever came to Moscow —"Ten Nights in a Barroom," Lincoln J. Carter's "The Defender," Barnum & Bailey's Circus, and a variety of minstrel shows.

Moscow wasn't the important city that Salem was.

It was a real frontier town when we moved there, with less than two thousand population. But it was an important trading center for a wide area, and that's why the circus and a few other shows came there. Idaho was still Indian country, the home of the Nez Perce tribe. Big reservations were located not far from Moscow, and it was commonplace to see Indians on the streets every day. They were not the noble redskins of the storybooks, and I felt no special thrill at seeing them. Later, when I visited one of the big reservations with my father, I met a few Indians who were closer to a boy's concept of what Indians ought to be.

Moscow's main street might have served as a set for a western movie. Frame buildings housed stores, the bank, and several gambling halls and saloons, as well as some licensed and legal establishments for lustier pleasures. Horses were tethered to rails along the street, and the only vehicles were wagons and hacks—except in the spring or after heavy rains, when even they could make no headway in the deep mud. Moscow was the kind of town with the kind of life that was disappearing from America during the years I lived there. When we first moved there, Idaho had been a state for only two years. Before I left for school seven years later, I had seen the first automobile make its appearance, the property of a doctor who was wise enough to keep his car in the barn during the muddy season and go back to his horse.

Our house in Moscow was big, roomy, and comfortable. Its outhouse was trim and painted, its cast-iron stoves ornate with leaf-and-flower decorations. Such facilities were adequate most of the year, but the winters were rough in northern Idaho, with the temperature dropping below zero frequently. A trip to the outhouse was a major undertaking in a twenty-below blizzard. It was about a mile to school, but I usually enjoyed the walk because I picked up friends on the way and we raced or had snowball fights. When we entered the schoolhouse with wet, freezing mittens, we all gathered around the stove, which the teacher had stoked to a red glow. On bitterly cold days, I took off my shoes and stockings and the teacher rubbed my feet until the circulation came back again and they stopped tingling.

The stoves in our house heated the downstairs only. We went into our freezing upstairs bedrooms on the run, to jump into beds that had been warmed in advance by bricks heated on the stove and wrapped in cloths. These stoves consumed unbelievable quantities of wood, and it was still my job to get that wood into the house. We lived on a hill, and the cordwood was dumped at the bottom, a good seventy-five feet below the house. I turned this obstacle into an asset by building a wooden chute-the-chutes that would just fit my wagon. It had a few dips and curves that made the ride down exciting. Any boy who hauled a load of wood up to the house could ride the wagon down again. It was sure-fire, and I never had any trouble getting wood into the house after that.

My gym in the barn was a big attraction, too, and in good weather we used the yard for races and jumping. I built some hurdles and standards for high-jumping, so we had eight or nine different track events as well as the gym work—enough to give me the idea of starting the Moscow Athletic Club, with close to a dozen enthusiastic members. I was about twelve years old at the time, and the club continued to grow during the next three years, until I went away to school.

Again I was lucky to be near a university, where I learned a great deal by watching the students practice and hold their meets. And at the University of Idaho I saw my first pole-vaulting. I thought it was wonderful, soaring so high in the air just by using a pole. They were probably jumping no higher than eight feet, but it seemed high to me, and I made up my mind to try it. Getting a pole was the problem—it had to be strong and straight, with a long grain and no knots.

One evening about dark a few members of the Moscow Athletic Club accompanied me on a walk out of town. Along the road were split-rail fences from which we appropriated a cedar rail that looked good. I suppose the farmer who owned that fence was angry at finding part of it missing, but he made an important contribution to a later world's record and an Olympic championship without knowing it.

There was a good deal of back-breaking and blister-raising work with drawshave and sandpaper before the fence rail became a vaulting pole. Since I didn't have a metal spike on the end of my pole, as they all did in those days, I dug a little hole in the ground at the base of the standards to slip my pole into. I don't think I had seen that done anywhere or even read about it, but it was the only thing for me to do in the circumstances. As

it turned out, holes for vaulting poles were later a burning issue in the most important event of my athletic
career.

I took a good many bad falls when I started practicing, but after a while I began to get the hang of it,
and the pole began to feel less like an encumbrance and
more like a help when I ran with it. I experimented to
figure out how fast and how far to run, where to put my
hands on the pole and so on. Pretty soon I was getting
over the bar pretty well, but I guess at not much more
than seven feet. I practiced a couple of hours a day after
getting the pole, dropping almost everything else for a
month or so to concentrate on vaulting.

The Moscow Athletic Club had its own meets
and contests regularly, boxing and wrestling matches,
gymnastic exhibitions, races, but we finally got tired of
facing the same old competition. That's when I decided
we ought to have a town Field Day. It was early in the
spring after my fourteenth birthday when I suggested
that the school kids of Moscow should put on a track
meet down at the town baseball field. It was quite a
promotion job, as I look back on it, for there had never
been anything like it in Moscow. We talked to all the
boys we knew, held meetings, asked our fathers for help
and advice. We called on teachers and principals, some
of whom encouraged their pupils to enter the meet.

We made our own medals for the winners, using
the backs from some old watches given me by a jeweler
in town, and my mother sewed a banner for the team that
won the relay. On the day of the meet, my father helped
me load the hurdles and standards and other equipment

in our hack and haul it to the field. Most of the kids in town showed up, even if they didn't all participate, along with some of the boys from the university and a sizable group of grownups. Some teachers acted as starters and judges.

The meet was a great success, but now that I think of it, I'm surprised that some of the other boys didn't get discouraged, because I won all but one medal out of six or seven events. My brother Harold was bursting with pride and said he wanted my picture taken by the professional photographer in town, Mr. Erichson. He took me and the other boy who won a medal and the captain of the winning relay team to the photographer's. I've still got that picture, but a funny thing happened about it a few days later when Harold got the bill for it. His enthusiasm had waned somewhat, especially in the face of a bill for one whole dollar, so he tried to tell me that I should pay for it, since it was of me.

A fight must have developed, because my father stepped in, and unless it was serious he always let us settle our own differences. He decided that since it was Harold's idea to have the picture taken, he had to pay for it. Now, of course, I wouldn't take anything for that picture showing me with my first medals from a track meet. And I'd give anything to have the medals themselves. When I went east to Yale a few years later, my mother cleaned out my desk and threw out all the junk I had collected, including the medals, which were technically junk even though I'd rather have them now than all the medals I won later.

I still have the medals I won at the second Moscow

Field Day held a year later. They're in my trophy case with the other cups and medals I've won in sports.

(The trophy case is built into the wall of the hall-way leading to A.C.'s room. Sliding glass doors protect the many silver cups of all shapes and sizes and scores of medals, chiefly of gold but a few of silver and bronze. A quick glance shows that they are for pole vaulting, wrestling, gymnastic work in general as well as specific fields such as horizontal bar, rope-climbing and Indian clubs. A couple from more recent years are for golf. A second glance shows that the winner of all these cups did not bother, in many cases, to have his name engraved on them after winning them. One gets the feeling that they are not very important to him, despite their prominent arrangement in a lighted showcase. The few that are most treasured, at any rate, are not associated with the greatest athletic triumphs. Among these are six small and almost black medals of amazingly thin bronze won at the second boys' Field Day in Moscow, Idaho, in 1899. A.C. looks at them, shakes his head, and laughs.)

Can you imagine a little fellow like me winning the shot put and the hammer throw? It's ridiculous, of course, but I was probably the only boy who ever prac-ticed, and I was stronger than I looked, even if I didn't have much heft to put behind the weights I threw.

The pole-vaulting medal is not surprising, but medals for the hurdles, and for fifty- and hundred-yard dashes are a little unusual. I was fairly fast, but never really took my running too seriously.

These were real medals, of course. For the second

Field Day we had no trouble collecting funds from the storekeepers in Moscow. The town officials, the schools and the university all got behind the Field Day, and it was a big success, with more events and many more boys entered than the first time. I went away to school before the next one was held.

Three

Indian Pony

(At the northern end of the Gilbert Game Preserve in Hamden, a small stream enters the property and wanders slowly down a gentle valley between two big fields where deer like to congregate about four-thirty every afternoon. Flowing through a culvert under a narrow road, it enters thick woods, almost loses itself in a short stretch of swampy ground, then gets its bearings and heads down a rocky defile, making considerable noise as it rushes around big boulders and tumbles over rocks, as if suddenly aware of important tasks ahead, where it will fill six ponds, the first stocked with rainbow trout and others serving as home for almost two thousand ducks.)

(Before it falls into the first pond, at a spot prized by two fat woodchucks, it must flow through half a mile of dark woods—oaks, elms, pines, maples, spruces, dog-

wood—rising above a thick growth of saplings and bushes, including dozens of laurel, green but rarely blooming in the half-light. For part of this stretch, the brook flows under a fifty-foot sandstone cliff which it has undercut. This cliff, worn by water into odd shapes and many small ledges, looks like a miniature wall of the Grand Canyon. Opposite it, the ground slopes up steeply several hundred yards to another road, but so thick is the growth that anyone standing on the slope and looking at the cliff, with the brook beneath it, might as well be miles from any road, a hundred miles from civilization.)

(Near by are four large foxholes, but no animals live there most of the time because A.C. and his head game-keeper, Alfred James, keep a close watch for the pretty beasts that are so deadly for ducks and pheasants. But no matter how often they kill off foxes, more foxes appear, despite the high fences around the game preserve. An expectant vixen knows this is a preserve and will clamber up an eight-foot wire fence as if it were a ladder, in order to have her young ones in a safe place.)

(The foxes will abandon the ancient holes when A.C. finishes cutting a trail down the slope, for they don't like humans so close. The chief purpose of the trail, however, is to enable people to reach this beautiful spot easily. Over the years, A.C. has cut more than thirty miles of trails through the woods in order to open up fine patches of laurel to the sun, to make comfortable hiking for hunters, and to bring lovely scenes into view. He has also built as many miles of narrow winding roads.)

35

(Almost every afternoon A.C. spends a few hours cutting new trails and roads. Dressed in heavy shoes, baggy trousers, a windbreaker, and a hunting cap, he wields an axe adeptly in chopping down a small tree, takes another look to be sure the path is progressing in the right direction, then calls to the men working with him, Archie Uren and Melville Roberts, suggesting a short halt for a cigarette. It is apparent that he feels good.)

I don't know of anything I enjoy more than this. Oh, I suppose a hunting trip to British Columbia or a camera trip to Alaska is more exciting, but it certainly is satisfying to get out here in the woods every afternoon and work to improve the game preserve. There's no end to a job like this, and that's one of the things that appeals to me. I'm happy so long as I'm building something up and improving it, whether it is some new half-million-dollar project at the plant or cutting a new trail here. Standing still is all that bothers me.

If you come right down to it, I guess I have a better time cutting this trail than putting over a big business deal, because I'm outdoors, I'm in the woods. That's easy to say, of course, now that the business is big and successful, but it wasn't that way in the early days. For nineteen years I didn't have any hunting or fishing or outdoor life. I dropped everything to concentrate on business until we were firmly established. During that time I couldn't even let myself think much about hunting or the outdoors—things that had meant so much to me ever since I was a kid.

Moscow, Idaho, was a frontier town with the wilds all around, and we often took camping and hunting trips to even wilder places. Our favorite spot was Priest Lake, in northern Idaho. I'm told it's a popular resort now, but then it was really wild. My mother was the first white woman ever to go up to the head of the lake. First there was a long and difficult trip by hack to the foot of the lake, over an old logging road. Then we took canoes or boats to reach the head of the lake, twenty-five miles further on. When we finally reached our camp, we had wonderful fishing and hunting.

One vivid memory of Priest Lake is the forest fire. Dad told me later that his family had never been in such danger, but at the time it was just fun for me. One of our tents caught fire, but we beat it out and carried all our stuff down to a point that jutted out into the water, and the flames just went past us.

Another exciting trip came when I went with my father to the Nez Perce Indian reservation at Lapwai, south of Kendrick, Idaho. His bank had the job of paying off Indian claims for the government, amounting to $626,000, and he had to stay at the reservation quite a few weeks while the Indians came in to get their money.

I got acquainted with a few Indian boys. I remember how they used to handle rattlesnakes. They weren't a bit afraid and would pick them up, hold them between their fingers—sometimes several in each hand. I never handled them, but I was never afraid of rattlers after that. Almost forty years later, when I built my cabin in the hills above Kent, Connecticut, I ran into another area with lots of rattlers. And there was an

Indian reservation there, too, for the Schaghticoke tribe. A handful of Indians—one or two families, I believe—still lives there, and the boys handled rattlers the same way.

The big event of my stay at the Nez Perce reservation was getting my Indian pony. My father bought him for me when the owner insisted that the animal was quite gentle. The truth is that he was one of the wildest horses you could find with a bridle on him, but I was so delighted to have him that I kept this from my father. The little devil threw me dozens of times, but never when my father was around.

Certain things seemed to make him go wild and buck like fury. After an hour of good riding, he'd suddenly make up his mind to get rid of me, and I was too busy hanging on to figure out what might have made him rebel. I grew to love him, but he could be as mean as the dickens.

In Moscow I kept the pony in the barn and rode him as much as I could, hoping that in time he would calm down. But he never really did. There was the time of the track meet in Pullman, Washington, for instance, when he ran away. Pullman was just across the state line, about nine miles from Moscow, the home of Washington State Agricultural College. Some of the schoolboys there had staged field days like ours and they challenged the Moscow Athletic Club to a meet.

I thought it would be fun to have the pony take us there in a wagon. Our buggy wasn't big enough, but we found a farmer who offered to lend us his wagon. The evening before the meet we took the pony out to the farm. I don't know if it was the smell of hogs being butchered or the idea of being hitched to a wagon, but that little devil gave one snort when I started to lead him into the shafts, bucked high, tore loose from me, and headed for the road at a gallop. It was useless to try to catch him on foot, so we trudged back to our place hoping he'd come back to the barn.

We had planned to camp out in the back yard all night so we could start for Pullman at dawn. We kept waiting for the pony, but he never showed up, and we had to walk the whole nine miles to Pullman, then compete in the track meet. I was in the mile run, but after a nine-mile walk, I didn't do very well. I managed to win the pole vault, but the Moscow Athletic Club made a rather poor showing, and we blamed it on the pony.

In about a week I learned that he had run back to the Indian reservation. My father, who just thought he had run away and still didn't know about the bucking, brought him back, and I kept trying to make the little devil behave. I finally got so I could stay on him pretty well, and the experience made a fairly good horseman of me, as I proved when the Ringling Brothers Circus came to town. They had a bucking pony that would meet all comers, with five dollars going to anyone who could stay on his back a certain number of minutes. After my wild Indian, I found him pretty tame. He reared and bucked for all he was worth, but he didn't have the determination or technique of my pony. I won the five dollars.

The time was bound to come, of course, when my father found out how wild my pony was. It almost happened one Sunday, when I decided to ride to church. The pony seemed meek and mild, and walked out of the yard as if he were the best behaved animal in the world and wouldn't dream of doing anything wild on Sunday on the way to church. About a block from our house there was a watering trough, and my pony headed for it, picking his way carefully through the deep mud of the street, which was even deeper and wetter around the watering trough.

While he was drinking, one of the reins slipped out of my hand and fell so that one end of it was touching the wooden sidewalk. At that moment a woman I knew was coming along on her way to church, all dressed up in a frilly dress and a big flowered hat. I asked her if she could hand me the rein so I would not have to get off in the mud. She smiled and reached down for the rein.

My pony, busy drinking with his head down in the trough, suddenly saw that big flowered hat out of the corner of his eye. He didn't wait for a second look but gave one snort and shot straight up in the air. I went up even higher than the pony, but I didn't come down where he was. I spread-eagled in the deepest and wettest mud puddle, showering the helpful lady from head to foot. By the time I picked myself up I was completely covered with mud as well as shame.

The pony headed for the barn, and the lady headed for my house with fire in her eyes, while I tagged along behind, dripping mud. She complained loudly and vociferously to my father, who just shook his head and promised to pay for having her clothes cleaned. Then

he asked me if the pony had ever thrown me before. I
said that he had once or twice, but always when there
was a good excuse. Dad seemed to accept this, but I
knew his suspicions were aroused.

A few weeks later the pony threw me again and I
landed on a rock wall. My back was hurt so badly that I
was laid up in bed for three days. When I got up I had
no pony. My father had sent him back to the reservation
for good.

But I was riding a horse again the next summer,
down on my Uncle George Hovendon's farm in Hubbard, Oregon. I worked every summer from the time I
was eleven or twelve, and two of these were spent at the
farm. The first year I picked hops in the hopyard, worked
on the threshing machine, and earned a little money.
But the summer that sticks in my mind was when I was
fourteen years old. I was a husky kid, and I'd had a good
deal of experience by that time. I looked on myself as a
regular farm worker, turning out just as much work as
the next man, and the other men felt the same way about
it. Every big farm had quite a few extra hands during
the summer, and my uncle's place was one of the biggest
farms in Oregon, covering a few thousand acres, with
vast hopyards, endless fields of wheat and other crops,
plus hundreds of acres of pasture for the animals. They
raised horses, sheep, goats, hogs, and cattle. A big dairy
farm was just one small part of the establishment.

I lived in the big house with the family, but that
was the only difference between me and the other farm-
hands. We all ate together in the big dining room—
family and hands. I got up with the others and was out

41

in the fields just after daybreak. I drove a pair of horses, getting the hay in. I cut bands on the threshing machine, and I cut just as many as the man on the other side of the machine. I knew what he was earning, and I figured I must be getting the same thing, so I expected to have around seventy-five dollars by the end of the summer.

My father visited the farm once or twice, and went to my uncle—he told me later—and said, "Aren't you working Alfred too hard? I like to see him work and he seems to enjoy it, but I think he's overdoing it." My uncle replied that I was a good worker, as good as any of the men, and he thought I could handle it all right. I did handle it, too, for almost three months.

Uncle George was quite a man, but from what I heard he was just a pale imitation of my grandfather, the forty-niner, whom I couldn't remember. They were both big, strong, hard-working men. They both loved horses, too, the wilder and more spirited the better. I remember my uncle handling some of the toughest horses I ever saw.

Sometimes Uncle George took me with him when he went to Grange meetings, and he always picked wild horses for the buckboard we rode in. I was scared to death, but my uncle always managed to keep the horses under tight control. Once we drove to a meeting in Butteville and had to cross a ferry on the way. The horses reared and twisted and tried to back away because they didn't want to go on the boat. The way my uncle managed to get those horses on the ferry was one of the greatest animal acts I ever saw, in a circus or anywhere else.

He always arrived a little late at these meetings, just as his father had done before him. Then he'd drive at a gallop into town, pull up sharp in front of the meeting place, and make his horses stomp and cavort around. Everybody knew when Mr. Hovendon came to town.

I had my regular horse on the farm, a good animal named Puss. We came to know and like each other a lot. I was very attached to two sheep-dogs, too, who were smart and well-trained. One became my particular pet and used to ride up on the saddle with me when he got tired.

Once I was sent out alone to move some sheep from one field to another. The dogs and I rounded up the animals and got them moving, except for one little lamb that would not budge. I finally picked it up and carried it to the new pasture in my arms. It was a long trip, from one edge of the farm to another, so it was late and almost dark when I got back to the house. My grandmother and uncle were worried, I could see. I explained what had happened, and my grandmother asked, "Tell me, do you itch?"

I did feel kind of itchy, come to think of it. My uncle cried, "Get that boy out to the washhouse right away!" She took me to a kind of laundry in a back ell of the house and told me to strip. I was covered with ticks. They were in my clothes, in my hair, all over my body. I got the best scrubbing anybody ever had, and my clothes were boiled. I don't know if those ticks were the kind that carry Rocky Mountain Fever, but anyway I was all right.

The last few weeks of the summer were the

hardest of all, and I worked like a beaver. By the time I went back to Moscow I was hard as nails, and happy about the pay I was going to get. It was a hot day when I left. I had packed up my things and was all ready. My favorite dog was beside me, as Uncle George had said he would give it to me. I'll never forget standing there in the heat, talking to my uncle.

"Well now, let's see," he said. "You're taking one of my dogs, so I think if I give you ten—no, I'll make it fifteen—dollars, we'll be square."

He didn't ask me. He just told me. And I was too flabbergasted to say a word even if I'd had the courage. I just took the fifteen dollars, said goodbye, and went home. But I was never so disappointed in my life. And mad, too.

One of the first things my father asked me was, "How much did your uncle give you for the summer's work?" When I told him, his eyes opened wide. He had seen me work and knew what I had done, but he didn't comment at the time because he didn't want to sell my uncle short when I was just a boy.

You can bet I didn't go back to work on the farm at Hubbard the next summer. I *had* to earn some money and be sure of it. Harold had gone away to school, to Pacific University at Forest Grove, Oregon, and I wanted to go, too. I wasn't ready for college, but Pacific University had a preparatory school connected with it, Tualatin Academy. I thought it would be wonderful to go to a school like that, with lots of other boys and a regular track team, football team, and an active sports program.

My father agreed but was concerned about the cost. The big depression of 1893 had hit the northwest hard, and its effects lingered in some fields for quite a few years. This was just about the low point of my father's financial history. We weren't really poor, but expenses had to be watched carefully. The school was not very costly, but whatever it cost was extra expense. Still, Dad didn't want to discourage me when I was enthusiastic about an idea. He told me that if I could earn good money at a summer job and bring in seventy-five or eighty dollars to help, he would send me to Forest Grove.

In the spring I heard that the Northern Pacific Railroad was going to make a survey up into the white-pine country of Idaho, preparing to construct a line for bringing out that best of all white pines. I applied for a job as back flagman on a surveying gang, which required no special skill but plenty of endurance. Later, I found out that my father went to the railroad offices and put on a little pressure for me, but at the time I felt that I got the job all by myself.

It was the most important job I'd ever had, and one of the most interesting. We were in the woods most of the time, camping out, and sometimes we got in a little hunting and fishing after hours and on Sunday. I was only fifteen, but I had my own .22. The men on the gang were real frontiersmen, tough and rough, but they were the salt of the earth, and treated me as if I were one of them, not just a kid. At the same time they never really forgot that I was just a boy. Once or twice we walked and climbed so far during the day that I was all petered out and had a long walk back to camp ahead of me. One of the axemen, a giant of a fellow, saw that I was about to drop and just picked me up and put me on his back for a mile or two.

They never made fun of me on such occasions. On the contrary, they thought I was quite a hero because of my wrestling. They found out that I was a good wrestler and they always delighted in matching me against any contender they could find. When we came to a little town, they always asked, "Any good wrestlers in town?" There was usually somebody who fancied himself as a local champion, and he never hesitated to enter the match when he saw the boy pitted against him. There was usually a winning stake of some kind—a caseknife or such—and often some betting on the side. I never lost a match all summer, so I was the pride of the surveying gang.

As back flagman my job was to hold the pole in position for the transit men to get a line on when they had gone ahead, sometimes as much as half a mile. I also had to carry the lunch. My pay was a dollar a day plus food and keep. Some of the men got $1.25, some $1.50. By the end of the summer I had a bit more than $75, so there was no doubt about my going away to school.

It was a big day in my life when I packed my things in a canvas bag and set out for Forest Grove. Harold and I said goodbye to our mother and father and younger brother and started out without a backward glance. My father told me, many years later, that this was one of the saddest days of his life, because he knew that I would never really be back again. I might come home on vacation once in a while, but the visits would grow shorter and farther apart as the years went on. He knew that I would be too busy doing too many things to have much time for home and family. He wouldn't have changed it for anything, because he understood me so well.

He was right, of course. I never did spend much time at home after that. I was too busy.

Four

Young Love and Tomfoolery

(The Gilbert home in Hamden has two names. A.C. calls it Mountain View, on the theory that there are two mountains to the north and the view southward is like that from a mountain top. Mrs. Gilbert, remembering the mountains of the west where she grew up, looks upon these elevations as hills and no more. Calling them mountains, she feels, is a little presumptuous. They are beautiful and she loves them, but that is no excuse for exaggeration. She calls her home Hilltop.)

   (This double name has become a family joke and is still the subject of an occasional good-humored argument. But each one goes his own way, calling it by the name he prefers, and everyone is happy, for it is a beautiful home, unpretentious, comfortable, hospitable, and satisfying.)

48

(*As you enter the red front door of the low, white-painted-brick house, you step into a large foyer. Ahead and to the left is the living room, with big windows at the far end looking over the same scene as that from A.C.'s room. Turning right inside the front door, you pass the trophy case, then walk down a hall toward A.C.'s room, his wife's room, and a guest room. The walls are lined with framed pictures that serve to carry out the athletic theme established by the trophy case. Here is a picture of the 1902 football team of Pacific University, with a very young A. C. Gilbert in the center of the group. Another shows him a few years older with Indian clubs as he performed at Yale. In another he wears the insignia of the United States Olympic team. The earliest picture on this wall is hardly recognizable, because the sixteen-year-old boy in it has his hair plastered down flat, and almost all you can see is the gigantic letter "P" covering the front of his track shirt.*)

(*"That's the way he looked when I first met him,"* Mary Gilbert *says. A.C. shakes his head as if he didn't quite believe it.*)

It makes you wonder why she ever looked at me again, doesn't it? And on top of that, she didn't really approve of all the shenanigans I was mixed up in at school. There was one rule she didn't mind my breaking, though. We were supposed to be in our rooms at eight o'clock, lights out at ten. But I sneaked out after eight sometimes to meet her when she finished choir practice. I hid among the trees and watched for her, then we walked home together.

49

Mary Thompson was her name, and she lived in Forest Grove and attended the Academy when I first went there. Her family moved to Seattle after two years and I didn't see her for some time, but I never lost track of her, as you can see.

The social life in Forest Grove was very limited. Aside from the fact that this was still the Victorian era, we attended a strict Congregational school, probably more strict than normal because it was co-educational. Dancing was not allowed. There was no drinking and almost no smoking. And there was no chance to indulge in these activities on the sly because Forest Grove was just a little town with nothing much in it except the college and the academy. It was just like its name—a village in the middle of a forest grove. We were surrounded by woods and farms, and the nearest city of any size was Portland, more than twenty miles away.

Because of the strict rules and isolation, some of us built up a lot of steam and had to let it off once in a while. We didn't wander off limits to taprooms because there weren't any. We went in for horseplay, for tomfoolery, and we used the things that were handy.

Chickens, for instance. Some of the people in town kept chickens, and all the nearby farms. Wanting something exciting and being a little bored with even good boarding-house meals, we readily thought of appropriating a couple of chickens on a quiet Saturday night and roasting them out in the country.

Not all of the students went in for this mild kind of hell-raising, of course. My brother Harold wouldn't have dreamed of breaking a school rule. He was serious-minded, hard-working, pious, and law-abiding. My standards were considerably more flexible. And I couldn't sit still any more than I can now. I could spend five or six hours in classes, do my homework moderately well, put in two or three hours of hard exercise in the gym or on the field, and still be ready for any likely suggestion for a little fun. If nobody else made the suggestion, I'd think of one myself, for I must admit I was a ringleader in a good deal of the horseplay, even during my first year. We had a sort of fraternity, called the Mysterious Ten, although there were more than ten in it before long. We never lacked for volunteers for the stunts we pulled.

Once we made a bad mistake about chickens. It was drizzling and chilly and we didn't want to go very far, so we took a couple of chickens from Mrs. Huckleby's chicken house. Now Mrs. Huckleby was a wonderful woman and we all loved her. She was in charge of the dormitory where many of the students lived and ate their meals, and she was like a mother to all of us. At breakfast Sunday morning, after we had taken her chickens, she came into the dining room and asked us all to listen to her a moment.

"Boys, I want you to have fun and all that. You're just full of life and don't mean any harm, I know, so I don't care if you take some of the farmers' chickens once in a while, but please, please, don't take mine."

We all felt terrible. We couldn't say anything, but we were mighty ashamed and she knew it.

It wasn't nearly so bad when we took the minister's chickens, although I was uneasy for a while the

51

next day. One Saturday night our gang took some chickens from the Reverend Josephus Clapp's coop. The next morning I went to church with Harold, as usual, and after the service the Reverend Clapp asked Harold and me to come to dinner. When we got there, the minister went into the kitchen to talk to his wife and came back looking embarrassed.

"I'm sorry, boys," he said. "I thought we were going to have chicken for dinner, but some ruffians broke into my chicken coop last night and stole two of my best chickens. So you'll just have to share leftovers with us."

On the way home, Harold suddenly asked, "Where were *you* last night?" I was very indignant and answered, "Why, you don't think I'd be mixed up in anything like that, do you?"

Harold didn't approve of the way I acted at school and wrote home telling my parents so. I had a dollar a month spending money, and he thought I was extravagant and spent it foolishly.

Perhaps Harold was right about my being extravagant, for the next year I moved from the dormitory, where board and room cost $1.85 per week, to a more expensive place. I had a room with Mr. and Mrs. Roe, and I boarded and spent most of my time at Mrs. Shannon's, perhaps because she had two beautiful daughters, Maud and Kate. Even though my meals cost $2.50 a week and many students thought I had gone high-hat, I never regretted switching to Mrs. Shannon's. The food was wonderful, and Mrs. Shannon was one of the finest women I've ever known. For three years she was a second mother to me, warm, understanding, and always help-ful.

Mr. and Mrs. Roe were fine people, too, and once Mrs. Roe saved me from a good deal of trouble with the school authorities. It happened this way: There was an old outhouse behind one of the college buildings that we had named Ferrin Hall, in honor of the president of the university, William N. Ferrin. As the top enforcer of strict regulations, he was an unpleasant character in my eyes, and I have no doubt that I was a considerable problem to him. Years later, he became an executive of the U.S. Rubber Company and came to see me when I was in business in New Haven. We got along fine, and I learned he was a wonderful man. He even enjoyed hear-ing the true story of "Ferrin Hall."

It must have been a particularly dull Saturday, or spring was in the air and in our blood, for ordinarily we didn't go in for pranks that might be dangerous. But this night we decided that "Ferrin Hall" had served its purpose and should be disposed of. We got some oil, poured it over the roof, and set fire to it. The blaze was much bigger than we expected, and we were pretty scared. The fire department came racing to put it out, and it was lucky that nothing else caught fire.

The next day the college authorities tried to find out who was responsible. They asked Mrs. Roe where the boys rooming with her had been the night before.

"Why, my boys were all here," she said. "They're good boys and are always in when they are supposed to be."

She may have thought she was telling the truth,

53

for she sincerely believed that all her boys were good boys. And we were, essentially. Most of our escapades were harmless, even if they broke the rules.

Once a few of us spent all one night trying to get the big bell out of the chapel tower. We got it out all right, but couldn't lug it out of the building. I forget where we intended to put it.

We had no better luck with the burro, which belonged to a peddler that came to town. At night we got the burro and led him to the chapel building. Some of the boys borrowed a wide belt from the livery stable, and others got the long rope which went around the athletic field, to keep the spectators out. We wanted to get the burro up into the chapel, which was on the second floor of one of the college buildings.

We put the rope over the top of the building and down on the other side. Some of the boys were to haul on the rope and hoist the burro up to the chapel windows, where I waited with two others to pull him inside. It was a hard job, and just as the burro came level with the windows and we reached out for him, he let out a long and loud bray. The boys on the rope heard him and started laughing so hard they could hardly hold on. Down slid the burro, two stories! We were laughing, too, but we went down and raised the devil with the rope-pullers for falling down on the job. Then we tried again. This time the burro didn't bray, but we expected him to, so we got laughing again and couldn't pull him inside.

I think the windows were too small anyway. We tried half a dozen times, wore ourselves out, and finally gave up. We had spent most of the night accomplishing nothing, but we had a wonderful time.

It may not sound like it, but I did not spend most of my time raising the devil. Most of my spare time was devoted to sports—track, gym, wrestling, football. I also entered every oratorical contest, and they were big events in those days. Several times I won first for delivery but my compositions did not come up to the standard required for first prize. There were also minstrel shows and exhibitions to raise money for the football team or the new gymnasium, and I usually performed as a bag-puncher, gymnast, or magician.

I never stopped practicing sleight-of-hand, so I improved steadily. I perfected the tricks Hermann the Great had shown me, learned new ones, and made up some of my own. And as I performed more, I learned a good deal about one aspect of the magician's art which is as important as technical skill—good stage presence. My magic hobby-horse was looking more like a thoroughbred every year.

Five

Chinning, Diving, and Other Sports

(A. C. Gilbert has tried to keep a record of his varied activities, in scrapbooks, diaries, and pictures both still and moving. The wonder is that during such a busy life he has found time to maintain any sort of running account of that busy-ness. There are gaps in the record. The business scrapbooks, for instance, are almost non-existent for the first seven or eight years, when he was too busy working to keep records. Hunting expeditions are well recorded in diaries and magnificent colored movies. Photographs from the early days in Oregon and Idaho, however, are jumbled together and have never been organized. Two scrapbooks about his athletic activities during college years are packed with newspaper clippings, pictures, and letters, but they show less organization as the years progress.)

(*Near the beginning of the first volume there is a yellowed handbill, like many others in the book, announcing:*

ENTERTAINMENT

VERTS HALL

Friday, February 1, 1901

MUSIC! ATHLETICS! LITERARY FUN!

Bring your family and leave your cares at home

Among the featured attractions is the following:

See the BOY BAG-PUNCHER

Traveled with the Idaho Colored Minstrels as a specialist. Said to be equal to Corbett. Punches the bag blindfolded.

A clipping from the Portland Oregonian bears the heading, "BREAKS WORLD CHINNING RECORD," and includes a picture of Alfred C. Gilbert in black gym tights and shirt, the latter adorned with several medals. The story reads, in part, "Alfred C. Gilbert, the Pacific University athlete, recently broke the world's 'pull-up' record by chinning the bar 40 times. Since 1888 the record of N. W. Mumford, of Cambridge, Mass., has stood at 39, and young Gilbert is the first athlete who has succeeded in breaking it.")

This is how I came to break the record: During my first year at Forest Grove, I used to take the train down to Portland about once a week to work out at the Y.M.C.A. The gymnasium at Pacific University was no real gym at all. I started doing something about that soon, but meanwhile the Y in Portland was a good place

57

to work, with an active gym program under the direction of M. M. Ringler.

After a few months, my family moved from Moscow to Portland when my father bought out the Wiley B. Allen Piano Company there. When I went down to the Y, I was able to have a visit with them, too.

One day in a meet at the Y there was a chinning contest. I had never heard of such a thing—and you don't hear much about them any more, either—but I tried to see what I could do. Most of the contestants pulled themselves up ten or fifteen times, and I did it thirty times. They exclaimed a good deal about it, but I just thought I had run up against a few fellows who weren't very good. But the next day there were headlines about it in the *Oregonian*. It said that I came within three of equaling the world's record, but it was wrong. The record actually was thirty-nine.

What set me up was that this was the first newspaper story about any of my athletic activities. I practiced a little more and at a college meet the following March, I broke the world's record. I didn't bother with it much after that. It was a pretty dull sport.

I should explain why the papers spoke of me as a Pacific University athlete when I was still in Tualatin Academy. Eligibility rules in those days were few and broad, so I was allowed to represent the university while I was still in its preparatory division. That's how I became a member of the track team while I was still two years away from being a freshman.

I vaulted for Pacific University in several meets my first spring, tying for first place almost every time with Millis, track captain. We were going a little over nine feet. Pacific had one of its best years in track, beating old-time rivals like McMinnville College and Willamette University and being rated second in the state.

I started agitating for a better gym during my first year. The college contributed some money and we raised more through exhibitions and shows, then took over a good-sized building and fixed it up. By my second year it was a fine place, except for the lack of an indoor track.

(*An editorial in* The Weekly Index *of Pacific University of December 17, 1901: "How many students realize that we have the best college gymnasium in the state? But we certainly have. Other schools have larger and better buildings, but an oyster is judged by its meat, not by its shell. Owing mainly to the efforts of A. C. Gilbert, this important department has been developed from a barn with a shower-bath and a few smashed lockers to its present condition."*)

During my second year at Forest Grove I had the first professional track coach I ever worked under. He was Bill Hayward, who had been assistant trainer at the University of California, and he went on to become one of the most famous track coaches in America. I met him again years later, when he was helping to coach Olympic teams. In addition to the pole vault, I entered the running broad jump in most of our track meets and did pretty well.

I became a sort of coach myself this year, in wrestling, when I trained a young fellow named Frank McKenzie, who was a year or two ahead of me in school.

59

I worked with him in the fall, and in December of 1901, he entered the wrestling tournament at the Multnomah Athletic Club in Portland and won the Northwest championship in the 125-pound class.

(*An article in the* Portland Oregonian *says, "McKenzie's success is largely due to the efficient coaching of A. C. Gilbert, who worked diligently with his protégé." And* The Weekly Index *wrote, "We wish to congratulate Mr. Gilbert on the ability he has shown as a trainer. McKenzie had no previous experience, and yet in less than three months Gilbert got him in shape to win against the Northwest. What Gilbert has done for one he can do for others."*)

Apparently I could not do it for myself, however. I lost to Edgar Frank, champion of the Northwest in our class, and well-known throughout the region. He was a fine fellow, a good wrestler, and a close friend of mine for years. He didn't put my shoulders to the mat—nobody did that in all my years of wrestling—but won on points. I was disappointed, of course, but not as much as my father who was in the audience. When I visited Portland the next week my mother took me aside.

"Please don't ever let your father watch any of your athletic contests," she said. "He was so upset when you lost that wrestling match that he has hardly been able to sleep since."

Dad wanted more than anything for me to practice hard, get a return bout with Frank, and beat him. That's why he was all for the idea of my going to Chautauqua when it came up.

The suggestion first came from J. B. Patterson,

Director of Physical Education at Oregon Agricultural College in Corvallis. I had performed there a couple of times with bag-punching, Indian clubs, and such, and Patterson had taken an interest in me. He thought that as an all-around athlete I should become a physical-education director. The idea had entered my head already, especially after the unofficial coaching I had been doing.

In the Spring of 1902 I performed again at Corvallis, where I broke the world's record for the running long dive with a mark of 15 feet 9 inches. Patterson again brought up the matter of going to the Chautauqua School of Physical Education that summer. He was going himself and thought I should come along. When my father heard that one of the teachers there was Charlie Mayser, a well-known wrestler, he volunteered to meet the expenses.

The School of Physical Education at Chautauqua, New York, offered a two-year course—or rather, two successive summer sessions—for which it granted a diploma. It was an excellent school, and its graduates had no difficulty getting jobs as directors of physical education. The head of the school was Dr. J. W. Seaver, Director of the Yale Gymnasium. Dr. W. G. Anderson of Yale was on the faculty, along with others like Dr. George May, Physical Education Director at the University of Michigan, and Dr. R. G. Clapp of the University of Nebraska.

The number of doctors there explains why it occurred to me that I should have a medical education. During my second summer, especially, when I became a good friend of Dr. Seaver and Dr. Anderson, both men recommended that I should have an M.D. if I wanted to be the best possible physical-education director, with a top job. Naturally, they suggested that I should get that degree at Yale. Several prominent Yale athletes attended the school, too—Knox, Moulton, and Jim Hogan, who as captain of the Yale football team was one of the all-time greats of Yale athletics. Dr. Clapp had graduated from Yale Medical School and had been world's champion pole vaulter in his day. He was the first man to vault 12 feet, but was not credited with it officially. The bar was set at 12 feet, but measurement by tape showed it to be an eighth of an inch short. Dr. Clapp invented the slide, in which the lower hand is brought closer to the upper hand in the pole vault, one of the biggest improvements ever made in vaulting technique.

The man who really fixed Yale most firmly in my mind was Mike Murphy, who was at Chautauqua my second summer. Mike was one of the most famous track trainers the country has ever had, first at Yale, then at the University of Pennsylvania, as well as with Olympic teams. He noticed me because I won first place in the pole vault at Chautauqua, beating some well-known athletes, including a few he had trained at Yale. Mike had quite a talk with me, showing me all the warmth of his wonderful personality. He said that if I would come to Yale he would make a world's champion out of me. Coming from someone like Mike Murphy, that statement made a deep impression and gave me a thrill.

I had a wonderful time at Chautauqua. There

were many good fellows there. My roommate, for instance, was Hirman Connibear, who became crew coach at the University of Washington, which sent many championship crews back east and to the Olympics. My work in gymnastics received a good deal of publicity in the papers back home because I was one of five selected out of several hundred to perform at the big show in the Chautauqua amphitheatre.

In wrestling, too, I had improved a great deal. Charlie Mayser was a good teacher and taught me, among other things, the scissors hold, which was then quite new. Even after my first summer, I had improved enough to beat Edgar Frank. The bout was a big event in Northwest athletic circles that year. It was held in Pacific Grove, and Edgar Frank came there from Portland with a contingent of rooters from the Multnomah Athletic Club. Frank won the first session on points, but I won the next two with falls, and so was considered Northwest champion. I was very happy, of course, and my father was bubbling over with joy.

My third year at Forest Grove was a big one in athletics. Aside from defeating Frank, I was elected captain of the track team—despite the fact that I wasn't actually in the university yet—and I played quarterback on the varsity football team.

I started out as a substitute, because I was still pretty small, and was used occasionally as quarterback on offense and end on defense. My big chance came in October, when the team traveled to Moscow, Idaho, to play the University of Idaho. There in my old home town something happened that reads almost like Frank Merriwell. I was sitting on the sidelines wishing I could get into the game. The regular quarterback, Day, was injured, and I went in. The only trouble was that I didn't finish the story quite right, for I didn't make several touchdowns and win the game. Pacific University lost, as a matter of fact, but not badly considering that we were outweighed fifteen pounds per man.

I played well, so Coach McFadden kept me in the quarterback position permanently. Two days later we went to Pullman, Washington, to play Washington Agricultural College. In those days teams made only one or two trips per season and got in as many games as possible each trip.

I was much more interested in beating Pullman than Moscow, because they were rivals from way back. It was a tough, hard-fought game, and I played every minute of it with great satisfaction, because we won 6 to 5. As you can see, football was scored differently in those days. We had some great men on this team. One of them, Philbrook, later went to Notre Dame and made Walter Camp's All-American.

During my fourth year at Forest Grove—I was then actually a freshman in the university—I was regular quarterback again, gained considerable experience, and thought of Yale more seriously than ever, dreaming of how wonderful it would be to play on one of the great Yale teams.

(*From a newspaper account at the end of the football season: "Pacific claims the best quarterback to be found in Oregon. Coach Tom McFadden, before he left for Stanford, spoke of Gilbert as the best quarter he had met in all his experience.")*

As captain of the track team again this year, I was especially proud when our team won the state championship—something that had never happened before. In most meets I entered six or seven events—dashes and hurdles in addition to my usual pole vault and broad jump. At the university field day I won two firsts—vaulting and broad-jumping—and four seconds in 50-yard, 100-yard and 220-yard dashes, and the high hurdles. At the meet with the University of Oregon, I broke the Northwest record for the pole vault, doing 11 feet, 3 inches, and won second place in high hurdles, low hurdles, and 100-yard dash. A couple of weeks later I broke my own record by vaulting 11 feet, 7 inches, and later raised this to 11 feet, 7¾ inches, a record that was not broken in the Northwest until 1910. At the Oregon Agricultural College meet I met Forrest Smithson, who was on the Olympic team with me years later and won the hurdles at London.

I was as busy as ever, these last years, with tomfoolery, oratorical contests, gymnastic exhibitions, and shows. And I enjoyed every minute of it.

Finally I decided that I would enter Yale in the fall. My father encouraged me, saying that he was doing much better and could afford it, if I would earn what money I could to help out.

Six

Cadavers and Competitions

(A. C. Gilbert often prepares his own lunch when he comes home from the plant at noon. First he lies down in his room for a half hour to an hour, then goes to the kitchen. He cooks with a casual air, lounging over the electric stove as if it were a campfire. And over a campfire is where he has done most of his cooking since he learned as a boy. He was always the chef for the stolen chickens in Forest Grove.)

(His family, which acknowledges his skill as an expert carver, finds it hard to believe that he can cook, for he never does when they are around. With a wife who is, according to his boast, the best cook in the world, why should he? Mary Gilbert laughs off this compliment by saying, "I've learned to cook the things he likes best, that's all.")

(When he finishes lunch, A.C. rinses the dishes

in the sink and places them in the rack of the dish-
washing machine. He drops empty cans down a hidden
chute to a barrel in the basement. When the maid comes
at three o'clock she will wash the dishes. He puts things
away in the refrigerator and leaves the kitchen tidier
than men are supposed to, according to tradition.)

It's my camper's training, I suppose, that makes
me clean up food things right away. And the routine
when I waited on table after first going to Yale. I got this
job to earn my board and kept it until the spring track
season started and I ate free at the training table. But
there were difficulties in combining medical studies with
being a waiter.

During the first year of medical school, our hardest course was anatomy, which I took under Dr. Ferris,
a wonderful teacher and for many years a close friend.
I spent a couple of hours a day dissecting first cats and
then cadavers—both of which are kept in formaldehyde.
Now, formaldehyde has one of the strongest and most
clinging odors in the world. No matter how I scrubbed
myself after anatomy class, I couldn't get rid of it. The
smell was in my hair, in my clothes, sticking to my skin.
When I approached a table with a tray of food, I could
see sensitive noses lift and twitch.

Schoolwork was hard, as the Dean of the Medical
School had warned me it would be. In those days, the
medical school was not a graduate school but a regular
four-year course, associated with Yale's Sheffield Scien-
tific School. Its students were eligible to participate in
college athletics, if they could find the time.

67

Since I entered Yale as a freshman after having had one year of college at Pacific University, I felt that I could handle the studies and go in for athletics, too. The Dean had reservations, but he said one thing flatly and firmly—no football. Or, if I went out for football, I couldn't possibly find time for any other sports. This was a big disappointment to me. I couldn't imagine giving up vaulting or wrestling or gym work, so I had to forego football. It was hard to sit in the stands that fall and watch the Yale games. I wanted to be out on the field so much that it hurt, but it really bothered me more a few years later, when it developed that I never made use of my medical degree. I had given up football for something I really didn't need in the business I went into.

But that's hindsight. At the time, I still fully expected to become a physical-education director. And I was soon convinced that the Dean was right about the difficulty of medical school, particularly the first year. I got by all right with average grades, but it was hard work and left me little time for other things. I managed to take some post-graduate courses at the Arnold School of Physical Education in New Haven because I could fit them into some empty spots on my schedule. This school was one of the best known in the country and could help me toward my goal.

Obviously, I didn't have any time for tomfoolery at Yale, even if I'd been interested. But I soon learned that the channels for having fun and letting off steam were entirely different from those at Forest Grove. There the nonsense had been typical of a small town and a small school. Yale was more sophisticated. It had 3,800 students compared with Pacific's 200 or less. I found myself in a different world.

I did manage to perform more and more magic, however. I had practiced steadily and my sleight-of-hand was approaching professional standards. I was good enough, at any rate, to join the Society of American Magicians that year. I met professional magicians and well-known amateurs, and learned a great deal from the many publications that were appearing about magic.

A few paid shows came my way. They didn't bring in much, but I can remember getting five or ten dollars for putting on an act at children's parties. Chiefly I entertained my friends among the students and faculty for the fun of it. It was surprising to find how many of the professors were fascinated by magic. Some of them began to come to my attic room at Mrs. Taylor's, on York Street, to see me perform. They became good friends, and I look back on my association with these wonderful men as a great and good influence in my life. I recall especially Dr. Bloomer, instructor in internal medicine, a great man who had been an associate of Osler. We were close friends for many years.

My constant practicing became a joke among the students and teachers in the classes I attended. At that time I was working hard to learn to back-palm a half dollar, one of the most difficult sleight-of-hand maneuvers, taking at least two years to perfect. One magician will often judge another by the smoothness with which he can back-palm a coin.

Well, I was soon practicing almost automatically and subconsciously. I kept one hand in my pocket or at my side, manipulating the half dollar over and over. I kept it up even when I stood up to recite. Once in a while, of course, I dropped the coin with a clatter and everybody laughed. If you should talk to any of my teachers or fellow-students of those days, they'd say, "That was Gillie, all right, dropping a half dollar in the middle of a lecture or recitation, a meal or a conversation. He was always at it."

(*Mary Gilbert has something to say about this. Apparently A.C. was still practicing the same trick three years later, for she says, "Alfred used to court me with one hand around my waist and the other in his pocket— back-palming a half dollar." A.C. does not deny it.*)

I suffered one big disappointment early in my first year at Yale. Mike Murphy, who had told me he would make me a world's champion if I came to Yale, didn't even know me when I went out for fall track! This was a terrible blow, but I didn't say a word about Chautauqua or remind him of what he'd said. He probably told the same thing to every likely young athlete he encountered. Anyway, he was such a warm and likable person that I soon got over being hurt.

I made a fair record in the fall track games but didn't startle anybody. At first I was a little discouraged. Yale had many great athletes—above all, several fine pole vaulters such as Ward McLanahan, the track captain, Walter Dray, Max Behr, and others. I didn't know how far I'd get against this abundance of pole vaulters.

When the spring track season started, I was sick for a couple of weeks and couldn't practice. I missed

70

some of the early dual meets, but I was in good shape and vaulting well by the time the Intercollegiates came around in Philadelphia. I was very upset that I was not scheduled to make the trip with the team. I went to Mike Murphy and told him I should have been included.

"They'll only let me take four pole vaulters," he said.

"But I've been beating all but one of those you're taking," I argued.

Mike wasn't sure of how I'd hold up after missing a good deal of early practice, but when I offered to pay my own expenses to Philadelphia, he said I could come along. In the preliminaries, only Walter Dray and I qualified, and Mike Murphy came to me and apologized for having made a mistake about me.

"Listen, Gillie, do you think you can take fourth place tomorrow?" he asked. "Because if you can I'll win the meet. But I've got to have that point."

"I *promise* to win at least fourth," I said.

Mike knew then that this was his last year at Yale —he was going to the University of Pennsylvania the next year—and he wanted more than anything to win the Intercollegiates. So he personally gave me a rub-down that evening and did all he could to pep me up, as though I needed it!

The next day I won fourth place and the point for him, but Tom Shevlin fell down in the weight throw-ing, so Yale lost to Cornell by two and a half points. But I won my "Y" and Mike gave me back the money for my train fare.

In gym you could get a "Y" only by winning the

Heaton Testimonial, which was awarded each year to the best all-around gymnast after strenuous contests staged half in the fall and half in the winter. I came in second. I could do more tricks than most of the other members of the gym team, but my form was not considered up to par. I did flyaways from a front giant swing and a back giant swing, flyaways from the parallel bars— generally considered circus stuff. While the horizontal bar was my best event, I was good on the flying rings, parallel bars, sidehorse, and with Indian clubs. Tumbling wasn't one of my specialties, but I could do a row of back somersaults, which only one other college man could do at that time. Back flips ending in a somersault were common enough, but a row of back somersaults was rarely seen and always made a big hit.

I had never paid much attention to form, always being more interested in learning new and difficult tricks. But when I lost out on the Heaton Testimonial because of form and one dropped Indian club, I decided that I would have to practice more. During the following summer, while I worked in the Portland Health Department as part of my medical training, I practiced regularly. In my sophomore year, I won the Heaton Testimonial, in the course of which I broke the world's record for the rope climb with a time of seven seconds.

(*From a newspaper clipping in the scrapbook: "In the eight events, Gilbert took four firsts, three seconds, and a third, winning seven cups out of a possible eight. His final score was 206.48 out of a possible 240. This is the highest score which has ever been made in a gymnastic competition at Yale. Out of the 3800 stu-*

dents now in the university, only four have, like Mr. Gilbert, won a 'Y' in two branches of sport.")

Actually, this was my third "Y" for I won two during my freshman year—in track and in wrestling. I won every wrestling match in dual meets and then won the Intercollegiates, getting my "Y" in this sport. I dropped wrestling after this year. I enjoyed it, but it took time, and there wasn't anything else I could do except win the Intercollegiate championship all over again.

Seven

New Heights, New Tricks

(*Mary Gilbert's room at Hilltop, or Mountain View, as the case may be, looks out upon the same lawn, laurels and rolling hills as are seen from A.C.'s room and the living room. Its walls are crowded with pictures of her prized trophies—a son, two daughters, and ten grandchildren. At the wide window is a feeding station, one of the most popular bird rendezvous for miles around. A few yards away, on the lawn, is a busy birdbath, and beyond it something resembling an old-fashioned street lamp, filled with birdseed and grain, a good deal of which gets scattered on the ground around the post. Some of the smarter birds—notably one or two bluejays —don't bother to peck at the grain in the container, but vigorously claw out a good supply, then fly to the ground and eat it in comfort. A chipmunk, who lives in the*

74

nearby woods, has heard about this and comes regularly to join the birds.)

(A.C. can watch all this from his window, too, but he admits that his wife knows more about birds than he does—"except game birds." He still cannot quite figure out how someone who loves birds and other wildlife so much, who enjoys so thoroughly the log cabin in the woods near Kent, who cooks venison and pheasant and rail so wonderfully, has never wanted to go hunting. So he accepts without really understanding Mary Gilbert's assertion that she could not bring herself to kill anything. So long as she does not object to his doing so, everything is all right.)

(They both object to anything that might kill the birds, so cats are banned from the game preserve. When A.C. builds and sells houses on land trimmed from the edges of his property, the deed provides that the buyers may not keep cats. Cats can climb fences and hunt the birds and small creatures in the game preserve.)

(Recently, during a few weeks of enforced rest, the birds came to mean more than ever to A.C. It was during the summer, and the deer rarely came up on the lawn because they found plenty of food in the woods and fields. Rabbits and woodchucks wandered into view occasionally, but the birds were always there, fascinating to watch. A.C. got out his movie camera and tripod, affixed a telephoto lens, and started taking pictures. Long an admirer of the patience of nature photographers, he found suddenly that patience had been forced on him. He took hundreds of feet of bird pictures with a few shots of their friend the chipmunk. Once he

waited two hours for the fat woodchuck to appear and stand up on his hind legs, looking around.)

(Mary Gilbert sighed with relief at this new activity. It is not easy for a man who has always been as active as A. C. Gilbert to sit quietly, even for a few weeks. "Why, he hasn't sat still five minutes since he was a baby," she says. "He's always doing something— sometimes several things at once. It's very exciting to be Alfred, you know. And he can remember so much about the things he has done. That's because he enjoyed them so much, I suppose. There's a favorite phrase of his— 'I look back on those years as the happiest of my life.' I've heard him say that about his childhood, about his years at Forest Grove, about Yale, about the first hard years starting his business. And he means it every time. Sometimes I'm amazed at the little details he can remember from fifty or sixty years ago. Why, he even claims he can remember the first time he kissed me. Imagine!")

Of course I can. It happened when I was on my way home after my first year at Yale. I stopped off in Seattle to visit her. I hadn't seen her for three years, but I found out right away that she was just as good company as she had been at Forest Grove.

I wore a blue jacket with my track "Y" on it and thought I was really somebody. Whether or not she was properly impressed, we had a wonderful day together. It was one of those days I'll always remember, because it was so perfect. When I left for Portland, I was sure that she was the girl I was in love with.

Before going to work testing milk for the Health

Department, I visited at home for a few days, then represented the Multnomah Athletic Club in the field games at the Lewis and Clark Exposition, winning the pole vault.

Back at Yale that fall, my medical studies demanded a great deal of time and effort, and magic performances took every minute of my spare time, aside from sports. I could have been twice as busy with magic shows if there had been thirty-six hours in a day. Regular practice and new tricks had improved my act considerably, and word spread that it was entertaining. I put on shows for clubs in New Haven, New York, Waterbury, Bridgeport and Boston. My fees went up and the engagements got better, so I was able to put a little money aside from this work.

In fall track I won the Willisbrook Cup for the pole vault, an award given in numerous sports based on handicap competitions. It was given by the Coxe family, for many years prominent in Yale athletics. During the winter I was busy with the gym team, entering every meet and giving special exhibitions, too, with bag-punching and illuminated Indian clubs. During the spring I was in most of the dual track meets, and I won the pole vault at the Yale-Harvard games. Then came the Intercollegiates.

I felt sure I would win the Intercollegiate pole vault, and hoped that I might set a new record. I was so confident that I did not hesitate to take a magic engagement in Boston the night before the Intercollegiate meet. The performance went off well, but only when I was on the late train from Boston did I begin to worry.

77

I was tired and I had caught a cold. The track meet the next day was on my mind, and I hardly slept all night.

What happened was just what you'd expect—I fell down badly. It was worse than just losing, because I did not mind losing to someone who vaulted higher, when I knew I had done my best. The loss at the Intercollegiates hurt me badly because I'm usually a tough competitor. I kicked myself for not using my head, for trying to do too many different things at the same time, and resolved never to make *that* mistake again.

A week later, I entered the games at Celtic Park, Long Island City, under the auspices of what was then the most important athletic group in the country, the Irish-American Athletic Club. Not only did I win the pole vault, but I set a new world's record at a height of twelve feet, three inches. I went home for the summer in considerably better spirits.

(*From the* New York World: *"When Gilbert, of Yale, smashed the world's record in the pole vault by two inches, there was such a volley of cheers from stands and field as must have caused atmospheric disturbances all along the North Shore of Long Island. The throng held its breath as the little athlete shot up into the air, and for a moment afterward there was silence. But the instant the announcement was made that he had cleared the rod by a vault of 12 feet 3 inches the storm broke loose."*)

After a short visit with my family, I went to Spokane to represent the Multnomah Athletic Club at the Pacific Northwest Championships, then to Seattle for a visit with Mary Thompson, and from there started on my last hunting trip for nineteen years. If anyone had told me it would be that long I would have said he was crazy. It turned out to be one of the toughest trips I've ever taken.

This is the way it happened: In New Haven I had become friendly with a young dentist, Dr. Frank Parsons. He had never been west at all, and was fascinated by some of my stories of the hunting trips I had taken with my father. He wanted to go hunting with me that summer, so I wrote Dad to arrange for a trip, get a guide and packhorses and so on.

Doc Parsons met me in Seattle, and from there we went to Portland and Forest Grove, where we took a stagecoach for some distance. We finally met our guide, with two burros to pack our stuff. We headed up into the Salmon River country of the Cascade Mountains, rough country that was hard to get into. It began to rain, and the going was worse than we expected. One of the burros fell off a narrow trail on the side of a mountain, and then the guide got lost. But Doc and I were determined to go ahead and get in some hunting. We took our grub and supplies and packed it on our backs. I can't remember how successful we were in bagging game. What sticks in my mind are the accidents, the weather and the hard going. Doc got the full treatment in his indoctrination into Cascade Mountain hunting, but he took it well.

Back in New Haven that fall, my friend Art Brides, who was in medical school with me and on the Yale football team—later he was on Walter Camp's All-

American—tried to persuade me to come out for football. Horatio Biglow, captain of the team, pressed me, too, and I would have liked nothing better.

(*The* Yale Record *said, "Through the shrewd judgment of Captain Biglow, the Yale football team is likely to secure a valuable man in Alfred C. Gilbert, the Yale gymnast, pole vaulter, and 'Y' man, who has been called by the captain for fall practice. Gilbert has had some experience at quarterback and is likely to try out for that position, in which event competition with Tad Jones would make things lively. He has great staying power and remarkable strength."*)

The Dean of the Medical School said no again, just as emphatically as before. If I went out for football, I'd have to give up pole vaulting in order to handle my medical-school work. And I had no intention of giving up pole vaulting. In fact, I had decided to give up gymnastics as well as wrestling so that I could concentrate on pole vaulting all winter. People were already beginning to talk about the Olympics, to be held in London in the summer of 1908, and there was nothing in the world I wanted more than to be on the American Olympic team. That would be the right kind of climax for my athletic career.

Walter Dray soon broke my world's record of 12 feet 3 inches, so I had something to shoot at. For a few years, we two Yale men passed the world's record back and forth. There's nothing like stiff competition to send a record up in a hurry.

During the winter I vaulted in several indoor

meets, winning the A.A.U. indoor championship. And on the first day that the weather permitted outdoor practice, I was on the field, working hard. On the second day I came down with the mumps.

The attack was not very severe, but I was laid up for a while, lying there fretting because everyone else was practicing while I couldn't. I had made up my mind to win the Intercollegiates this year, to make up for my poor showing the year before, but I had tough competition to beat—the toughest coming from my Yale teammates, Walter Dray, Frank Nelson, and Charlie Campbell.

The first day I was permitted to go out I went to the field and started vaulting. It was a foolish thing to do, of course, because I had a relapse, and this time the sickness really was severe. I felt terrible and was laid up for a long time. I was out of school as well as sports, and missed every spring track meet. It was a big disappointment, and on top of that my studies were twice as hard because of the classes I had missed.

I was getting a little worried about some of the requirements for graduation from medical school. My studies were all right, even though difficult, but certain special assignments required full-time work that I had not been able to do because of my sports activities. For example, there was regular work, for a specified period, in the hospital and the dispensary, similar to the sort of duty an interne goes through today. In addition, the school then required that every student work for one full month as a pharmacist in a regular drug store.

This chore I took care of when school ended that

Spring of 1906, before going back home. I worked in a drug store at the corner of Chapel and York, in New Haven, but I spent far more time behind the soda fountain than behind the prescription counter, where I was supposed to be. I became one of the most expert soda jerkers in town and enjoyed myself immensely. If I had had any serious intention of practicing medicine I would have paid more attention to the work I was supposed to do, but my plan was still to become a physical-education director.

When I finally got home to Portland, I had been there only a few days when a telegram came from the New York Athletic Club, inviting me—at their expense —to come back east and participate in several meets while living at Travers Island. I went to my father to see what he thought about the idea.

"What's the matter, Alfred?" he asked, a little sadly. "Don't you enjoy being around home?"

Of course I did, but this was a good opportunity. I would get back east without expense, live for the rest of the summer at no cost, and get plenty of chances to practice and compete in the pole vault, which would certainly improve my chances in the Olympic tryouts the following spring. Dad saw that I really wanted to go, so he finally agreed.

It was a good summer, and I did a creditable job in the meets I entered, even though I didn't win the national championship. I had a good amount of spare time, most of which I spent practicing new magic tricks. The previous year at Yale had been quite successful so far as magic performances went. I boosted my fee considerably and still got more requests than I could possibly fill. What made me feel good was getting asked back over and over again to the same places. That meant people liked the show I put on, but I could not give the same show each time. So I dug out new tricks, worked up a few of my own, and branched out into mind-reading and spiritualistic acts, which were great favorites in those days.

As a result of all my practice and work, my fourth year at Yale was just as busy and successful in the field of magic as in sports. I was getting as much as a hundred dollars a night, and that gave me a little capital for other ventures in connection with magic. One of these developed out of lessons in magic that I gave to some of the students and other people in New Haven. (The famous Ted Coy was one of them.) I learned right away that almost none of them would really practice and have the patience to perfect sleight-of-hand manipulations. They wanted tricks that they could master in a half hour or so, to fool their roommates or friends. There weren't many such tricks available on the market then, so I decided I would have to have them made.

That's how I came to meet John Petrie, who was my business partner for several years. He was introduced to me by Professor Parsons, prominent music teacher in New Haven at that time. On the side Parsons was a magician and dealer in magician's tricks, known all over the magic world as Henry Hardeen. He sold magic and spiritualistic secrets.

Professor Parsons was a good friend of mine, chiefly through our common interest in magic, and I spent many evenings with him. He had not only two names, but two distinct personalities. Never have I seen anyone so close to a Dr. Jekyll and Mr. Hyde. In his salon and music studio he was a quiet, talented, gracious, and suave gentleman—the center of a circle of the most prominent people in the field of the arts. I've called on him and found him in such a group, as polished and charming as anyone could wish. Then we went back to his room together, and he became a different man. His frock coat was stripped off, he pulled out a chew of tobacco, his talk and even his tone of voice and his facial expressions changed completely. I always felt that he was the happiest when he let himself go and acted natural—when he was the magician. But the other half of him was real, too, and I suppose that a musician would have felt that Professor Parsons, not Henry Hardeen, was his true personality.

Anyway, through him I met John Petrie, who worked as a mechanic in a factory in New Haven and was interested in magic and magic tricks as a hobby. His father was a locksmith and had a little workshop behind their home in Westville, a suburb of New Haven. John thought he could manufacture the little tricks I wanted to sell to my magic students. We worked out a few tricks, got them made, and boxed them. I sold the boxes to my students, charging five dollars a lesson with the tricks included.

Some of the students came back for more boxes to take home as presents. Others came just to buy the boxes without bothering with my lessons. John Petrie and I even then started talking about going into the magic business and getting out a catalog, but we were both too busy to do much about it at the time.

The climax, or what should have been the climax, of my magic career in college came with a performance at the Hyperion, the big theater in New Haven run by the Shuberts. I rented the theater, hired a small orchestra, trained two assistants, and put on a full evening's entertainment. I was really becoming another Hermann the Great, I thought.

(In one of the scrapbooks there is a theater program announcing that on Tuesday Evening, February 4, 1908, Charles Dillingham presents Elsie Janis in the Newest Musical Comedy, "The Hoyden," with Joseph Cawthorn, and with music by John L. Golden and Robert Hood Bowers. Following this is the program for Wednesday Evening, February 5th, 1908—GILBERT, assisted by Madame Darsone and Will Green.)

Madame Darsone was a girl I had used in some of my club acts to help in mental telepathy and other stunts. Will Green was really a Yale student named Paul Titus. He was in medical school with me and had always been interested in my magic. He became Dr. Paul Titus, one of Pittsburgh's most prominent citizens and a president of the National Association of Gynecologists. But I will always think of him as he was that night, blacked up with burnt cork for the role of Will Green of New York, assistant to the great magician, Gilbert. I will never forget, either, how frightened and nervous he was. This was the most elaborate show I had ever put on, so we

85

had practiced carefully, but as curtain time drew near, Paul began to get stage fright. A little something to quiet the nerves seemed only to inflame them. When the show began—but I think the review in the *Yale Record* can tell it better. It hurts me to recall it.

(*The review reads in part:* "*All those wishing to see a large flock of ambidextrous manipulations, mental telepathy, illusions, Oriental caskets, second sights, spiritualistic phenomena, etc. etc., stepped into the big tent at the Hyperion last night and watched 'Gil' Gilbert, the Yale pole vaulter and gymnast, tear off a number of Asiatic favorites. Oh! and by the way, he was very much assisted by Madame Darsone, she who reads the soul without putting on her glasses, and by 'Will Green of New York,' who holds the intercollegiate title for awkwardness. We will come to them later, but let's rave about 'Gil.'*")

("*Some thought that because 'Gil' is a pole vaulter he would appear in linen mesh, therefore the dress suit was vigorously applauded. 'Ladies and gentlemen, I will roll up my sleeves to show you that I am not tattooed.' And the show was on. Take three bandanas, mix well, stir to a frazzle, and you have—one American flag. Marvelous!*")

("*'Now let me distribute a pack of cards among the gentlemen (if there are 52 in the house). Hold it tight. Don't let me see it. You, sir, have the ace of hearts. Right? You have the nine of clubs. Time presses, so I cannot tell the remaining gentlemen what they have.'*"

(*Measles, diphtheria, stuporous melancholia.*) *Wonderful! Wonderful!*)

("*Act II: Scene, dark room. Time, present. In this throe was introduced the flying cage, fishing by magic, Sebastus blocks, and the Oriental casket. Let us pass over these minor things, however, and get to 'Will Green of New York,' who became as popular as malaria a moment after his appearance. Will's right name is Paul Ti— well, that's a secret, but he was hired to black up and help Professor Gilbert in the tricks that were too hefty for one spirit to handle. Did he help? Gracious yes! He alone transformed the show into a circus and came near putting the entire Orient on the bum.*)

("*To gain an idea of Paul's gracefulness the reader is requested to imagine a camel trying to shin a tree with a crutch—that's Paul. Well, the professor is taking about two tons of bunting from an empty jar. Astounding, but Paul dropped the fake bottom out of the can in taking it from the field. Here we have a bird in a cage. Place it here, put a cloth over it and—but Paul bumped into the string and held up traffic. If looks could kill, the glance that the professor tossed at 'Will Green' would have singed him beyond recognition.*)

("*We now have the magic clock. It will tell the time and is assisted by two glass bells that ring the hour on the slightest provocation. This trick worked, Paul being out in the wings and too busy to queer it. He arrived a moment later, however, and knocked over one of the bells just to show that he was still on the payroll. Now here is a big barrel with the ends knocked out. We place it in the center of the stage, assisted by 'Will Green of New York,' and place paper on either end after the fashion of a drumhead. All ready! 'Will Green of New York,' however, put his foot through the paper and showed Madame Darsone rolled in a ball and attempting to sing 'March Down the Field' with a barrel stave in her throat.)*

("Now for the last shock. Professor Gilbert will stand in a frame and allow himself to be tied by two gentlemen from the audience—and 'Will Green of New York.' The gentlemen tied the professor until he couldn't stir, stopping all circulation and endeavoring enthusiastically to break a few bones—assisted materially by 'Will Green.' A screen was placed before the professor and a moment later he emerged smilingly and swung the Indian clubs in neat style.)

("The show throughout was interesting and cleverly conducted, and would have been on a par with any professional performance had it not been for the artistic work of 'Will Green of New York,' who bumped into everybody present as a guarantee of good faith.")

I didn't lose any money, but the performance at the Hyperion certainly didn't add anything to my reputation. I was glad to forget it and busy myself with athletics for a while.

During my fourth year I concentrated entirely on the pole vault. One interesting development came at this period when I started experimenting with a bamboo pole. I liked it right away. It was much lighter and stronger than the old poles. If it should break it would not leave a long sharp splinter, often quite dangerous, as the old poles did. Some of the other vaulters on the Yale team didn't like bamboo at first, but I kept using it and the others finally came around to it when they saw how it was helping me to vault higher. In the Yale-Princeton meet, for instance, Walter Dray and I tied for first place, jumping off the tie later, which I won. In the Harvard-Yale meet I beat Dray with a jump of twelve feet, three and a half inches, barely missing the new world's record he had set some time before.

Then came the Intercollegiates, held in Philadelphia in a downpour. All four Yale jumpers appeared with bamboo poles, the first time such a thing had happened. Mike Murphy, who was then at the University of Pennsylvania, protested, but the referee ruled that there was nothing to prevent the use of bamboo poles.

We started vaulting in the rain. When Walter Dray, Frank Nelson, Charlie Campbell, and I had all reached eleven feet easily, we found that we were the only ones left in the event. So we called it quits, knowing that none of us could come anywhere near a record in the rain, and the event was declared a four-way tie. It was the only time in the history of the Intercollegiates that all four places in any event have been won by men from the same school.

Since we four were going to try out for the Olympics in about a week, we agreed that the jumps at the tryouts would settle the tie among us so we could distribute the four medals.

This was the big moment for me, so big that I even let it postpone my graduation from medical school.

There was a certain amount of required work that I had been unable to complete—the most important being regular duty in the dispensary and hospital. I could not get these assignments finished that year while busy with track meets all spring. The Dean, knowing how important the Olympics were to me, agreed that if I wished, I could return to Yale for a while the following year in order to complete all requirements for my degree.

So I went off to the Olympic tryouts in Philadelphia, after a good spring, feeling excited and confident that I could make the American team. That year the tryouts were held in three places simultaneously—Philadelphia, some place in the Middle West, and Portland. While I was vaulting at Franklin Field, my father sat among the spectators in Portland, watching the tryouts there. One of the chief features of the western meet, advertised in advance, was the effort of several pole vaulters to break the Northwest record which I had set in 1904 with a leap of eleven feet, seven and three-quarters inches.

One after another the vaulters in Oregon failed, and the announcement was finally made that "the Northwest record set by A. C. Gilbert still stands." This was followed shortly by another announcement: "We have just received a telegram from Philadelphia saying that in the Olympic tryouts there, A. C. Gilbert has broken the world's record for the pole vault with a leap of twelve feet, seven and three-quarters inches, exactly one foot higher than his unbroken Northwest record."

You can imagine what a thrill this was for my father. For me, it was the biggest day of my life.

Eight

Hatchet-Man of the Olympics

(*In the trophy case in A. C. Gilbert's home there might well be an honored vacant space, in the center of the dozens of cups and hundreds of medals, for the Olympic medal that is not there. But such a gesture would never occur to A.C. He can still get worked up, however, when he talks about the 1908 Olympics.*)

There were probably more boos, protests, arguments and instances of poor sportsmanship at the 1908 Olympic games in London than any before or since. They were the biggest Olympics since the event had started in 1896, with more countries sending teams than ever before. The American team was certainly the largest this country had ever sent. The host nation, England, was determined to win, and she let her strong desire for victory becloud her usually perfect sportsmanship. I

91

know it's hard to believe in these days when the English athlete is the epitome of the perfect gentleman, as well as an excellent competitor in sports. In later years, I was the *Chef de Mission,* or manager, of three American Olympic teams, and I have been host here to several Oxford-Cambridge teams that came to compete at Yale and Harvard. In all these instances, the Englishmen have been wonderful. But in 1908—well, the contestants were all right, in the main. The complaints of most participants, other nations as well as America, were leveled against the judges and officials.

Thirteen feet was my goal at the Olympics. I wanted to be the first man to vault that high, and there was good reason to expect that I might be. During the last week of practice at Yale, I had made it, and Mike Murphy, who coached the Olympic track team, predicted in the newspapers that I would go thirteen feet.

On the ship I shared a cabin with two other Oregon boys, Forrest Smithson and Dan Kelly, with whom I had often represented the Multnomah Athletic Club in the Northwest. There were quite a few New York policemen on the team—Matt Sheridan and John Flanagan being the most famous—and they almost tore the boat to pieces having a good time. I put on a magic show that was well received, but enjoyed most the shuffleboard contest of the S.S. *Philadelphia,* which the boys on the Olympic team entered, although most of us had never played it before. I teamed up with Paul Pilgrim and won. I've still got the cup, although I don't prize it as much as the one presented by Isadora Duncan, the famous dancer, on the return trip.

When the ship neared Southampton, a tug came out to meet us, bringing some welcoming officials, reporters and photographers. One of the reporters said that he wanted to see Tewanima, the American Indian entered in the Marathon. Indians were still sort of fairy-tale characters to most Englishmen at that time. Mike Murphy went downstairs to look for Tewanima, ran into me, and told me to play the part of the Indian. I was as brown as a berry from the sun, and in those days I had plenty of very dark hair. I mussed it up, grabbed a fire-axe off the wall, and raced up on deck letting out war-whoops and dancing around the reporter and photographers with wild brandishings of my axe. The photographer busily snapped pictures, but the reporter couldn't say anything but "My word!" I don't think they ever found out that they had not seen a real Indian.

At Brighton, where we trained, I felt more confident than ever, because once more I jumped thirteen feet in practice. The Mayor of Brighton heard about this and came down to the hotel to meet me. But he was a little confused. In England they call it pole *jumping* instead of vaulting, and he apparently did not notice the word "pole," because he asked to meet the man who had jumped thirteen feet. He didn't believe such a thing was possible, but he met me, shook my hand, and believed.

Then came the first blow. The night before the meet was to begin, James E. Sullivan, head of the American Olympic Committee, notified us that the English had ruled we could not use a hole for the pole in vaulting. Now, I had vaulted with a hole for the pole to fit into for years, along with all other Americans and most other vaulters in the world. Only the English still use spikes in their poles, and one Canadian on whom they had pinned their hopes for victory in this event. The only way we could interpret this last-minute ruling was that the English officials were trying to insure the victory of Archibald, the Canadian.

All of us felt terrible, and I wondered if this prize I had wanted most for so many years was going to be taken away from me at the last minute. It was too late for me to begin practicing with a spike and get in good form. I made up my mind that I wasn't going to take the rule lying down. I looked up Olympic and English rules and found not one word against holes for the vaulting pole. In view of this, I decided that direct action might get results.

The next morning, before going out to Shepard's Bush, the scene of the Olympics, I stopped by an iron-monger's and bought a small hatchet. When I went to the field, I hid it under my sweater. The meet had been in progress several days, and considerable ill-feeling had already developed as a result of arbitrary rulings by the judges.

The pole vault was divided into sections or heats, and I was in the first section, so I went out on the field a bit early, before there was anyone near the area for the pole vault. When I reached the base of the standards, I took out my hatchet, bent down, and began to chop a hole in the ground. I was very considerate, for I dug it to one side so that it could not possibly get in the way of those few who wanted to vault with spikes.

Well, somebody saw me right away, and there was an uproar! Police came running and grabbed me, the pole vault judges rushed over, and the ground's-keeper confiscated my hatchet and started to escort me off the field. Jim Sullivan came to my rescue and stopped them. We had it out right there on the field. The English were all for barring me from the field and disqualifying me from the vault entirely. I insisted that the rules—the English rules—be read aloud, and I got my way. One of the judges read the rules from beginning to end, and there wasn't a mention, as I knew, of hole or no hole.

When he finished reading with an air of complete satisfaction, I pointed out that holes were not barred, that it was perfectly permissible to use holes. I added that if they put it up to the contestants, most of them would not object to a hole. The ground's-keeper spoke up at this point and said *he* would object to a hole in his fine English turf, more than a hundred years old. Very carefully he put the sod back and patted it down with loving care.

The judges finally declared that no matter what the rules said or did not say, it was English custom to vault without a hole and English custom must prevail. We had a long and futile argument about it, and I learned then and there that you can never win an argument. I didn't win that one and neither did Jim Sullivan. If I wanted to vault at all I had to drive a spike in my pole and vault that way. So I had a spike driven in, feeling so dejected that I hardly wanted to vault at all. As I look back on it now, I think it's a miracle that I performed as well as I did. I didn't know where I was when

I took off, and I felt as awkward as a calf. It was just bull strength that made me an Olympic winner.

When I came down after my first leap, I almost jolted my ankles out of joint, for I had landed on hard ground. Then I noticed that only for a short distance on the far side of the standards was there any soft ground for landing. This was all right for the English vaulters, who couldn't go much above ten feet and thus landed fairly close to the standards, but for most of us, it was rough going. We protested but as usual got nowhere.

I won my heat with a leap of twelve feet even. The second heat was won by E. T. Cooke of Cornell, with a fine leap of twelve feet, two inches. The finals were held in the afternoon, and Cooke could not come up to his performance of the morning, eleven feet, six inches being his best jump. We kept going to eleven feet nine inches, and four of us got over all right. They set the bar up to twelve feet and I was the only one who could make it. None of the others could get above eleven, nine.

Well, I figured I had won, of course, and I was very happy that the ordeal was over. I turned to go back to the dressing room when the English judges said, "What's the matter? Don't you want to try to win?"

I asked what they were talking about. I had won my heat and then I had won the finals. What else did I have to do to win the event? They replied that I would have to jump at least twelve feet, two inches, the top mark set in a preliminary heat. I had never heard of such a thing, and neither had anyone else, but I didn't feel like arguing. It was embarrassing because the other man was Cooke, another American, a good friend of mine, and a fine competitor who had made a wonderful jump under conditions that were just as difficult for him as they were for me. I didn't have much heart left for more jumping.

They put the bar up to twelve feet, two inches. The first time, I missed. The second time, I missed. On my third and last try, I made it by the skin of my teeth. Well, I thought I had finally won, even according to the judges' strange way of looking at things. But I did not realize how angry they were about my hatchet work and my protests. There was nothing they could do about *some* American winning, but they were certainly making it as hard as possible for one particular American to win. They now told me that I had tied for first place, and didn't I want to try to win all by myself? I said I didn't think I could go any higher without a hole, but I would give it a try. They set the bar up—not just an inch, but to twelve feet, six inches. Of course I didn't come anywhere near getting over.

The event was declared a tie, the first, last, and only time in Olympic history that a performance in a heat in the pole vault counted equally with performances in the finals. At the time I was annoyed at the officials, but not nearly so disappointed as I have been since. I was too pleased with myself for doing as well as I did, under the circumstances. Looking at it from the team angle, which was most important, the Americans did very well, winning all but one third of a point in the pole vault.

Since there was only one gold medal, Cooke said

that I should receive it, so I went through the ceremony in which the Queen presented it to me. But it must have carried a jinx, because it was stolen soon after I got back to the United States.

It's funny how, as the years go by, I get more upset about that Olympic business. One reason, I think, is that in retrospect I realize that it was the one time in my life in sports that I didn't get a square deal. That one time just happened to be the most important athletic contest of my career. Then it was more of a joke than anything else, because there was plenty of kidding about my digging the hole with my little hatchet.

Feeling happy but tired, I turned down invitations to appear in some meets in Paris and instead took a short sight-seeing trip with two friends from the Olympic team. We went to Germany, Switzerland and France, and we climbed the Jungfrau, which caused some papers to comment that this was a new high for a pole vaulter. In Paris an incident occurred which had quite a bearing on the future.

I happened to pass a store that sold bamboo furniture, and stepped inside to inquire if they had a supply of bamboo poles. They did, and took me to their warehouse, where I selected fifty poles that would be excellent for vaulting, for which I paid $1.25 each after a good deal of dickering.

I managed to get them shipped back to the United States free as a part of our Olympic equipment. From New York I had them sent to New Haven, and when I went back to Yale in the fall I carried out my first real business venture—as quick and profitable as anyone could wish. First, I printed up a letterhead with the name, "The Yale Bamboo Pole Vaulting Company." It also carried the pictures of the four men who had won the Intercollegiates with bamboo poles the preceding spring—Gilbert, Dray, Nelson and Campbell.

On the letterheads I wrote schools and colleges around the country, offering these fine bamboo poles for $25.00 each. Orders poured in, and I could have sold three times as many as I had. When I tried to order more there was difficulty about getting them from Paris, and by that time A. G. Spalding & Company began importing them. Still, I had made a neat profit of more than $1,100 in a very short time and with very little effort. That modest capital helped determine my course of action later in the year—and for the rest of my life.

Incidentally, I have several important associations with bamboo poles. I was one of the first, if not the first, to use them in vaulting. I started the first sale of them here. And I continued to use bamboo poles in many ways—in climbing, hunting and picture-taking. I found that a short bamboo pole made an excellent staff in the mountains. It was fine to steady a gun against in shooting. And when I fixed a small socket to the top, it made a steady mount for my moving-picture camera—not as good as a tripod but much better than holding it in the hand. Often, when I'm in the woods or mountains, I walk with the camera screwed in place ready for action. Many good shots would have been missed without my bamboo pole.

To get back to the Olympics, they were all over but the shouting—and the shouting lasted a long time.

When we landed in New York there was a ticker-tape parade up Broadway and presentation of medals by the Mayor of the city. We were put up at the best hotels, wined, dined and feted. Then came a trip by excursion boat to Oyster Bay for a special reception by President Theodore Roosevelt at Sagamore, his home and summer White House.

It was the President who singled out the three Oregon boys—Smithson, Kelly, and myself—for special attention, although the Portland papers, of course, had been waving the state flag for all they were worth. This was the first time that many winning athletes had come from the West, and in this instance it was not California that walked off with the honors. Oregon athletes had won more points at the Olympics than the men of any other state except New York.

(*A newspaper article in A.C.'s scrapbook quotes from T.R.'s talk to the assembled athletes: "All parts of our great country are represented among you, but it gives me special pleasure to notice that Oregon, that splendid state bordering on the mighty Pacific, possesses three sons among the finest bunch of athletic talent the world has ever seen. Ah! that is a great state, Oregon, and well may she be proud of Smithson, Kelly and Gilbert!"*)

After the New York welcome, we three Oregon boys had a kind of triumphal tour back home. The Portland newspapers hired a special railroad car to take us across the continent, and sent W. J. Petrain, sports editor

100

of the *Oregonian*, to escort us. We stopped over in Chicago, Denver, and Salt Lake City for receptions and festivities. In Portland, all business shut down for the day, and the school children pulled us through the streets to the city hall. There were banquets and speeches and hand-shaking and cheering till I thought we three would drop. We were all made life members of the Multnomah Athletic Club, among other things.

Finally I got a chance to say hello to my family, take a deep breath, and think about the biggest prize of all—marriage to Mary Thompson.

Nine

Little Acorn in Westville

(*With some hesitation, A. C. Gilbert takes a half dollar from his pocket, limbers up his fingers, and prepares to demonstrate the back-palming of a coin. This is not a magic trick, but true sleight-of-hand. A.C. expresses some doubt about his present dexterity, since he has not back-palmed a coin for a long time.*)

(*He holds the half dollar up for all to see, makes a slight motion with his hand, and the coin disappears. Another wave of the hand—and there it is! A slight smile and the crinkly lines around his eyes show his inward pleasure at finding he can still manage the trick fairly well. He places the half dollar in the palm of one hand with a pointedly deliberate gesture, as if to make certain that no one will possibly miss what he is doing, then blows lightly on the closed fist—and there is no*)

102

coin. He picks it delicately out of the air with his other hand, bends over and apparently passes the half dollar through his knee, from one hand to the other. All this is done effortlessly, as if it were the simplest thing in the world.)

(Taking up a deck of cards, A.C. demonstrates how much simpler it is to back-palm a large, rectangular, and lightweight card than a heavy, round coin. Deftly the card is made to appear and disappear as he talks. Suddenly, as he makes it reappear, it turns into five cards fanned out as you would hold them in a poker game. He smiles broadly at the expressions of surprise, and launches into a series of card tricks, obviously warming up to his impromptu performance. A different manner, different gestures, even a different way of standing become apparent, and you get a glimpse of the polished and graceful young performer of forty years ago. He is still as delighted with his tricks, when they go well, as when he first learned them.)

(In fine form by this time, A.C. wishes he had a few props for other tricks. "I think there are a few in the box of toys we keep for when the grandchildren come," his wife says. A.C. disappears for a few minutes and returns with several handkerchiefs of different colors and two hollow cylinders of cardboard. Handkerchiefs change from red to blue, disappear entirely after being stuffed into one cylinder, only to reappear in the other cylinder. Then, as A.C. turns to the table for another gadget, everyone sees a little black cup on an elastic cord hanging below the bottom of his short jacket. He laughs and decides that his act is finished.)

This is one item in the boxes of magic tricks which started my whole business back in 1909. John Petrie and I had begun on a small scale even before I went to the Olympics, but when I came back to Yale in the fall of 1908, I soon got into it much more seriously. For one thing, I had a good deal more time, because I carried only about half the normal work of medical school, and I was no longer eligible for athletics. For another, I was now a married man.

After the hullabaloo over the Olympics had finally died down, I had gone up to Seattle where Mary and I were married. Then we came back to New Haven and set up housekeeping in an apartment near the medical school.

John Petrie and I got together again right after I returned to New Haven, started turning out boxes of magic tricks and working on a mail-order catalog for professional tricks. We made professional equipment for my own performances which I still gave as often as I could. Some of the paraphernalia was devised by John, who was clever at that sort of thing, and some by me. Other magicians liked them and wanted to buy them. Finally, we turned out all the standard equipment needed by a professional.

At the beginning, however, I concentrated on the trick boxes. We used the name of the Mysto Manufacturing Company and put out three different boxes, priced at twenty-five cents, fifty cents and a dollar. Each box contained several tricks—cards, coins, rings, vanishing apparatus—with instructions on how to use them.

A little before Christmas I made the greatest sale

of my whole career. I was able to make it, I'm sure, because I had no idea about the discounts retail stores were supposed to get. I went to a bookstore down in the middle of town and suggested to the manager that for the last few weeks before Christmas I should put on a magic show in the window of his store and sell my magic boxes.

"How much will I get out of it?" he asked, and I could tell he was interested.

"I'll give you ten per cent," I said, graciously. For a man who averaged around 40 per cent discount, he did well not to blink. He did even better to agree. I'm sure he felt more interested in the crowds I would attract to his store than in any profit on the boxes. He realized that I was well-known in New Haven and had put on many shows.

Medical school ended for the Christmas holidays and I went into the window of the bookstore. I enjoyed myself and sold lots of boxes—so many that John Petrie and his father had a hard time keeping up with the demand. When Christmas finally came, I totaled up our sales and found that we had disposed of more than $600 worth of trick boxes. I was deeply impressed. I sat right down and multiplied this figure by all the bookstores, toy stores and department stores in the United States, and knew that I was soon going to be a millionaire, all right.

Of course, it didn't turn out that way. I could put on a show in only one store at a time. When I didn't put on a show, there were no sales. That meant I had to hire other people as demonstrators, and they were hard to find. A really good magician could make more money giving performances. A down-and-out magician was usually not a very good salesman. A good salesman was not a magician and was hard to train. In time we did find a few very good men but not enough to cover all those stores I had totaled up.

We put more effort into our mail-order business, and the reputation of the Mysto Manufacturing Company began to grow fast among magic people. John Petrie and I got along fine and made a good team. He was enthusiastic, completely absorbed in the magic business, an excellent mechanic and workman, and a clever inventor. He actually worked out more new tricks than I did, though I made some good ones myself. My performances and my contacts with magicians were of great value to the partnership, of course, but I don't think there would have been a business—at least a business that grew so fast—without both of us working together.

We did a little advertising that first year. I remember that the line we took with our trick boxes was, "Be a Magician. Learn to entertain. Earn money giving Shows." This was the path I had followed, so I expected it would work for others. It did, too, but not in the quantities we had hoped for. Still, it was a good idea. It certainly kept us busy, including Mary, who helped with the bookkeeping, wrapped packages, and kept me company when I had to work late. I concentrated on the magic business just the way I had concentrated on athletics, except that during this year medical studies did not take as much of my time as before.

I had a class or two, but the most important work came in the hospital and dispensary. Although I had always made it plain that I did not intend to practice medicine, several of the doctors at the medical school argued with me during that last year, trying to get me to change my mind. They all said I would be a good surgeon, that I had surgeon's hands. I knew that what they were talking about were my magician's hands made nimble and strong and steady by years of practice at sleight-of-hand, on top of the fact that I was naturally ambidextrous. All this resulted in good hands for a surgeon, I suppose, but I didn't feel I had either the temperament or a strong enough desire for it.

(*"They came to me, too," Mary Gilbert says. "They tried to get me to persuade Alfred to become a surgeon, and said he could be one of the great surgeons of the world. I said no, he couldn't. He would worry himself sick about every patient, and if one of them ever died—which was bound to happen some time—he could not stand it. I knew what he was like. People are apt to think that because he has so much fun doing almost everything that he doesn't worry. But he is a terrible worrier, especially when he feels responsible about somebody else's life or welfare. So I told the Professors I wouldn't try to change his mind at all."*)

My father had always hoped that some time during my medical studies I would become so interested that I would decide to practice medicine. When he and my mother came East for my commencement that June

107

of 1909, he still hoped that would happen. And Dr. Seaver told him that I would make a great surgeon, so he was more eager than ever. Dad told me that if I would come back to Portland after graduation, he would set me up in a fine office and get me started there.

I could see how much it meant to him, so it was not easy for me to tell him that I already had a business started in New Haven and that I wanted to go on with it. He knew that I had been putting together the trick boxes and selling them, of course, but he didn't know John Petrie and I had a shop and a really going business. He thought it was just another hobby out of which I made a little money. He was right, in a way, for magic had always been a hobby, even though I was a kind of semi-pro in the field. But the hobby was turning into my business, while the business I had intended to go into—in the field of athletics—became in time just a hobby.

The news about my new career was not broken fully to my father until I took him to the shop to meet John Petrie and to show him some of the wonderful tricks we had made. I was particularly proud of one I had just devised, in which a huge bouquet of roses suddenly appeared in an empty vase. The flowers were carefully made of feathers so they could collapse into a very small space and blossom out full and fresh when released. Mary and I had spent many an evening making them at home, and they were beautiful.

My father was impressed all right, and seemed to be delighted with all the tricks I showed him. Then I went through our new catalog with him, and he inquired about our business, orders, financing and manufacturing.

He knew then that I would never go back to Portland and be a physician. He was so disappointed he could hardly stand it, but at the time he did not give me the slightest hint of his feelings. Years later, when the business was very successful, he admitted that the scene in the workshop had been one of the low moments of his life. Here I was, a young man with a fine medical education, spending my time and efforts on gadgets for magical tricks! As I look back on it now, I can't blame him for the way he felt. It must have seemed completely crazy to him.

But to my face he acted just as enthusiastic as I was. He brought into play his old attitude of backing me in anything I really wanted to do. He covered his own disappointment completely, raved about my tricks, complimented me on my business, and told me to go ahead full steam. He backed me with more than words, too, for he offered me then and there $5,000 as a loan so that we could build an adequate factory. As a business-man and banker, he saw that we did not have proper facilities. The little shack was cramped and overcrowded already, and we had barely started our business. I had some capital, of course, from my bamboo-pole venture and shows I had given, as well as the boxes and tricks we had sold so far. But we needed that capital for operating expenses, to buy new materials for making more boxes and tricks.

Nothing my father ever did for me meant as much as that loan, for it enabled me to get started as a manu-facturer instead of a young fellow with a nice-paying hobby. I signed a note and paid him interest at 5 per cent, making sure that the deal was thoroughly business-like.

Then I graduated leaving behind my medical studies, athletics and hunting. Everything was business, and so far as that was concerned, nothing could stop me. I was on my way.

Ten

"Hello, Boys! Make Lots of Toys!"

(The office of the president of The A. C. Gilbert Company, at Erector Square, New Haven, Connecticut, is large and comfortable. With its walls paneled in fine dark wood, its imposing fireplace, a huge Oriental rug on the floor, it still has an atmosphere of casual naturalness that characterizes anything A.C. is closely associated with. The big desk is situated at one end of the room like that of a commanding general, but in this case the general has his jacket off and his feet in a lower drawer. A kind of mild disorder shows that the room is used for work, not just for pushing buttons or for overawing visitors. On a table you may see half a structure made of Anchor building blocks, part of a new Erector model, the sample of a new toy or appliance someone is trying to sell the company, and unidentifiable odds and ends.

111

In the middle of the floor you may on occasion find a circle of railroad track, locomotive and cars, transformer, and the working model of a new accessory for the Gilbert American Flyer line.)

(Above the fireplace hangs an oil painting by Gordon Soper, which millions of grown men would instantly recognize as the painting that for many years advertised Erector. It shows a Life-with-Father father and mother watching their two boys build—right in the living room in front of the fireplace—a gigantic structure of Erector girders.)

(The location of A.C.'s office in relation to the rest of the plant is hard to figure out without a map, for the factory is one of those that has, through the years, sprouted wings, ells, extra floors and an offspring in Branford about twenty minutes away. Actually, it is pretty much in the center of things. The engineering department—A.C.'s greatest love—is around one corner, and stairways near his office lead quickly to half a dozen of the most important manufacturing sections. A.C. is probably out of his office more than he is in it, however, seeing his engineers or executives, checking up on a new machine or process, or walking briskly through the plant to see how things are going. It is a big place, but he knows every inch of it.)

It's not much like that first plant out in Westville that we built in the fall of 1909. That was a small wooden building of two stories, put up on the lot next to John Petrie's house on Valley Street, under tall West Rock. Mary and I moved to an upstairs apartment not far away, on Barnett Street. We had shared a cottage with Charles and Mary Tillotson during the summer, down at Rocky Beach, after giving up our other apartment. In back of the cottage I had fixed up a pole-vaulting place so I could keep on practicing. I thought I might compete in some meets, but the business grew so fast that I could not take the time after the first year. I did go into a few meets near New Haven at the beginning, the most important being the celebration of Westville Day. Here I jumped thirteen feet two inches, setting a new world's record. It was measured by A.A.U. officials who were present, but was not allowed because I was not in competition with anyone else.

It was a good thing we lived close to the new factory, because I was there most of the time, except when I was out selling. Every evening I came down to work after dinner, and usually Mary came with me to help. Sometimes she brought a lunch down and we ate together, then got to work. She did the bookkeeping and helped wrap mail-order packages. My salary was then $65 a month, and we paid $25 a month rent for our apartment, so she had a pretty tough time making both ends meet.

(*"I certainly did," Mary Gilbert says. "This is one of the periods about which Alfred says, 'I look back on it as one of the happiest times of my life.' I can't quite understand it, because it was hard work and we had to watch every dollar. I think I was much happier when things became a little easier. I remember how Alfred used to bring home five or six men for lunch—magicians*

113

THE MAN WHO LIVES IN PARADISE

*or men from the factory. I had a little kitchen no wider
than a doorway. It had been made out of a closet, and it
was hard enough to cook for two there. But I found out
how to stop that. I began giving them cream cheese and
jelly sandwiches."*)

It was hard work, all right, but it was exciting because I could see the business grow from week to week,
from month to month. I have no idea what the volume
of business was in 1909 when we had been going less
than half a year, or even in 1910, our first full year, because we were not incorporated yet and do not have any
books. It could not have amounted to much, but it was
growing, and kept on growing through the spring of
1910.

That summer we combined a vacation with a selling trip—my first big selling trip. My father invited us
to come out to Oregon, so we went west and stayed for
about two weeks at Gerhardt Beach, where they had a
place for the summer. Mary and I, my brother Harold
and his wife, my younger brother Wellington, my father
and mother were all together, which certainly made my
father happy, and we all had a wonderful time. Then
Mary went up to Seattle to visit her family while I
started on my selling trip—showing our new line of
magic-trick boxes. My first stop was Portland, which got
me off to a good start because old friends and people
who knew who I was gave me encouragement. I remember getting very good orders from M. Seller and Company, and from Meier & Frank.

114

I worked down through the big cities of California and then headed east by way of the Southern Pacific, selling the department stores in the important towns. In the South it was hot as the devil and I worked mighty hard, but I was enthusiastic and doing well. I did not get turned down in a single store I called on, I know that. For the first time I was coming in contact with the toy business, because the buyers who handled my magic boxes in most stores were the toy buyers. I met salesmen of some of the other toy manufacturers and remembered even then being struck with the fact that there weren't very many good toys and that most of them were made in Germany.

From the south I worked my way up through Washington, Baltimore and Philadelphia, finally arriving home with such a big batch of orders that I had to borrow some money from a bank to finance the manufacture of stuff I had orders for. The loan was paid back that fall.

I sold the New York stores, of course, but in addition we opened our own store in the fall of 1910. It was under the Weber and Fields Theatre around Twenty-ninth and Broadway. I met Weber and Fields and negotiated the lease with them. The rent was not large, I know, but John Petrie would have been scared to death if he had heard the figure, so I kept it from him. To manage the store I hired Clyde W. Powers, who had been stage manager of the old Hippodrome. He was a magician and a good magic man, with many friends among the professionals. The store was a success from the moment it opened and made money from the very beginning. The first magic store on Broadway, it attracted a steady crowd of customers, amateur and professional.

The year 1911 was a memorable one for me, personally and in a business way. My first child, Charlotte, was born, a big event which caused me to come home evenings a bit more.

Just after Charlotte was born I had a letter from my father. It showed as much as anything could what a wonderful man he was, and how well he understood that we would welcome financial help but would not feel easy about accepting an outright gift. You'll recall that I worked on a surveying team of the Northern Pacific in the summer of 1900 to earn money to help me go to Forest Grove. I turned over $55 of that money to Dad, and of course he used it to pay some of my school expenses, because at that time he wasn't doing too well himself. Well, now he pretended that he had put it away and saved it for me. The reference to 1903 in his letter means a time he was in difficulty because of his brother's going into receivership.

(*My dear Alfred,*
September 15, 1900, just 10 years and 8 months ago to a day, I gave you a note for $55 due on demand, drawing interest at 8 per cent per annum. I believe this was surveying money. I realize the same is outlawed and by law you can't collect a cent, and from my own personal knowledge it was a crime after 1903 for any palouses to pay an honest debt, and as I was afraid of being strung up if I paid it I just had to keep out of sight. But now I

*guess it is safe for me to uncover, and in the meantime I
have struck pay dirt, so want to get this debt off my mind.
I am enclosing herewith check for $102.00 as follows:*

Principal	55.00
10 years, 8 months interest	47.00
	102.00

*You put the note in my hands for safekeeping, so I am
enclosing that also and will ask you to mark it paid and
return.*

*(Well, this cleans up all my indebtedness except a debt
of gratitude to my Lord and Master which I can never
pay, for giving me three of the best boys in all this world,
and the next best thing to this, a grandchild. With much
love to both Mary and yourself,*

Father)

Aside from the good feeling of that letter, you
have no idea how welcome the $102 was! My salary
stayed the same for some time even though our business
kept going ahead. On January 5, 1911, we incorporated.
The incorporators being A. C. Gilbert, John A. Petrie,
and F. N. Gilbert. The first record of a directors' meeting is dated January 10, 1911, with A. C. Gilbert as
president, John A. Petrie as treasurer, and Clyde W.
Powers as secretary. Assets taken over from the partnership were listed as follows: Real estate located at 159
Valley Street—$2,870; Merchandise and raw materials
—$3,993; Machinery and tools—$3,340; Assets receiv-
able—$2,297; Furniture, fixtures and merchandise, New
York Store—$1,000. These figures look far from im-
pressive, but the banks were already warning me that I

was growing too fast and that I should be more conservative, take things a bit slowly. I could not see why, when more business kept coming in. We were already cramped for space in the new building and were thinking about ways of getting more.

The New York store was moved early in 1911 up Broadway close to Times Square, near the old Knickerbocker Hotel. The rent was very high, and once again I didn't dare tell the actual figure to John Petrie. But business boomed in the store, which made money right away. Clyde Powers was at his peak in those days. He was a good magician and had a winning personality. I've seen him do a standard card trick so well that even professional magicians were baffled and thought it must be a new trick. He sold lots of stuff, and the profits on magic things in those days were high.

After only about a year below Times Square, we lost our lease and moved to 255 West 42 Street. We did less business at this location, but the rent was less, too. Meanwhile we had opened retail stores in Philadelphia and Chicago, but the latter had a sad history. The store was just off State Street, and we took a two-year lease from the United Cigar Company. The young fellow we put in charge was not a magician, but had become very interested in magic, and we thought he ought to do pretty well. The store had been open hardly a month when I got a telephone call from the United Cigar people in Chicago asking what was wrong. A truck had moved up to the store the day before and moved everything out—stock and fixtures.

Our man had absconded, that's all, with all the

money and everything in the place. Even the police couldn't locate him. This was disastrous, and I could see only one solution. We had to give up the store and get out of the lease somehow. I went to see the United Cigar people and they were very nice. I must have done a good selling job then, for they let us out of the lease and we tried to forget that unpleasant experience.

About this time I was riding back and forth from New Haven to New York a good deal—the section being electrified by the New York, New Haven & Hartford Railroad. I looked out the window and saw steel girder after steel girder being erected to carry the power lines. I found it interesting to watch their progress from week to week, and most other travelers did too. It seems the most natural thing in the world that I should think about how fascinated boys might be in building things out of girders. My increasing association with the toy business set me thinking in that general direction, too. Anyway, that's where the idea for Erector came from. Sometime when you are riding on the New York, New Haven & Hartford, you can see that the girders supporting the wires look a good deal like Erector girders.

I suppose the idea was germinating in my mind during several trips, but it seemed to come to me all of a sudden in the fall of 1911. I went right home and got some cardboard to cut out girders. I fiddled with the cardboard until I had several different lengths and shapes out of which many things could be built, then I went to the shop and had one of the machinists make a set out of steel. When I saw that sample I knew I had something.

I got a box of bolts and nuts and started putting

119

my pieces together. When I tried to put four girders together to make a square girder like those on the railroad, I found it wouldn't work until I made a kind of lip along the edge of each piece. This little invention was probably the most important single factor in the success of Erector, although the principle of action and motion in a toy was a close second. With the groove along the edge of the Erector girder, I could fit four pieces together with two small bolts and I had a square girder. The groove also helped keep single pieces steady and firm when bolted together.

It would take a long time and a good deal of expense to get Erector into production, I knew, for we had to get heavy presses, make dies, and do a good deal more experimenting before we had a top-notch product. Nevertheless I was so enthusiastic about its possibilities that I did not see how we could miss. I was astonished but not really discouraged when my two associates in business were not even interested in Erector.

They were both magic men and were happy to remain magic men. They had a good business that was increasing, and they were content with that. It's true that I was a magic man, too, but I was interested in many other things. Even though the magic business was going well, I could see its limitations. There were just so many magic-trick boxes you could sell in the country, just so many professional pieces of apparatus. Even when you reached the top you would not have a really big business. The toy business, on the other hand, was potentially as big as the young population of the United States—or the world.

120

I can see now why John Petrie and Clyde Powers did not want to branch out into anything new in 1911. The Mysto Manufacturing Company was successful, growing so rapidly that the banks had advised caution, and had gained a pre-eminent position in the field. As I look at our two-hundred-page catalog from that year, I see what a good business it was. The writings in some magazines, to the effect that I got out of the magic business and into toys because magic was a failure, are just not true. Business in 1911 totaled $37,272 with a net profit of $366.37. This was on top of very modest salaries, of course, but I was quite disappointed. My father, however, was very encouraging, pointing out that we had built up this business in just two years, had constructed a new plant, bought new machinery, all of which was completely written off, and had invested in machinery and tools for new products not yet manufactured. He thought we did well to show any profit at all. The next year, 1912, while we were still selling nothing but magic, total volume rose to $59,610.42, with profits of $7,437.

The catalog shows why we did that much business, for it describes and illustrates hundreds of tricks. Starting with our magic boxes ranging in price from twenty-five cents to twenty-five dollars, it goes on with page after page of card tricks, coin tricks, handkerchief tricks, disappearing and multiplying billiard balls, and a great variety of containers such as bottles, vases, cans, tubes, boxes, hats, glasses, decanters that changed milk to coffee or water to ink and sometimes sprouted rabbits, birds, bouquets, flags, coins, or cards previously selected by the audience. We sold professional equipment like

121

wands, tables and even curtains, as well as the professional tricks ranging in cost up to $95.00. We had even more expensive tricks made on individual order, and the catalog merely lists them with the note "Price on application." Among these were pieces of apparatus made for famous magicians of the day or manufactured by us with permission of the magicians who had developed them. There were Houdini's Paper Sack Escape, Houdini's Milk Can Escape, Kellar's Levitation, Germain's Great Water Trick, and many others. There was a huge glass casket to be suspended in the air, in which a lady mysteriously appears after everyone could see the casket was empty. As the descendant of a witch, I was particularly proud of our Witch's Caldron.

(*The catalog description reads as follows: "This master illusion and apparent miracle heads the lists of modern witchcraft, as it is certainly the most spectacular and by far the prettiest and most attractive illusion ever invented. It will positively bewilder the most intelligent audience. This great caldron hanging off the floor is filled with water in full view of the audience, first having been shown to be unmistakably empty, and the absence of compartments clearly demonstrated. A fire is then built under the huge kettle and soon dense steam rises from the surface of the boiling water. Into the steam the performer throws dead rabbits, fowls, etc., and a few minutes later he reaches into the steam, bringing out the rabbits alive, and they run off the stage. Soon, white doves fly from the kettle. The fire is then put out and as a climax a lady emerges from the kettle. Note: The kettle*

"HELLO, BOYS! MAKE TOYS!"

stands off the ground during the entire act and is well to the front of the stage, with no back drops or draperies, no stairs pushed to the kettle before or after the production. Recommended as pre-eminently the stellar illusion we offer for sale.")

In the back of the catalog we had a special section —also put out as a separate catalog—of jokes and puzzles. They were advertised by one of the earliest uses of comic cartoons for advertising purposes. The cartoonist who drew a great many of these strips for us, as well as other illustrations for our catalog, was a young fellow just getting started on the *New Haven Register* as both cartoonist and reporter. He later gave up the drawing and concentrated on writing, becoming the famous syndicated columnist, H. I. Phillips.

(*"We used to meet at the Hofbrau for lunch,"* Mr. Phillips says, *"to go over the illustrations I had made and sometimes argue as to whether I rated $2.50 or $3.00 apiece for them. Once in a while he would phone me and say, 'Let's meet for lunch. I've got a new idea.' He was always full of ideas, but I never would have dreamed that he'd turn out to be a big industrialist. He struck me as being a young fellow having a lot of fun with a crazy new business."*)

I had a lot of fun, all right, but the magic business, which had its heyday in the year 1911, was not enough to satisfy me. I made up my mind to push into the toy field, and my father encouraged me for all he was worth.

123

I knew that John Petrie would not want to go along with me on this venture when the matter of additional space for the plant came up that fall. We needed space for the installation of machinery making Erector, in which John was not interested. I had found a bigger plant that we could take over, the Kirchoff Carriage Works on Foote Street in New Haven, but John voted against our acquiring it. The other directors wanted to go ahead, however, so on November 23, 1911, I was authorized to lease the Kirchoff plant under a two-year lease for an annual rental of $900, with an option to buy at $8,500, together with property next door which rented for $125 a month, with an option to buy at $12,000.

In view of my partners' lack of enthusiasm, my father advised me that I should try to buy them out. There was no difficulty with Powers, for when I offered to turn over the New York store to him, he agreed at once. He had only a small amount of stock, anyway, and he loved that store. It was making money, and he felt sure that he could continue to build it up.

John Petrie was approached by my father, who offered to buy out his interest in the Mysto Manufacturing Company. He said he knew that I would like to have John stay with me, and I would certainly have no objection to his going on with the manufacture of magic stuff. There had never been any friction between us— not even over leasing the Kirchoff place—and there was no reason why we could not settle the matter easily so that each one could work in the field he wanted. The banks offered to lend me enough money to buy John Petrie out, but I was pleased to have my father in the

124

business, and he wanted to do it so he would have an excuse to come east often to see me. He and John Petrie finally agreed on a price of $4,500. John stayed on for some time, as we continued to make magic. Eventually we kept the magic-trick boxes only—we still put them out today—but gave up the professional apparatus. John went into the business himself, under the firm name of Petrie and Lewis, and was one of the country's outstanding quality manufacturers in this field, up to his death at the age of eighty-three, in February, 1954.

My father and I owned all the stock of the Mysto Manufacturing Company, and my enthusiasm soared— with his not far behind. Once or twice a year he came east for a visit to go over the books, to advise about the business. He was always a great help, too, and I enjoyed every single minute I ever spent with him.

The year 1912 was a good one, with business increasing considerably and profits much more. We were still selling only magic. Most of my hard work went into the planning and tooling up for Erector, though I kept busy selling, too. At that time, we began to hire a few more people, after moving to the Kirchoff plant on Foote Street. We took on two salesmen, one of whom, Al Richmond, stayed with the company occupying several important positions and becoming a director, until he retired at the age of sixty-five. One of Rich's favorite stories for years concerned the salary we paid salesmen in those days. They received $25 a week and had to pay their own expenses. Of course, they didn't make long trips, going to Bridgeport, Hartford, Providence, New York, and places not far away. But Rich came to me and complained, saying that all other salesmen had their expenses paid by their companies.

I used to get pretty annoyed at this, Rich says, and would accuse him of listening to big talk of other salesmen who were just bragging about how much they got and were trying to act more important than they really were. Instead of spending his time listening to such talk, he ought to be working. That would be the only way the company could grow, make more money, and in time pay better salaries. At that time, as president, I was still getting only $125 a month.

Well, you can call it a sweatshop if you want, or anything else. We all worked hard as the devil and didn't get much, I know that. But I know this, too—everybody associated with me shared my enthusiasm. I will never forget their loyalty. Al Richmond stayed with me as long as he worked, and so did many others who began in those early days.

In 1912, for the first time, I showed my trick boxes at the Toy Fair at the old Broadway Central Hotel. Those were the days when the word "toy" meant the flimsy-flamsy gimcracks marked "Made in Germany." A few American manufacturers were in the business, some of whom kept on and grew with the American toy industry, but at that time close to 70 per cent of the toys sold in this country were foreign-made. The toy business was known as the "bedroom industry" because of the Toy Fair at the old Broadway Central Hotel, where manufacturers rented rooms and displayed their wares on beds. In 1912, the Mysto Manufacturing Company had not a very large room or a very big bed to show its products, but I knew that the next year would be a different story.

It *was* a different story, too, for at the Broadway Central Hotel in 1913 I showed Erector in all its glory. After more than a year of work, it was good, although not nearly what it is now. But you could build scores of models with it, and many of them moved. It had wheels, axles, gears, and pinions in addition to its girder parts of different sizes, its angles and plates. Most important, it had an electric motor. It was in pieces, and the boy had to put it together, but it really worked and it made a windmill go round, made a bridge lift up, hoisted an elevator.

To be honest, Erector was not actually the first of all construction toys. First there was the Richter Anchor Block line made of pieces of stone with some steel parts. It was good, but there was a limit to what you could build and no motion. We bought out Anchor Blocks a few years later.

More important as competition was a steel construction set called Meccano, produced in England by a big company with world-wide sales organizations. Meccano was made of strips of steel, flat and not shaped like girders, that could be put together with bolts and nuts. It was good, but it had no gears or pinions at that time, and no motor. From the first, Meccano was the chief competitor of Erector and became stiffer competition within a few years, when the company opened an American plant. Half a dozen other construction toys

127

appeared, too, after the success of Erector, but none offered the competition of Meccano. Years later, we also bought out the American Meccano Company.

The two things that made Erector stand out even at its first showing at the Toy Fair were its square girder, put together with only two bolts, and motion—things going around and up and down. Erector attracted attention and drew crowds. Some of the biggest buyers in the toy business gave me encouragement and advice and— more important—big orders.

From New York I went to the Chicago Toy Fair, and Erector repeated its success. I came home with such a stack of orders that it was obvious I could not possibly finance the manufacture of enough sets to take care of pre-season demand, let alone reorders and regular orders from the smaller cities. So I went to the bank with which I had usually done business, and they turned me down on a loan. They said I was moving too fast, taking on too much. I showed them my orders, showed the cost of merchandise and manufacture, to prove that there would be a handsome profit at the end of the year. They still said no.

I had heard about a Mr. William H. Douglass at the Mechanic's Bank in New Haven, so I told him my story. He got right in a car and drove out to the Foote Street plant, looked over my orders and figures, and asked me how much money I wanted. I told him what would be needed.

"You've got it," he said. "I'll have to go through the formality of having my directors approve the loan, but you've got it. You can start production right away."

I don't know if it was my enthusiasm that sold him, or his own big heart for helping enterprising young men, but that loan made it possible for me to go into full production that first year of Erector's life. The loan was completely paid off that fall, much to my relief and Mr. Douglass's satisfaction.

I was busy every minute that year, and I spent my evenings making and trying out new Erector models. With each set there was a booklet of instructions, and I wanted to put into it as many different kinds of things for boys to build as possible, although the hope was that after a short while an inventive boy would start making his own things instead of just copying models from the manual. At the beginning, however, all the ideas had to be mine, and they had to work. I put together hundreds of things, some of which worked and some of which didn't. I've often said that I have put together more bolts and nuts than any man alive or dead. And I had fun doing it, too.

With a new product I decided to do a new kind of advertising. We had spent some money on ads for the magic sets, but now for the first time a toy manufacturer went into big space in magazines with national circulation.

To plan my advertising campaign I consulted with a young man who had just started an advertising agency in New Haven, Charles W. Hoyt, beginning a long, happy, and profitable association. Charlie Hoyt was enthusiastic, full of ideas, worked well with me, and eventually became a stockholder and director in the company, after moving his agency to New York and

129

building it up to a big organization. During the fall of 1913 we took big space in *The American Boy, St. Nicholas, Boy's Magazine, Good Housekeeping, Saturday Evening Post, Youth's Companion* (my old friend from whom I had won premiums as a boy), *Popular Mechanics, Cosmopolitan,* and others. Almost every ad carried a headline which remained Erector's slogan for many years—"Hello, Boys! Make Lots of Toys!"

As I look back at those magazines, I realize another striking thing about those first ads—their personal note. I may not have realized it at the time, but it was something new in advertising, as I see when I look at all the other ads in those same magazines. The ad's copy was a direct personal message from me, A. C. Gilbert, to the boy reading the magazine. Sometimes there was a picture of me, with a caption about my having been world's champion pole vaulter. The ad might start, "I built Erector because I know what boys like." It would go on to urge, "Send for my free book today," and "If your dealer hasn't it, please write me." And the coupon on the ad was addressed to A. C. Gilbert, President, Mysto Manufacturing Company.

I wanted the ads to read as if they were personal messages from me to the boys. It was not just good selling, as it turned out, but I meant it. This same theme was carried out in a newspaper we published called *Erector Tips.* It carried a personal message from me, a story about some athletic event I had engaged in, and other personal items. I was convinced that boys became interested and excited when a *person,* not a corporation, spoke to them. And I must have been right, for the letters

130

began to flood us that first fall. We printed the best letters in *Erector Tips,* and sometimes pictures of the boys who sent them. The paper was sent free to any boy who wrote in for it, whether he owned an Erector set or not.

We used *Erector Tips* as the chief medium for promoting our prize contest. We offered prizes for the best original models boys made and sent in pictures of. There were two purposes here—to get boys interested in experimenting with Erector, and to get new models we could put in our instruction manual. To this day, a great many models in the manual are those that were contributed in prize contests over the years.

Nobody had ever advertised a five-dollar toy before in this country, and it really took courage. We had sets ranging in price from a dollar to twenty-five dollars, but we featured the five-dollar set. People in the industry, who had thought that a dollar was a lot of money for any toy, believed we were crazy. But it worked, and started a new trend.

Even before the Christmas season was under way that year, I knew we would not have enough space, so I gave a contract to Charles and Auger for $7,000 for building an addition to our Foote Street plant, although it was not ready until the spring of 1914. Also, that fall the family moved from Westville to an apartment on Norton Street, not far from the factory. The young couple who lived below us, Mr. and Mrs. Arthur B. Alling, soon became good friends of ours. Alling was with the Hendryx birdcage people in New Haven but it wasn't long before he came with me, first as book-keeper.

This was one of the most rewarding and heart-warming associations I have had in a long business career. A. B. Alling was a good friend, an excellent financial man, and he became a pillar of the company. From the first, I had complete confidence in him and his judgment, and his coming meant that I could get away from the plant for a day or two now and then, something that had been impossible.

My salary at the end of 1913 was just $125 a month, but the directors voted me a bonus of $1,500 for that year, and raised my salary, as of January 1, 1914, to $350 a month. This was made possible by a total volume that year of $141,000. We spent $12,000 on advertising, and showed a net profit of $45,619. It was a good year, all right.

Eleven

Five Dollar Breeze

(*A machine about twenty feet high and half a block long in the A. C. Gilbert plant puts zinc plating on millions of pieces of Erector every year. It can best be described as a huge conveying machine with an endless chain, to which are attached steel arms carrying huge metal baskets. One operator feeds hundreds of Erector parts in a basket, then the arm moves along the conveyor line and plunges each basket into various chemical solutions and cleaning preparations. The huge baskets, shaped like barrels, slowly rotate as they travel along, causing the Erector parts inside to tumble about so that every part of each piece comes in contact with the various solutions. The arms automatically rise, lifting the baskets from one solution to another, still rotating so that the liquid drains off the Erector girders as they come*

133

back to the starting point. Then each basket automatically tips and spills out into a trough all the Erector pieces, which now gleam like silver.)

(A.C. takes an almost personal pride in this huge plating machine, as he does in all the unusual devices in the plant, in many of which he has had a hand as to concept, design, or adaptation to the special needs of this demanding manufacturing business.)

It's surprising how many of our products call for brand-new special machinery. That's the part of the business that fascinates me. Lots of the things we put out here were never made before, or made in this way, so we've had to figure out how to produce them as we went along. Take Erector, for instance. It was not just a new toy, but a new kind of toy. There were no precedents we could follow in manufacturing the many pieces of an Erector set, and as sales boomed, we had to work out machines that would increase the quantity produced.

There has never really been any letup in the sales of Erector, except during war years when we couldn't get material and turned over our plant to war work. When you stop to think of it, you can't find many toys that were big successes in 1913 and are still being sold, let alone being sold in big quantities. Altogether, we've sold about thirty million Erector sets since they were first introduced.

In 1914 sales continued to mount. Total business that year was $375,626, with the startling net profit of $97,569. My father came east to see me at the end of the year, and when he went over the books he was more excited than I've ever seen him. "Your business has taken in more money this year," he said, "than I've earned in my whole life up to now. And you're just thirty years old!"

We spent $47,000 in advertising that year, using big space in the same magazines, plus a full page in the *Literary Digest*, the top news weekly of that time and for many years after. We went into a great many farm magazines, too, because we figured that boys on the farm were natural builders, anyway, and would enjoy Erector during the long winters.

We put out a booklet designed to help dealers sell Erector. One section, called "A Hint to Parents," contains some ideas and words which in those days were new and startling. In that year there was no such thing as progressive education, and the very concept of "child psychology" was one that most Americans had paid no attention to. I was emphasizing fun in education considerably before most educators thought of it. The pioneers of that idea in the school system were running up against stone walls of opposition at the time, and for some years thereafter.

(Quotation from the booklet for dealers published in 1914: "Our new educational idea, which is the result of a study of child psychology, is developing a new angle of vision upon education. We find that the element of fun and pleasure has a wonderful effect in stimulating the inventive faculties which lie dormant in the child. Why not develop them in a sort of subconscious way?")

135

When schools became interested in our construction and educational toys, we discouraged them as much as we could. For years our schools seemed to be conducted on the theory that real learning was painful, and anything enjoyable couldn't possibly be instructive. We were afraid that if kids saw our things in school, they'd think they were just as deadly dull as the rest of school and would have nothing to do with them.

In 1914 our prize contest became the biggest thing of its kind the country had ever seen. Nowadays fabulous prize contests are so common that people hardly notice one unless it promises to make them rich. But back in 1914 and 1915 they were rare, and prizes were small. We offered the things most boys wanted more than anything in the world—a Shetland pony, a real automobile, a motorcycle, bicycles, canoes, camping outfits, and scores of lesser items. By 1915, the contest was so big that we could not handle it and had to call in outside help. That year we received sixty thousand entries, and each entry was a photograph of an original model which some boy had built. They showed the most amazing ingenuity and cleverness, too. I loved the contests myself, for I found it the most encouraging thing in the world to see the thousands of ideas boys had and the wonderful way they worked them out. Even greater possibilities were offered in Erector by this time because every set that sold for $3.00 or more had an electric motor, ready to run.

We opened a New York sales office in 1914, in the American Woolen Building at Eighteenth Street and Fourth Avenue, and an office in Chicago the next year, in the North American Building. Before 1914 ended, we knew that we had to have more space for the factory. My father advised me against trying to add any height to the buildings on Foote Street and thought we ought to buy a plot of land, put up a new plant, and have room for expansion. As usual, his advice was sound. On December seventeenth we bought from Abraham Lander a piece of land on Fox Street for $5,000. My father said that if we didn't want to take the money out of the business for the new building, he would lend the company money for its construction. We were growing so fast that despite high profits we needed to plough a great deal of money back into the business to keep moving ahead at the same rate.

Mary and I bought our first home at this time, too, on Everit Street. Up to this time we had always rented, and it was a wonderful feeling to have a home that was really ours. We must have bought our first automobile about then, too, for I remember driving in the middle of the night, on February 1, 1915, to the Foote Street plant after being telephoned that it was on fire.

The fire was in what we called Number Three Building, which was the original three-story structure of the old Kirchoff Carriage Works. It burned completely to the ground, and everything in it was a total loss. I'll never forget the terrible feeling as I stood there watching it go up in smoke. The only consolation was that I was completely covered by insurance—or so I thought. Afterwards I learned one of my hard business lessons when I found out that I was operating under a co-insurance clause which I had not fully understood. It meant that the company had to stand a certain percentage of the loss, which was quite a blow.

We had to keep moving ahead, however, because business was still going great guns. By the middle of February we had awarded a contract to Louis A. Miller of Meriden to build a new plant for $25,000 on the land we had bought on Fox Street. It was finished in May and still stands right next to our present plant. We never dreamed, as we moved into the new factory that spring of 1915, that in less than two years we would have outgrown it.

Our export business had increased so much that I thought we should look into the possibility of opening an office abroad, so I sent John M. Saxton, one of the best men in our sales department, to London to survey the situation. He returned in April, 1915, with a very favorable report, so we decided to go ahead at once, sending him back to England, with his family, to take charge. But while he was in New Haven conferring with me, he came down suddenly with pneumonia and despite the efforts of the best doctors in New Haven, he died within a few days. It was a terrible blow to me, to the company, to his family and friends, for he was a fine man, intelligent and loyal. We postponed immediate plans for a European office and then dropped the idea because of the war already raging there, a war in which our country would soon be involved.

This year of 1915 set the pattern that we have followed, or should have followed, ever since—the manufacture of educational toys and products involving the use of fractional-horsepower electric motors. Almost every time we have deviated from this program—except when forced to by war or other emergencies—we have made a mistake. Fortunately not many of our mistakes were very costly and some actually made money.

Early in 1915 I began working on a line of educational toys, many of which were not in production for another four years. The first was a fascinating electrical experiment set, and the second was our first chemistry set. I had taken six years of chemistry and spent some time brushing up on it so that I could work out this set myself with the help of an engineer brought in for the job.

About this time I encountered a serious industrial problem. All our products were toys, and the toy business was probably the most seasonal business in the world. Ninety per cent of our toys were sold at Christmas time. Then there was a period of at least a few weeks before we could start production of the next year's merchandise. I had several hundred workers by this time, and I hated terribly to have to lay them off for this period. I hated to see a factory standing idle, machines quiet and unproductive. I wanted to build up a working force that would be loyal, happy, and interested in the business. Men and women could not feel that way unless they had the security of steady employment, as well as good wages and pleasant working conditions.

I had to find some product that we could manufacture which would fill in the gap in the working year, when we were not making toys. Naturally, something involving small electric motors came to mind first. That's when I had the idea for the Polar Cub fan. In those days electric fans were pretty expensive, and I knew there must be a big market for a good, moderately priced fan.

In 1915 we launched the first five-dollar fan in the country and advertised it widely with the phrase, "A Big Breeze for Little Money."

It was a big success right away, but we had a good many problems with it at the beginning. For one thing, the motors at first were wound with cotton-covered wire, and this made them too bulky. We tried silk-covered wire, which reduced the size but put the cost up too high. That's when I turned to the idea of enamel-covered wire. No commercial motor had ever used such wire, and many people had tried to make it. One of America's largest manufacturers of electrical equipment had experimented and failed. A big wire company, which we consulted, said it could not be done. I suppose I should have given up at that point. If those firms with all their resources and experience thought it was impractical, why should I, a toy manufacturer, believe I could do it?

Fortunately, I had an engineer at the plant then —John Lanz—who said the job could be done. I had confidence in him because he was a man of real ability, and he didn't hesitate to break away from the conventional any more than I did. Maybe he was just as stubborn as I was, too, when it came to something he really wanted to do.

Anyway, I told John Lanz to go ahead and work it out and that I would stick with him until we made it. It took a good deal of sticking, too, because there was plenty of trouble for a long time. He kept working and experimenting until he'd get discouraged, then I'd try to pep him up and start him off again. Finally he had a wire that he thought was right, and we wound motors,

140

put them in fans and got so many returns that some people in the plant insisted more came back than we ever manufactured. Even then I urged Lanz to keep on working, and he did. Finally he made an enameled wire that was really good, and an automatic machine for winding the armatures, which had never been done before. One girl could operate three machines and produce more than 350 armatures a day. That machine has never been improved on since.

After the product was finished and proven, we still had our troubles. The Underwriters' Laboratory wouldn't pass our enamel-wire motors, and we almost had to bootleg Polar Cub fans for a while. But the fans worked, and people knew it. Other firms, great big ones, started making motors with enameled wire, and then the Underwriters accepted them. Today just about all small motors in the world use enameled wire, of course.

I don't think many people know that it was the A. C. Gilbert Company—then still known as Mysto Manufacturing Company—which developed enameled wire for motors. But I want to tell you that this was a mighty important contribution to the appliance and electrical industry—certainly the most important contribution our organization ever made in this field. Somebody else would have done it in time, of course, because it was a development that was bound to come. But we did it when everybody said it couldn't be done, when the best electrical wire experts told us we were foolhardy to try. We did it because John Lanz had courage and initiative, and because I insisted that he try, and backed him until he succeeded.

141

Polar Cub also had an air-gap commutator invented by one of our engineers, William G. Viall. The fan was successful, but it did not contribute much to the business in its first year, 1915. Erector was going so big, however, that we more than doubled the preceding year's figures, doing a total of $800,887, with a net profit of $133,956. We spent $124,000 on advertising that year, and Erector won a Gold Medal at the Panama Pacific Exposition in San Francisco.

The next year, 1916, was one of the most eventful and successful in the history of the business. We went over a million dollars for the first time, brought out several new products, introduced new promotion methods, extended our activities to the entire toy field, bought a new plant, changed our name—but the year always will be indelibly fixed in my mind as the year in which I lost my wonderful father.

He had become terribly interested in the business, much to the benefit of the company and the pleasure of all who came in contact with him. His advice was invariably sound, and his enthusiasm was continually helpful to me in the new work I was doing. He encouraged me on the series of educational toys, the first of which came out that year. The electrical set had wire, bells, buzzers, and other apparatus that a boy could put together to learn about electricity and have fun doing it. We also brought out that year a 110-volt motor—our previous ones had run from batteries—and a transformer. One new toy was Brik-Tor, which we called the missing link in toydom, the younger brother of Erector. We were aiming for what I called the pre-screw driver set, the

142

boys who wanted to build things but were too young for Erector. It was a sound idea, but Brik-Tor was not the right answer. It was moderately successful, but it lacked the flexibility and motion of Erector.

In June we changed the company's name to The A. C. Gilbert Company, as Mysto didn't really fit the business any more. Arthur B. Alling became a director at the same time. We sold the old Foote Street plant for $20,000, and in December bought the plant of the Maxim Munitions Works, at Blatchley and Peck Streets, for $150,000. This is the site of our present factory.

During 1916 we spent $144,746 on advertising, but the most significant new promotion and advertising idea was the Gilbert Institute of Engineering, which many writers have delighted in pointing out, had no faculty and no campus. While this is true, I insist that it helped promote more genuine education than many an accredited school. It *did* give diplomas, anyway, certifying that the holder was an Engineer or Master Engineer of the Institute. The boys didn't get these diplomas just by asking for them. They had to work and work hard for them, no matter how much they enjoyed the work. Diplomas were given for great ingenuity and inventiveness in making Erector models.

Local branches of the Institute were started all over the country. I have in my scrapbook an account of a meeting in the town of Olean, New York, at which six hundred boys showed up and several hundred more were turned away for lack of room in the hall. An educational movie, produced by our company, was shown, followed by a talk given by a prominent boys' club leader.

143

The whole affair was backed by the Miller Hardware Company, which of course sold Erector sets—and lots of them.

It was for many years a very effective selling idea, but I still think it was more than just that. From the civic and recreational point of view, the branches of the Institute accomplished the same purpose as that now set for boys' clubs and athletic groups which aim to keep young fellows off the streets and occupied with worthwhile work and fun. The commercial aspect of it didn't make the boys get any less enjoyment and instruction from playing with Erector sets. If you had read the hundreds of letters I have received from engineers who tell me that their interest in their profession started with an Erector set, you would know that I had done something besides make money. It is not an accident that in World War II the first model of the Bailey Bridge, designed for rapid crossing of European rivers, was made from an Erector set. Nor that in a recent television program, Dr. Roy K. Marshall, who handles the excellent Ford commercials, demonstrated the principle of the camshaft with a little gadget he had built with an Erector set. I'm prejudiced, of course, but there are dozens of examples like this, showing that Erector did a great deal of good, that it filled a deep need.

Sales figures in 1916 proved that point. Although other products contributed something to the total, Erector brought in the major share of our volume of $1,285,463 that year, with net profits of $233,131.

The most important thing I undertook in 1916, I believe, was the organization of the toy manufacturers of the United States into an association. There had been one or two attempts earlier, but they had not so much failed as they had not even got started. The war in Europe gave the American toy industry its great chance, I felt, to become a real industry. German toys, which had for long dominated our market, had difficulty reaching our shores. I wrote letters to a great many toy manufacturers suggesting a meeting. Most of them liked the idea, and we began to formulate plans. But this is another story that I'll keep for later.

Evidence that the A. C. Gilbert Company was getting somewhere came when Dr. Elwood E. Rice phoned me for an appointment. I don't know if you are familiar with the name, but this prince of salesmen had attracted a great deal of attention. I first noticed the name when I saw in New York a huge animated electric sign—one of the first, I think—on top of the building at Twenty-fifth and Broadway and Fifth Avenue, which later became the Gilbert Hall of Science. This sign advertised the Rice Leaders of the World Association.

This was an association of many prominent industrialists in the country who stood for Honesty, Quality, Service, Strength, Fair Dealing, and other universally acknowledged virtues. Elwood E. Rice, LL.D., had founded this group to "foster the practice of right principles in business." When he deemed a corporation worthy of membership in his group, he honored them with a certificate and asked them for a contribution. Just exactly what he did for them in exchange for this, I could never quite make out, beyond his big sign which mentioned the names of members occasionally,

145

and advertising which promoted the Rice Leaders of the World Association as much as it did the members of it. It was a kind of Seal of Approval of business organizations. In this case, however, they paid substantially for it.

Dr. Rice may have heard of my business figures and decided that I should become a world leader. Or he may have run out of names in the top brackets—many of whom he had sold—and descended to lower levels. In any event, he wanted to come and see me. My father was in my office at the time of the appointment and happened to be looking out the window. He saw a very imposing figure in striped pants, frock coat and tall hat, descend from a handsome rented limousine with uniformed chauffeur. He turned to me with a cry. "Alfred, lock the safe! Here comes P. T. Barnum!"

I rushed to the window and stared, and the eminent Dr. Rice really looked the part. My father roared with laughter, told me to watch myself carefully, and retired. Of course, when Dr. Rice came into my room with his very British secretary, I could not possibly take him seriously. After sitting down, he mentioned that he had asked for just twenty minutes of my valuable time, then placed on the desk a beautiful gold watch. It was square—the first square watch I had ever seen—which served its primary purpose of attracting attention.

At one point in our talk, he asked his secretary for some paper. The young man took from an alligator-skin briefcase several sheets of beautiful stationery with lettering printed in about seven colors. I never saw anything quite like it, and thought it was a crime to write

146

on it. Finally, in spite of Dr. Rice's generous offer to make me a Rice Leader of the World for only $10,000, I disappointed him by insisting that I was not important enough to travel in such illustrious company.

What I remember most about the incident, of course, is my father's slant on the whole thing, the wonderful good fun with which he looked at it, and the underlying sharpness of his observations. His wit and gaiety were as enjoyable as his advice and encouragement were helpful. That's why it was doubly hard, a few days later, when he suffered a severe and painful attack of gallstones. I got him to the hospital at once, and called in the very best surgeon in New Haven.

He was operated on, and in a week he was gone. It was a tragedy that I've never really gotten over. Losing him was like losing a part of myself, and I couldn't quite believe that he had gone. With my mother and younger brother, we took his body back to Oregon where he was buried.

Twelve

Statesmen at Play

(In the winding department of the A. C. Gilbert plant, thousands of miles of fine copper wire are used for the making of electric motors and the coils of transformers. Much of this wire is so fine that it does not appear to be much larger than hair, and most of it is coated with an invisible covering of enamel which insulates it.)

(Along one side of the room, near a bank of windows, stands a row of small machines for winding this wire on the cores of armatures for fractional-horsepower motors, of which the A. C. Gilbert Co. makes more than any concern in the world. These are the tiny motors that fit inside locomotives for toy trains, the slightly larger motors that run vibrators and small mixers, and the next size motors that run electric fans, drills, large mixers, and many other appliances. The winding machines

148

*themselves are run by electric motors, and look quite
simple. One girl can handle several machines. She pushes
a button and the armature core whirls around so fast
that it becomes nothing but a blur, winding the fine wire
on it. After a certain number of turns, the winding automatically stops.*)

(*Near by, A.C. stops to watch a girl tying the fine
ends of the wire so rapidly that one can hardly see her
fingers move. As she finishes one piece and reaches for
the next, she looks up at him and smiles. He smiles back,
asks about her sister, who also works in the department
but has been out sick. The girl answers, then goes on with
her swift tying, as A.C. watches for another minute or
two.*)

It fascinates me to watch her do that tying job.
I can imagine how I'd fumble it. Come to think of it,
my sleight-of-hand work should have made me pretty
good at it, with a little practice. But I didn't even keep up
my magic during the years I was so busy with the growing business. I did put on a magic show at one of the
banquets following the anual meeting of the Toy Manufacturers Association. For several years I helped plan
the entertainment at these meetings, and they were a
lot of fun. The Association has always meant a great deal
to me because of the good it performs for the entire
industry and because of the many good friends I made
through it.

It was established at a crucial moment, too, for
with the coming of World War I, the toy industry might
have received a fatal blow except for the strenuous ef-

forts of the Association and its members. The American toy business was just starting to grow up into a major industry, stimulated by the cutting off of German toys, which had for many years dominated the field. Then curtailment of materials and manpower caused by our entry into the war threatened to stop its development, and after the war the flooding of our markets with cheap foreign goods might have killed it off. Luckily, the Association was there to take vigorous action in both instances.

Previous efforts to establish a trade association had failed either because they had included wholesalers, creating two warring camps, or because they tried primarily to enter into restrictive agreements in support of price maintenance. In planning the new group, I insisted that neither of these obstacles be put in our way. The Association was to consist only of manufacturers, and there was to be no attempt at price fixing or anything that might be thought monopolistic. It was essential, too, that we set up permanent offices and hire a secretary from outside the industry. At the organizational meeting, sixty-eight manufacturers took part in founding the Toy Manufacturers of the U.S.A.

(*From a booklet issued by the Toy Manufacturers of the U.S.A. on its thirtieth anniversary: "While we cannot be too sure today as to who was the first to conceive the idea of an Association, we are quite confident A. C. Gilbert played a tremendously important part in the organization of our Association. He was a leading figure at the initial meetings, and served as the first President.")*

They elected me president when I was in Oregon as a result of my father's death. Harry C. Ives, of the Ives Manufacturing Company, which made electric trains, was made vice-president. A. D. Converse of the famous Toy Town was second vice-president. Leo Schlesinger, one of the real old-timers of the American toy industry, became treasurer. All of these men later served as presidents of the Association. As executive secretary, we hired Fletcher D. Dodge, who did a remarkably fine job in that position for the next fifteen years.

It was a good group, active and vigorous from the start. Many new members came in right away. Offices were established in the Flatiron Building, although they moved to the Fifth Avenue Building, where so many toy firms have their offices, a few years later. A credit bureau was established, a news bulletin was issued, and within two years there was a collection service and a Washington representative. It was fifteen years, however, before the Association took over the sole management of the annual Toy Fair.

I served as president of the Association for two years. At the banquet following the 1918 meeting, when I retired from that office I was presented with a silver cigarette case, which I carry to this day.

(From an article in Toys *and* Novelties, *a trade magazine: "Toward the close of the banquet came one*

*of the finest incidents of the two crowded days and eve-
nings. It was the presentation of a silver cigarette case
to A. C. Gilbert, founder and first president of the Toy
Manufacturers of the U.S.A. The presentation was made
by Leo Schlesinger, and had the double charm of coming from his warm heart and silver tongue. The case bore
this inscription on the inside, which Mr. Schlesinger
asked Mr. Gilbert to read:*

*Alfred C. Gilbert
Founder and First President
of the
Toy Manufacturers of the U.S.A., Inc.
as a token of esteem from the members,
New York, December 19, 1918*

*Mr. Schlesinger then asked Mr. Gilbert to read
what was engraved on the outside, and he read, 'A.C.G.'
Mr. Schlesinger, turning to the members, said, 'A—
always ready to serve our association. C—consistency
in every undertaking for our welfare. G—good fellow-
ship which he has shown to all the members. These are
the three great principles of Alfred C. Gilbert.")*

My most important undertaking for the Association during these years was the hearing in Washington
before the Council of National Defence. There was a
great deal of talk about whether or not toys were essential during the war. There had been restrictions on many
materials, of course, and difficulties about manpower.
Many toy manufacturers who had the facilities, as we

did, were occupied largely with war work of one kind or another, but we wanted to keep at least a skeleton crew to turn out some toys and maintain some continuity of American toy production. Then the Council of National Defence considered placing an embargo on the buying and selling of Christmas presents. This was when the toy association decided that it must present its case. A committee was formed to go to Washington, I was asked to make the presentation before the Council, and Fletcher Dodge arranged an appointment for us.

The Council of National Defence was made up of certain key members of the President's Cabinet. I remember that at our hearing there were Secretary of War Newton D. Baker, Secretary of the Navy Josephus Daniels, Secretary of the Interior Franklin K. Lane, and Secretary of Commerce William C. Redfield.

Our group from the Association got together some of the best educational toys in the country, and a few of the most popular toys of all kinds, and set out for Washington. I gave a great deal of thought and careful planning to the presentation of our case, for I knew we had a difficult job ahead of us. We were given fifteen minutes to tell our story—not much time, but as it happened, this hearing turned out to be one of the happiest and most successful undertakings I ever participated in. I was earnest, I was honest, and I was sincere. I had a real story to tell, and I had the toys to prove my point. The amazing thing was the interest those men showed in the toys the minute they were displayed. The doors were closed and instead of a very formal hearing, it became informal indeed, with the cabinet members down on the

153

floor playing with toys. And the fifteen-minute time limit was forgotten entirely.

(*The* Boston Post *carried a long story on this hearing, with a picture of A. C. Gilbert bearing the caption, "The Man Who Saved Christmas for the Children." The story read, in part: " 'Make me a boy again just for tonight!' In the old song it didn't come true, but down in Washington very recently it actually happened to some of the greatest and busiest men of the nation, the members of the President's own Cabinet.*)

(*"The man who did it says it didn't take a bit of magic to bring these dignified, grey-bearded men, grown serious with the burdens of war, right down to playing with toys on the floor like the little lads they used to be long ago.*)

(*" 'I didn't do it,' A. C. Gilbert of New Haven, Conn., the man who really did do it, denies when he is asked about it. 'The toys did it.'*)

(*"It all began to happen when the toy men of the country, who had been working for months to fill Santa Claus' orders, heard that the Council of National Defence had decided that there should be no Christmas shopping or giving of presents this year. Immediately the toy men went to Mr. Gilbert, who is chairman of the Toy Association War Service Committee, a maker of toys and a lover of children, and asked him to go to Washington and tell the Council of National Defence just what the loss of their Christmas toys would mean to the children of America.*)

("*First Mr. Gilbert collected from all the toy men samples of the various kinds of toys which they had ready for Christmas and then he went right to Washington with them. The hearing was held in the Navy Building, which is heavily guarded. No parcels of a suspicious nature are permitted to pass without being opened. So there was an amusing ten minutes' delay while the guards searched Mr. Gilbert's bundles and brought forth toy steam engines and rocking horses and puzzles and tin soldiers, etc.*)

("*In the office with its stiff leather davenports and its group of dignified and very serious men who had been spending long weary hours in hearing the complaints of many people who objected to their plans, Mr. Gilbert and the men who had come with him grew a bit awed and decided that the toys were out of place. So they put them behind a big couch and Mr. Gilbert waited his turn to plead the cause of the little ones. He was called upon last, which made it look even more doubtful that the lovely toys he had brought would ever come out of their cases, for it had been a long hard day and the members of the Cabinet were tired.*)

("*'The greatest influences in the life of a boy are his toys,' said Mr. Gilbert when he finally had his chance to stand before the Council. 'A boy wants fun, not education. Yet through the kind of toy American toy manufacturers are turning out he gets both. The American boy is a genuine boy, and he wants genuine toys. He wants guns that really shoot and that is why we have given him air rifles from the time he was big enough to hold them.*

155

It is because of the toys they had in childhood that the American soldiers are the best marksmen on the battlefields of France.')

("There was a marked change in the attitude of the members of the Council. It was evident that they were coming his way.)

(" 'America is the home of toys that educate as well as amuse, that visualize to the boy his future occupations, that start him on the road to construction and not destruction, that as surely as public school or the Boy Scouts, exert the sort of influences that go to form right ideals and solid American character,' continued Mr. Gilbert in a gentle but very earnest way.)

("The interest grew steadily and came to the point where the other toy men brought Mr. Gilbert the toys they had hidden and from the moment he opened them out on the big library table, the secretaries were boys again. Secretary Daniels was as pleased with an Ives submarine as he could be with a new destroyer. 'There's no use trying to deny that toys get every one of us,' he said as he kept fast hold of the submarine and inquired if they were on sale everywhere in the country.)

("How the boys and girls of America would have laughed if they could only have been concealed in that room and, peaking over the tops of the davenports, seen the Cabinet playing with the toys! Secretary Redfield wanted the steam started in one of Mr. Ritchie's Weeden engines as soon as he set eyes on it. 'I learned the rudiments of engineering on a machine like this,' he said. Secretary Lane became buried in an aviation book just issued by McLoughlin Brothers and wanted to know

where he could get more books just like it. Every one of the 40 or more toys they laughed over and played with. 'Toys appeal to the heart of every one of us, no matter how old we are,' said another Cabinet member.)

(*"And it was because they did, and because the words of a man who makes them, a man who believes in them, a man who loves them, appealed too, that the boys and girls of the United States are going to awake this Christmas morning upon a day as merry as Christmases past."*)

Nevertheless, all of our main plant was turned over to war work. We made parts for machine guns and gas masks, but the most important job was making Colt .45 automatics under sub-contract from Winchester. And we had a good record, proving that we could turn out top quality precision goods, although some people had doubted that a toy manufacturer could do it.

Before the United States had actually entered the war, I began to be somewhat worried as to whether or not we had overextended ourselves. Buying the Maxim Munitions plant had really taken a lot of courage. Now that I'm older and more conservative, I wouldn't dream of taking such a big step as that was then. Our growth had been almost incredible, of course, especially in view of the fact that no substantial outside money had ever been put into the business and all our moves and increases had come from funds the business earned itself.

Early in 1917, figuring that we might have moved too rapidly, we sold the Fox Street plant to Frank H.

Trigoo for $82,000, for the manufacture of Liberty Motors. We made a fair profit on the plant, of course, but it changed hands several times in subsequent years for much higher figures.

We opened a sales office in the Phelan Building in San Francisco in 1917, and brought out several new products in spite of the war situation. The most important of these was our Chemistry set which has throughout the years been one of our best items. It was perfectly safe, and yet a boy could do hundreds of interesting experiments with it. I worked hard on the manual or book that went with it, making sure that it would be fun. It was chockful of fascinating experiments and tricks, so boys liked it and learned a lot from it.

I might as well mention right now the wonderful endorsement our chemistry set received many years later, which proved that I had been on the right track when I started our educational toys and made them so they would be fun first of all. During World War II, when we were contemplating abandoning the production of chemistry sets for a while, Professor Robert Treat Johnson, head of the Sterling Foundation at Yale—who was later to redesign our whole Chemistry line—insisted that it was our duty to continue to put them out. He said that one of the biggest factors in the growth of the chemical industry in the United States had been Gilbert Chemistry sets. Years before, during the late twenties and thirties, he had been astounded at the great increase in the size of his classes and had conducted a survey over quite a period to find out why so many more students were taking chemistry. He found that in a majority of cases the first interest in chemistry had been aroused by our chemistry sets.

Another interesting development in 1917 was a kind of prophecy of things to come—the Polar Cub Home Motor, which sold for $10 with a four-legged metal base with rubber feet. The motor could be tilted to various angles to take different attachments, each of which cost a moderate amount extra. The motor could be hooked up to run a sewing machine—they were all foot-treadle affairs in those days—or to sharpen knives, polish silverware, beat eggs and whip cream, massage with a vibrator attachment, or blow cooling air with a detachable fan blade and guard. This was certainly a forerunner by a full generation of the home drill with its stand and numerous attachments, as well as the precursor of the electric kitchen mixer and beater, of which we made the first a few years later.

We also brought out a drill press, wood-turning lathe, and scroll saw. They were the real thing and did a good job, but were not full-sized. We called them industrial models. They sold fairly well, but there were two things wrong. One was that we were a few years ahead of our time—a common failing—and the other that boys old enough to use such equipment could handle full-sized machines, and wanted to.

We brought out a few toys suggested by the war. Most significant was a nurse's outfit, with cap, arm band, bandages, adhesive tape, scissors, and a bottle of soda-mint tablets. This was the first nurse's outfit ever offered for sale in this country. A submarine with a periscope, conning tower, and torpedo tube, which dove, discharged its torpedoes, and rose again, sold for $1.50 and was quite popular. Our machine gun was good-sized, and an accurate copy of real guns then in use.

When metals became scarce we turned to wood for the first time and put out a toy called Kiddikins, aimed chiefly at the pre-school age group. This was a construction toy similar to Tinkertoy. In recent years we redesigned it, made it in colored plastic, and called it Erector Junior, with great success.

Our sales dropped during 1917, of course, because of the war work we were doing, but we made out well just the same, with total volume of $870,937 and the handsome profit of $112,909, after spending about $82,000 on advertising. My salary as president was now $20,000 a year, not particularly large in view of the volume of our business but enough to make things considerably more comfortable than they had been in the early years of the business. Our second child, Lucretia, was born in April, 1917, and our son, Al Jr., two and a half years later in December, 1919.

War work occupied the greater part of our capacity during 1918, so our sales figures really meant nothing. We did manage to keep on producing small quantities of our established toys and appliances and to introduce a few new items. Our Phono Set was like a small intercommunication system with two phones, run from batteries. Teleset was a telegraph set with key, buzzer, wire, and a manual with telegraph codes.

Most significant of our new products, in view of its subsequent history, was the Polar Cub Vibrator. This was the beginning of a series of important motor-driven

160

appliances that were lightweight and attractive and that could be used by a woman in the home. It was to become one of the steadiest sellers in the appliance field.

During the war everybody worked hard at the plant, and many of us were active in outside affairs. I put in a great deal of time and effort in the Liberty Loan drives in addition to my work with the Toy Manufacturers Association. Around that time, too, I began taking part in the activities of the National Metal Trades Association, of which I became a director, in time, as well as head of the New England division. In July of 1918 I accepted a directorship in the Mechanics Bank in New Haven. My father had always warned me never to become a director of a bank unless I gave a good deal of time and attention to the bank's affairs and attended meetings regularly. Remembering this advice of a man who had been a banker for many years, I turned down all such requests for some time. But finally all the directors of the Mechanics Bank, the institution which had given my company its first sizable loan when Erector was launched, called upon me and asked me to serve. So I consented, though I was to wish many years later that I had followed my father's advice.

With the war over, we converted to civilian production with great speed, as shown by the figures for 1919—total volume of $1,729,000, and profits of $155,169. We spent $108,000 on advertising. A Paris office was opened under the direction of R. R. Hutton, who had served as interpreter for Herbert Hoover when he was in charge of relief work abroad. A London office and showroom were finally opened, too, under the direction

161

of H. H. Silliman. Our toys proved very popular abroad, and we considered these foreign offices quite successful, although they did not show an actual profit.

Personally, I profited considerably from a subsidiary activity that came about as a result of my occasional trips abroad—profited not in a financial sense but in terms of pleasure. It was through my English visits that I became interested in Elizabethan furniture with which we have furnished our homes, but I'll go into that when I tell about the building of Maraldene.

After the war was over the Alien Property Custodian sold properties that had been taken over from their German owners. One of these was the F. Ad Richter Company, which had a factory in New York for making their famous Anchor Blocks, probably the first construction toy ever made. These stone blocks were heavy, beautifully designed, and came in a variety of shapes that made possible the building of some wonderful structures. We decided to put in a bid for the property and submitted our offer along with another firm that wanted to acquire Richter's patent medicine line. Our bid was accepted, so we took over the stock and machinery of Anchor Blocks for $25,000, and put them on the market in 1919. They sold very well for many years. Last year we redesigned and revitalized Anchor Blocks and they are having a new life.

We spent a small fortune in 1919 advertising a new toy for which we offered a prize of $100 to the boy supplying the best name. We didn't get any inspirations, really, and wound up with the rather obvious name of Gilbert's Wheel Toy. It was a big construction outfit, with four rubber-tired wheels and an assortment of other carefully designed pieces which enabled the boy to build a number of different vehicles—a wagon, a truck, a coaster, a scooter, a wheelbarrow, and other things. But there was one flaw with Wheel Toy that none of us foresaw. The boy who was old enough and big enough to construct these vehicles properly was too old and too big to ride in them. We learned that important fact after the toy was on the market, but it sold fairly well and we lost no money on it. There was no repeat sale, however, so we dropped it after a while.

We changed our war tank into a caterpillar tractor and put it on the market in 1919, and brought out a soldering set, our first tool chests, which we then called Manual Training Sets, and a variation of this called a Designer and Toy Maker, which had tools, material and plans for making small wooden and metal toys. Another toy, which we called Air-Kraft, was the beginning of the model airplane hobby in this country, with light-weight planes driven by rubber bands.

The most important new development in 1919 was radio. We had made wireless sets for a few years, but with the end of the first World War, radio got started and we were in it right from the beginning. Much of our work in this field resulted from the fact that a young man associated with us, Clarence D. Tuska, returned from the army with a good deal of experience in the Signal Corps behind him. We put him to work on our wireless and radio products at once, bringing out our first crystal sets in 1919. But the whole story of radio and broadcasting comes a bit later.

163

In spite of these many new products, in some of which I played an important part, I worked hardest during that year on the new line of educational toys which made their appearance the following year. Late every evening I worked on the books and manuals that went with the toys, and during the day I worked with the engineers on the construction and planning of the sets themselves. I had a great deal of help, of course, but in those days I was really the creative engineer of the company as well as its president. And I loved every minute of it.

Thirteen

Radio and Circus Car

(*The word "Erector" had become part of the language
even before 1920, as shown by a clipping in one of the
business scrapbooks of The A. C. Gilbert Company. In
a newspaper story the word was used without a capital
letter to mean any boy's construction set. Some officials
of the company wanted to write the newspaper and have
it print a correction so that the trade name would receive proper credit. A.C. realized the significance of the
incident, which was repeated many times in subsequent
years, and knew that his invention had really succeeded
beyond his most ambitious dreams. When a trade name
becomes so much a part of the language that it drops its
capital letter to become just another word, a product has
received its highest recognition.*)

(*Some years later the United States Post Office*

165

and the city of New Haven officially designated the area near Blatchley Avenue and Peck Street as Erector Square. But the visitor does not need to wait for a glimpse at the street signs to know that he is near the factory that makes Erector, among other things. If he has traveled on the main line of the New York, New Haven & Hartford Railroad, he has seen the giant display windows and signs along the rear of the plant, advertising Erector, Polar Cub Fans, American Flyer Trains, and other Gilbert products. Around New Haven he probably has seen the big trucks painted almost like circus wagons. And many blocks from the plant he can see the tall tower on top, which looks as if it were made of Erector girders. It bears the word "Erector" in huge letters, but originally it was put up for more than just advertising.)

That tower held the antenna for our radio broadcasting transmitter—the sixth licensed broadcasting station in the United States, Station WCJ. Not many people today know that we were pioneers in radio because we did not stay in the business long, but for a while we were in it up to our necks, both in broadcasting and in manufacturing receiving sets.

We had put out a wireless set for several years, of course, and then when Clarence D. Tuska came back from the Signal Corps, we speeded up our activities in this field. Our first real radio sets were what they all were in those early days—crystal sets with headphones. We originally intended them to be just toy sets for boys to put together and operate, but when the vacuum tube came into use, our sets were the equal of almost any on

166

the market and were bought by many grownups. The manuals accompanying our sets, written by Clarence Tuska under my direction, were really models of instruction in a new and very complicated field.

The one-hundred-and-twenty-page book put out in 1922, for instance, took up the history and theory of wireless and radio, gave complete instructions in building simple receiving and transmitting sets, then went into that newest and most fabulous development, the vacuum tube, or the "audion."

During the early twenties we listed dozens of wireless and radio items in our catalogs, from parts, antenna, and tubes to complete receivers and transmitters. The most significant thing about them was this—we were the first concern in the country to put our sets in cabinets. Up to that time and for quite a few years afterward, most sets were uncovered and open, for people seemed to like to look at all the apparatus they were trying to operate. We put our sets in nice-looking wooden cases with attractive fronts, and were a few years ahead of the public in doing it. I still think I was one of the first to see that radio sets would become pieces of furniture in the living room.

As early as 1920 we were broadcasting from our plant in New Haven, although at first our transmission was in wireless code. Under the name of "Gilbert Radio Press," we sent out regular news reports.

(*From an announcement in 1920: "We have established a high-powered radio transmitter in our plant here in New Haven under special Government license, and*

167

will send daily press messages and matters of general interest. The plant we have established is unique in itself, and to our knowledge the only one of its kind in the country. It is of the very latest design and is similar to the sets installed for the Navy Department. With the large umbrella antenna which is 125 feet high, an average range of over 1,000 miles is expected. The operator in charge of the Gilbert Station will transmit the daily news twice every day except Saturday and Sunday. The first bulletin starts at 4 P.M. Eastern Time, with five-minute periods, and ten-minute intervals between these periods. The second bulletin starts at 7 P.M. and is sent in the same way. Each of the periods will be used to transmit at different speeds. This will give the beginner, as well as the experienced operator, an opportunity to copy the press bulletins.)

When voice transmission began to come in, we were among the first to broadcast. We were on the air only a few hours a day, of course, and our programs were of uneven quality, to say the least. In addition to news broadcasts we had quartets made up of people in the plant, speakers from Yale and other well-known guests, and whatever the more imaginative people in the company could dream up. In other words, our station was just about like all other stations in those days. We had built the transmitter ourselves, and we had strength if not accuracy. We blasted everything else off the air for miles around, and we had a hard time keeping it steady on our supposed frequency. But none of this bothered the listeners of those pioneer days. They were delighted to hear anything—even a garbled sound—from a new station somewhere.

After a few years we gave up all of our radio business—broadcasting as well as manufacturing. Why? Well, the assets of great value were not of any value yet. The broadcasting license itself would have been worth a small fortune a decade later. But we became involved in litigation over our use of vacuum tubes. RCA was suing everyone who used the Fleming tube, as infringing on their patents. I felt sure that we would win out in time, and the owners of the patents under which we operated insisted that we would win. But litigation, meanwhile, cost a great deal of money in legal fees and I could see no end to it. I was right, too, for it took years to reach a settlement. In time, we would have been all right, for RCA finally had to buy the patent rights they claimed were infringements of their own. But with all the costs and time of lawsuits, added to the fact that we were getting away from the fields we had set for ourselves, I decided we should get clear of the whole thing and return to the business we really knew. Maybe it was a mistake, but I have always tried to ride in too many directions at once as it is. Radio was not just another by-path, but a main road. And I already had one laid out for me.

I just gave the whole thing to Tuska—all our rights and everything. He tied in with Maxim, inventor of the Maxim silencer, and founded the Tuska Radio Company. They went out of business, as did so many of the early firms, but Tuska joined one of the big companies. He has been an important witness in many law-

169

suits over those early patents, for he was in it from the beginning.

Our radio broadcasts made one of the most effective stunts in connection with our Demonstration Car—probably the best promotion and advertising idea I ever had. We hired a regular railroad car from the New Haven Railroad, pulled everything out of the inside and re-fitted and redecorated it completely, then painted the outside like the gaudiest circus car you ever saw. We fixed up shelves and display cases inside and installed our best Erector models in all their glory. Our Chemistry Sets and all other educational toys were on display, our radios, fans, and other appliances. Above all, it was a toy car arranged to make a spectacular show for kids as well as advertise our products.

In 1922 "Mr. Gilbert's private car," as it was sometimes called, went on the road. We figured out an itinerary just as a circus does, and had our advance man placing ads and making necessary arrangements in the cities on its tour. We made tie-ups with the big toy stores, department stores, or hardware stores in the different cities, ran big ads in the local papers about a week in advance, with pictures and news stories. The stores offered free tickets to all boys who would come and ask for them, tickets to visit the Gilbert Circus Car when it came to town.

The car attracted a tremendous amount of attention right from the start. Newspaper reporters and photographers came down to meet it when it arrived in town and was shunted on to a convenient siding. Boys and girls flocked to the store by the thousands to get the free tickets. With the car on the siding, our men hung out banners and streamers and made a real circus look about the whole thing. Inside there was a magician doing magic tricks, a man showing how all the moving Erector models worked, another doing chemistry experiments. But the feature of the show was reception of a broadcast direct from the plant in New Haven.

This was exciting stuff, almost as exciting for the boys of that time as the balloon ascension and parachute jump I witnessed as a youngster in Salem. It was something new, and very few of them had ever seen radio sets, let alone listened to a broadcast. The transmission of a voice over the air without any wires was still considered mysterious and miraculous, and people didn't quite believe it who had not actually heard. And here were boys everywhere being given a chance to listen in, on the Gilbert car, to a broadcast from the Gilbert plant many miles away! They loved it.

This was fine in Bridgeport and Waterbury and Meriden. It worked well even in New London and Hartford, and fairly well in Worcester. But when the car got as far away as Boston, and later Albany or towns in Pennsylvania and New Jersey, the feeble receivers of those days just couldn't pick up the signals from our transmitter in New Haven. The stunt had made such a big hit during the first few weeks that we could not imagine giving it up just because we traveled beyond range. So we staged the receiving of the broadcast just the same. Each day the station wired to our car in advance the broadcast it was going to put on at the right time. Then we hid one of our men in the toilet of the car, with a microphone, and he read off the broadcast just as the station sent it out.

It wasn't quite honest, of course, but it made a wonderful show. And what the kids heard was exactly what went over the air from New Haven—we saw to that. If you could have seen the wide shining eyes of those boys and girls, you wouldn't have deprived them of the thrill for anything. It got to be quite a joke among people in the company, naturally, because one poor soul had to stay locked up in the washroom for several hours a day, and nobody else could visit it during that time.

The demonstration car kept traveling for about two years. It went through New England, New Jersey, New York, Pennsylvania, Delaware, Maryland, and then crossed the mountains and covered Ohio, Michigan and other states of the Middle West. It continued to get front-page attention everywhere it went, attracted tens of thousands of children and their parents and store buyers. It was certainly one of the biggest things the A. C. Gilbert Company ever did; it built up the company's reputation tremendously as an outfit that did new and different things in a big way.

It cost a lot to run the car and keep it moving around, but I think it was worth every penny of it. After two years we figured that it had accomplished about all it could, so we stopped it. But I'm convinced that we could have kept it going for years more, covered the rest of the country and come back for repeat performances with new products. It might even be a great promotion stunt today, except that now railroad yards are often not as convenient to reach. I suppose we would have to use an airplane now to keep up with the spirit of the times.

The biggest feature of the demonstration car, aside from Erector and the radio broadcasts, was our new line of educational toys. I had been planning these for years and had spent many a day, night, and weekend on them during 1919, getting them ready and into production. They were put on the market in 1920, and I made a special trip all around the country to talk about them, demonstrate them, and publicize them in addition to the work of our regular salesmen and the presentation at the Toy Fairs. There were eleven new items in this line, which when added to Erector, chemistry sets in several sizes, electricity, wireless, telegraph, and telephone sets, gave a pretty thorough education in the physical sciences.

Among the new sets was one called Hydraulic and Pneumatic Engineering, which sold for $15 and enabled a boy to construct miniature water systems, make water guns, raise sunken toy ships and perform scores of tricks. Magnetic Fun and Facts was one of the most popular, with magnets, parts for a small motor, an electric shocker, magnetic jackstraws, and a complete book explaining magnetism and giving plenty of tricks to keep a boy busy for a year. In writing the books that accompanied the sets, I found my magic a great help. I outlined tricks that would amuse, mystify, and educate at the same time, tricks that held a boy's interest while illustrating a law of physics. That's why these educational toys were so successful. In the manual that went with the Sound Experiments set, for instance, I showed boys

173

how to make a lead weight *ding* inside a closed bottle by means of "thought waves." In the same book I also told the story of the famous Fox Sisters who started a great spiritualist religion at the turn of the century, and how they managed to perform the table-rapping of "departed spirits."

There was a Civil Engineering set for $25 that taught surveying, primarily. The Weather Bureau was really a beauty, although the best of the three sizes sold for a terribly high price for those days, $37.50. It had to cost that much with an aneroid barometer. The smaller set for $15 lacked this but had plenty of interesting things, thermometers, anemometer, recording devices, etc. I had a great deal of fun myself in preparing this set, for I erected a whole weather bureau on top of the plant. I found that I could write the manual much better if I actually went through the process myself and understood it thoroughly. Our weather bureau was as good as any in Connecticut, and we later sold most of it to the city of New Haven.

During 1920 there were also sets on signal engineering, astronomy, mineralogy, and glass blowing. The last was later incorporated into our chemistry sets on a less elaborate scale.

There had never been anything like this series of educational toys before and there has been nothing like it since. All of the sets were planned with the greatest of care, and they were well packaged in hardwood cases. Some were more successful than others, of course, as we expected, but the line as a whole received great acclaim and brought us a lot of business, a lot of prestige, and a great deal of satisfaction as well. Dozens of times in the last fifteen or twenty years I have met engineers of one kind or another who have told me that they first became interested in their professions through the educational toys we put out.

The books that went with these sets were often sold separately and made a fine library. They were written and illustrated so that a boy could do many experiments without the special equipment in our sets.

Later we added a few more books to our line of publications, some of which were given away free for publicity and others sold for small sums. There was one called "Boy Engineering," for example, that contained an article by Walter Camp on "How to Become a Football Star," one by Eddie Rickenbacker on "My First Flying Over German Lines," another by Johnny Mack, Yale track coach, called "How a Boy Should Train to Become a Champion Athlete," an interview with Thomas A. Edison, and a piece by me on pole vaulting. Another booklet we issued was called "A. C. Gilbert's Olympic Sports Book," and contained articles by myself, Lawson Robertson, Olympic coach, and Harry Hillman, track coach at Dartmouth.

We produced several other new toys during the early part of the twenties, but one in particular is worth mentioning, just because once more we were quite a few years ahead of the times. A child's phonograph was nothing startlingly new, but the combination books and records that we also offered were. They were called Bob-o-Link Records and Books, and did back in 1921 what so many companies have been making money at

175

in recent years—putting together a story book, nicely illustrated in color, along with a phonograph record. Some of our illustrators later became famous in the children's book field, notably Maude and Miska Petersham.

Those first three years of the twenties were up, down and up. The year 1920 itself was our biggest up to that time, for we went over the two-million-dollar mark. With the many new products of that year, the company required more capital, so at a special stockholders' meeting in March, 1920, ten thousand shares of common stock were authorized at a par value of $100 a share, and ten thousand shares of 8 per cent preferred stock at the same par value. You can get an idea from that high dividend rate of what sort of thing led to the post-war depression. Three new directors were elected in May that year. Charles W. Hoyt, who had always handled our advertising, Tracy Lewis of the Beacon Falls Shoe Company, and Frank Frisbie, president of the Mechanics National Bank. Each bought fifty shares of common stock at $100 a share. The next year, during the depression, they were rather discouraged about their investment, but seven years later, when a financial reorganization of the company took place, those who held on to their stock realized about $75,000 on their $5,000 investment.

During these years my younger brother, Wellington, began to play a more important part in the business. He had come with the company in 1916, after graduating from Yale, starting work in the factory and working into more and more important positions. He was particularly good in the field of machine-tool engineering, and

176

played a big part in the development of new machine tools required in our varied and complicated manufacturing processes.

During the twenties, F.W. became factory manager. He was a hard and conscientious worker and did an excellent job. In 1928, he became a vice-president of the company, in 1929 a director, and later secretary and treasurer for a few years. Finally, in 1944, he resigned to enter business for himself, still being retained as factory and engineering consultant. He bought into the Chellis Company in New Haven, which in time became Gilbert and Richards, machine-tool brokers.

It was good to have him with the company for so many years, and it was especially nice when his children and mine became good friends. We all used to get together for Christmas and Thanksgiving dinners and other festive occasions when the children were young. Having a big family together reminded me of the times I used to go to the farm at Hubbard, when the house would be filled at Christmas with cousins, uncles, and aunts, all having a good time.

I don't like to think about the year 1921. My father had been through a bad depression, but I had never experienced it. I put in a year of sleepless nights and worried days, but I learned some important lessons in financing, even if I had to learn the hard way. If there is a person in the world who doesn't like to borrow money, I'm the one—and we had to borrow plenty that year. The trouble was that we had been dealing with only one New Haven bank, and in bad times one bank couldn't lend what we needed. It was a difficult job to go out and

177

get new banks to help us, but we pulled through all right, paid off all our debts, and made some excellent banking connections. Arthur Alling, the treasurer of the company, was a tower of strength during this trying period.

About that time I followed rather unconventional methods, at least in one instance, in getting a much-needed loan. I used my magic—and it worked. Here's what happened. I gave a party at the Quinnipiac Club in New Haven for some banking friends, among whom was A. L. Aiken, then president of the National Shawmut Bank in Boston. I had known Mr. Aiken for several years, and he had once said that the resources of his bank were at the command of the A. C. Gilbert Company. But in a depression things were different. Still, he had come to New Haven to discuss a loan with me, and our conference was scheduled for the next day. I knew that our books and figures would make a good case, but maybe not good enough in bad times. Sometimes the situation calls for unusual measures.

My act took some careful planning. I got in touch with Mrs. Aiken, without the banker knowing about it. I explained what I wanted to do, and she fell in with the plan readily, telling me a few incidents from her husband's past—nothing intimate or embarrassing, but the sort of thing that I would not conceivably know anything about. Then I hurried back to New Haven and arranged things at the Quinnipiac Club.

What I did would not seem very mysterious today with radio and television so common. But at that time radios were rare and an understanding of them rarer. I put a small speaker in the bottom of a vase I had used in magic acts years before. It stood about twenty inches high, had two handles and a strange spout. I laid out an induction coil that could not be seen, under the rug, and placed a man with a microphone in the room below, giving him the proper clues and script.

I knew they would call on me after dinner to do some magic tricks, and they did. I explained that my magic was getting a little rusty, but I still kept in contact with spiritualists, and if they would relax and concentrate I was sure I could get in touch with the spirit world. Looking around the room, I casually picked up my vase, which, of course, I had planted there before the dinner as a piece of normal bric-a-brac. There was nothing to make anyone suspicious of it. I set it in the center of the dining-room table, putting it close to Mr. Aiken, announcing that my spirits would speak through it.

I went through the proper amount of serious hocus-pocus to get in contact with the spirit world, and finally said I had communicated with a spirit who wished to speak to Mr. Aiken. At the right cue, a thin hollow voice whispered from the spout of the vase. Mr. Aiken leaned forward to catch the words. At first he could not understand, the spirit faded away, and I called it back again. Then it identified itself as the spirit of an old college friend of Mr. Aiken, and proceeded to recall incidents from their youth.

Mr. Aiken was dumbfounded, of course—bewildered, mystified, and fascinated. Then I said that the spirit was going away, that I could keep it there no longer. But at that moment the voice returned and said,

"Oh, before I go, I want to tell you something—something very important."

A pause, and complete silence in the room.

The spirit voice spoke again. "If A. C. Gilbert asks you for a loan, give it to him. He's good for it. I know!"

Well, that did it! They all took it in the right spirit and knew it was a hoax, of course, but some of the people there, as in almost any gathering, *wanted* to believe in spirits. And the others had no idea how I had managed to do it. Mr. Aiken, above all, couldn't figure out how I knew these facts out of his past.

The next day, at the end of our conference, the company got the loan. Mr. Aiken said that our figures warranted it, but he added, too, that anyone who could put on that stunt was smart enough to pull through a depression.

And we did, of course. Although our business in 1921 dropped to $747,000 and we were in the red $63,605, we made a great comeback in 1922, with total sales of $1,340,844. The profit column showed only $2,997 in the red, and the following year we were going great guns. The salaries we had cut in 1921 and again in 1922, from the president on down, worked their way back up again.

The year 1921 brought other worries besides depression. Foreign goods were flooding the market again, toys made with underpaid labor and even child labor. The American toy industry, which had just organized itself, was seriously threatened. It had to have tariff protection to survive. So once more the toy association called on me to head a committee for a trip to Washington. We

180

appeared before the House Ways and Means Committee to present our case, and we brought along a great many fine toys.

The hearing was almost a replica of that before the Council of National Defence in 1918, and even more successful. I went to Washington asking for a tariff of 60 per cent and came away with a tariff of 75 per cent on toys. What pleased me particularly was the reaction of John N. Garner, then Representative from Texas and later Speaker of the House and Vice-President of the United States. Mr. Garner was an ardent free-trader, but after listening to our story—and looking at our toys—he said, "I must admit that this is one industry that needs tariff protection to survive—at least for a while."

That tariff saved the industry, without any doubt, and enabled it to continue growing to its present size and strength, and to give to American children the most imaginative, educational, and enjoyable toys in the world.

181

Fourteen

New Places, Products, and People

(Drill presses, punch presses, die casters, injection mold-ers, screw machines and automatic mechanisms of a dozen different kinds carry on many of the multitude of manufacturing operations in the Gilbert plant. A.C. him-self is fascinated by new techniques, new tools, new methods, and especially by machines that turn out prod-ucts efficiently, rapidly, and with as little human atten-tion as possible. He looks fondly, for example, at a small and relatively simple machine that makes wheel and axle assemblies for toy railroad cars. Two big hoppers on either side contain the wheels, which slip down into place one at a time. Thick wire for the axles feeds from a big spool into one side; it is cut the right length, after which two wheels slip over the ends. And there you are —axle, axle, axle, axle almost as fast as you can say the words.)

(Another machine keeps busy all day long, minding its own business and bothering no one, turning out small bolts. Most factories would buy their bolts and nuts from a concern specializing in such things, but the Gilbert plant uses so many millions in connection with Erector sets that it makes its own, on machines that require no more than an occasional supervisory glance and replenishing of materials. The company also makes its own paper clips—the flat metal kind. Millions of these are used in packaging, to fasten girders, wheels, puzzles, magic tricks or other items to cardboard trays.)

(Whenever someone gets an idea for a new and better machine, A.C. will be the first to encourage his engineering department to go after it. And he will enjoy it as much as a boy with a new Erector.)

We had some fine machines back in the early twenties for making our line of mechanical toys— wind-up cars and trucks and such. We shipped them all to Austria, along with the tools and dies, and opened a plant there in 1922. It was a beautiful plant just outside of Vienna, and we put in charge Hugo Klagsbrunn, who had been a professor at the university of Vienna. He did a fine job. The operation started out well, and we had high hopes that a big business would develop, with the Vienna plant as the center from which we could sell our toys throughout the world.

After a short while, however, serious troubles began to develop. Austria, like many European countries, was going through a far worse post-war depression than we suffered in America, and theirs was made more severe by political difficulties that erupted in riots and violence of many kinds. It was here that I had my first encounter with trade unions, and it was not a favorable introduction, by any means. It was bad enough that there were sitdown strikes and riots in which workers broke windows and machinery in the very plants which might be able to give them work and wages. But when the union leader involved in our factory approached us during the height of the troubles and stated that for a certain sum each month, payable to him, he would see that the workers did not damage our plant—that was too much for me. I saw no reason to bribe anybody for the chance to manufacture goods and provide jobs. If I had to give out extra money, I would have wanted to give it to the workers directly, in the form of higher wages, rather than to a political union leader of those workers for the lining of his own pockets.

I won't go into all the details of the two years the plant was going in Austria. By 1924 it had become an impossible situation, and it looked as if the government might try to take over our plant and all of our machinery. Quickly and quietly we just loaded all our most valuable equipment in trucks and got it out. It was a costly and disillusioning experience. Only one pleasant thing came from it—my connection with German Shepherd dogs, about which I'll tell later.

We maintained our offices in London and Paris, of course, but Mr. Silliman resigned in 1924 and Mr. Hutton went from Paris to take charge of the larger London headquarters. Oh yes, I forgot to mention that in 1920 we had moved our New York offices to the Fifth

Rather skinny but proud of my muscles, I posed in our back yard in Moscow, where I really started my sports activities in earnest.

but one of the home-made medals adorned chest after the first boys' Field Day in Mos- v, Idaho. In my hands is the vaulting pole I ved from a fence rail.

In my barn-loft gym I practiced until I was good enough to run away with a traveling minstrel show and be billed as "The Champion Boy Bag-Puncher of the World."

The glowering young man with hands on hips was the regular quarter-back of Pacific University's football team in 1902 and 1903.

My shoulder muscles had developed considerably since my boyhood days in Moscow. This picture was taken during my first year at Yale, when I won the Intercollegiate wrestling championship.

At Yale Field, starting my run in pole-vaulting practice and using one of the first, not the first, bamboo poles.

Clearing the bar to win the pole vault at the Olympic Games, held in London in 1908.

Winning a place on the American Olympic team was the climax of my athletic career. In the tryouts I broke the world's record for the pole vault.

In 1928, when we sponsored the first sports broadcasts ever heard on a national hookup, I acted as master of ceremonies and interviewed many stars. Here I was with Babe Ruth.

When I raised German Shepherd dogs, in the twenties, I had many champions, but the dog I loved and admired most was Alf, shown with me here.

This circus car demonstrating Erector and other Gilbert toys toured the country in the early twenties and entertained thousands of boys. Its antenna received broadcasts from our transmitter in New Haven, the sixth licensed broadcasting station in the United States.

*The trophy room of my log cabin in the game preserve out-
side New Haven contains many of my prize heads.*

One of my family's favorite spots is the log cabin I built on the grounds of the Preston Mountain Club near Kent, Connecticut.

The battered hat and heavy beard cannot conceal the pride I felt over a record moose shot on a hunting trip to the Kenai Peninsula, Alaska.

One of our most successful promotions for Gilbert American Flyer trains was the Boys' Railroad Club and its series of television programs. This scene shows clearly the realism and accuracy we have always insisted upon in our trains.

On a hunting trip to Alaska in 1939, with Watson and Electra Webb, Mt. Veniaminoff erupted, sending smoke and ashes up 30,000 feet and covering the snow and sea for miles around. Our camp was on a shore of a small lake, seen in the foreground, less than ten miles from the volcano. Electra Webb took this picture.

Avenue Building, which is still one of the chief centers of toy manufacturing firms.

When the business had made a good comeback from the post-war depression and got over the cost of the Austrian venture, it was in excellent shape. By 1926 it reached the two-million-dollar mark again, and kept going up, with profits generally holding up very well. It was a firmly and solidly established business, and I was able to spend a little more time in other affairs. I was busy building our own house, which led to the construction of other houses. I was active in Yale athletics and in the affairs of the Amateur Athletic Union, Intercollegiate A.A.A.A., and American Olympic Committees. I raised dogs, and I finally started going hunting again, after nineteen years. Since each one of these activities was an important part of my life for several decades, I'll have to tell about them separately. When you lead five lives, you can't write about them all at once without getting mixed up. For the moment, I'll stick to the business, which was always Number One.

During the twenties, there were many new products, several new people of importance, and basic changes in the structure of the business. In 1923, I see from the records, Arthur Alling was Secretary and Treasurer, and later in the year was made a vice-president. Also made vice-president was George Adams Wood, a real super-salesman, one of the best I've ever seen. He had been in charge of the very important circus or demonstration-car operation, which was so successful.

One of the mainstays of the company came to New Haven as Sales Manager in 1924. This was Herman

L. Trisch, who had started with the Mysto Manufacturing Company as a supervisor of demonstrators back in
1915. The next year he became a salesman in the northwest territory, and then in the Pacific Coast territory. It
was during this time that I almost made a serious mistake
without realizing it. The sales department had grown too
fast and needed some pruning, so I went over the list of
the personnel with Mac MacCready, who was then sales
manager.

Looking hard for someone we could eliminate, I
came upon Herman Trisch's name on the list. I had met
him at sales meetings, of course, but he was such a quiet
person that I had not noticed him especially. Since he
was little more than a name on a list to me at that time,
I suggested to Mac that perhaps he could be eliminated.

"Now wait a minute," Mac said. "Trisch may be
quiet and sort of retiring, but I think he's just about the
best salesman we've got. If you doubt it, just try writing
a few of the accounts in his territory and find out what
they think of him."

I was willing to take Mac's word about the man,
but his statements aroused my curiosity. I was also eager
to find men in the company with outstanding ability and
to push them along to more important positions. So I
wrote half a dozen accounts on the Coast, and the re-
plies I received really impressed me. Every single store
manager went out of his way to tell me that Herman
Trisch was the best salesman from any firm that called
on them, and that he grew on them the more often he
called.

Well, that had something to do with the fact that

186

in 1917, when we opened an office and showroom in the Phelan Building in San Francisco, I put Trisch in charge. Two years later he moved to Chicago as District Manager of the Middle West. Then in 1924, when we needed a new sales manager, it was Trisch I called on. From that time on he has been increasingly important, increasingly valuable—a real Rock of Gibraltar in this business. I don't see how we could have got along without him. He became a director in 1930, a vice-president in 1940, first vice-president in 1944, and executive vice-president in 1948. An optimist, but a realist, too, he always helped carry us through when things were difficult and worked hard to make good times even better. I've been mighty fortunate to have working with me a few men, devoted and loyal, like Herman Trisch, in whom I could place complete confidence. This is the sort of thing that has made my business so successful and my business life so rewarding, and I can never properly express my appreciation to such men.

During the twenties some important new products were put out, especially in the appliance field. Somehow or other we got into the heating line, starting with an electric heater, a cigarette lighter, and going on later to a toaster, a waffle iron, a heater-fan, a percolator, a corn popper, and a heating pad. This last item was unusual in that it was the first electric pad with which wet heat could be supplied.

As the years went by, however, we found that we could not really merchandise our heating line properly. If we wanted to sell such appliances well, we had to have a whole series of toasters of different sizes and prices, a line of waffle irons and percolators, and so on. It was a separate business in itself, really, so we finally sold the entire group of appliances and kept out of that business.

In 1923 we brought out our first—and I think the first anywhere—portable electric kitchen beater of the Dover eggbeater type. This was done in co-operation with the Wesson Oil people, for there was an attachment on the beater that allowed Wesson Oil, as a shortening, to drip at the proper rate into the mixture being made. Although various improvements were made on this in later years, we were prevented from being the first to bring out the modern type of mixer-beater by another very important tie-up.

This was our juice extractor, which we brought out first under the name of Polar Cub in 1927. But the next year we made a connection with the Sunkist orange people to manufacture for them the first big-selling electric juice extractor, called Sunkist Junior. This was advertised in very big space all over the country and sold millions in the next few years.

The inevitable happened, of course. Somebody thought of combining into one appliance our juice extractor and mixer-beater. We could not do this because of an exclusive arrangement with Sunkist. So others came along and stole that market away from us. Later, of course, when our contract with Sunkist ended, we were able to market such appliances, the first being one called Kitchen-Etta, in 1934, with four power outlets enabling the appliance to beat, chop, extract juice, sharpen knives, sift flower, crush ice, or grind coffee. Ever since that time we have put out mixer-beaters, and today have the only one whose attachments fit easily into place without tipping the machine upside down or changing its position in some way. I have a patent on this type of power outlet for attachments.

Another operation similar to the Sunkist extractor deal, but not nearly so big, was made with the Thompson Malted Milk firm in 1928, using an electric drink mixer we had put out under the Polar Cub name in 1925. In 1931, we made a drink mixer on a stand, and later a regular soda fountain mixer.

All these products used fractional horsepower motors, which meant that they really fitted in with our manufacturing program. That is why they have remained in the Gilbert line, in some form or other, all these years. Another such appliance brought out in the twenties was the first Polar Cub electric hand drill. We've made drills ever since, and have a line of them today.

One interesting experience in merchandising came in connection with our vacuum cleaners, which also use small motors. In 1927 we made a small hand vacuum, and the next year produced a full-size cleaner. At that time most vacuum cleaners were sold by house-to-house canvassers, and there was a very big mark-up. We found out that we could make a perfectly good vacuum cleaner, capable of meeting just about any competition so far as performance was concerned, for a retail price of $10. Since most cleaners sold for around $75 then, we thought we would sweep the market and make a fortune. Who wouldn't want a good vacuum cleaner for $10 instead of $60 or $75?

Well, people just wouldn't believe it. They'd look

189

at it, look at the price, and ask, "Does it have a motor in it?" In big department stores, when a salesman couldn't switch the customer from our cleaner to a more expensive one—on which he made more commission—he would even go to the customer's home the next day and do a real selling job against our vacuum, his argument being mainly that anything selling for so little must be a piece of junk. Actually, after very careful tests, it proved itself to be the equal of just about any vacuum cleaner on the market and longer-lasting than any. But you could not prove it to the stores or a lot of the public. It was priced *too* low, that's all. It taught us a good lesson in pricing, of course. We no longer put out a full-sized vacuum cleaner, which requires rather special selling methods, but we still have the small hand-cleaner that can be sold easily in appliance and department stores.

The A. C. Gilbert Company went on the air in 1928 with the first sports review program ever heard on a network. This was during the fall season, when we did most of our advertising of toys for the Christmas rush. I thought that boys would love a sports program, especially if they could listen to some of their favorite sport stars. So we started a once-a-week program over the National Broadcasting System network. I acted as master of ceremonies, talked about sports, and interviewed big-name guests like Babe Ruth, Chick Meehan, Lawson Robertson, Grantland Rice, and other favorites of the time. During those weeks that we were on the air, Mrs. Gilbert and I came to New York, where we stayed in an apartment, so that I could handle the broadcasts easily. I never thought of it at the time, but somebody recently pointed out that this is probably one of the few instances of a president of a company acting as his own master of ceremonies on a radio series. I enjoyed it, and the program was very popular, judging by the number of letters we received. They poured in by the thousands, asking questions of the stars we announced in advance.

We kept these sports broadcasts going every fall for several years, and when we gave them up, a big beverage company continued them with Grantland Rice as chief commentator. That was really the beginning of sports broadcasts.

In 1932 we went on the air with a series of programs featuring Frank Buck, whose book "Bring 'em Back Alive" had just been a great best seller. I would introduce Frank, and then he'd tell some story about his experiences hunting for wild animals and capturing them. I remember once his telling about a battle between a python and a tiger. The python had wrapped himself around the big cat, but then it turned out that the tiger had been brought back to the States for some zoo. Well, we got a deluge of letters after that one, and most of them asked the same question. "It looked as if the python really had that tiger," they said. "How did he ever get away?"

Frank answered on the next program. "Well, this is kind of embarrassing," he said. "The boys are right— the python did have that tiger dead to rights, and he was a goner. But from a business point of view the tiger would bring me a thousand dollars, and the python was worth only twenty. So I had to shoot him before he killed the tiger."

191

Before the end of the twenties, the company underwent a major financial re-organization. In 1928—significantly just about a year before the beginning of the world's worst depression—I finally succumbed to the arguments of my bankers and several directors of the company that I should diversify my holdings. As it was, everything I had in the world was tied up in the A. C. Gilbert Company. Now that it was so firmly established and approaching the status of a big business, the public would readily take the opportunity to invest in it. And no man of sizable financial holdings, I was told, should have all of his eggs in one basket.

It was a difficult decision to make, because this particular basket was one I had built myself and I had all the confidence in the world in it. I couldn't imagine any place I'd rather have my money invested. But the experts finally persuaded me that spreading my holdings was the sensible thing to do. The Wall Street firm of Shields & Company agreed to buy and to market a minority of the stock of the company using ten times the average earnings for the past ten years as a basis for figuring the price. At the time, I held the big majority of the common stock, with 4,264 shares, while Frank Frisbie had 100 shares, Arthur Alling 300 shares, my brother F.W. 200 shares, George Adams Wood 2 shares, Herman L. Trisch 10 shares, A. L. Richmond 10 shares, and Charles W. Hoyt 88 shares.

The company, which now became legally a new company incorporated in Maryland, issued 100,000 shares of common stock and 25,000 shares of preference stock. The company (the "old" Connecticut one) received 60,000 shares of the common. The preference stock and the other 40,000 shares of common went to Shields & Company. The "old" company then dissolved and the money from Shields was distributed to its stockholders along with the 60,000 shares of common stock of the "new" company. Shields & Company sold the preference stock to the public through the New York Curb Exchange, today the American Stock Exchange. They offered a package deal of one share of preference with one-half share of common for $55.75. Then, as the market was created, they eventually sold the balance of the common.

The issue sold readily because of the excellent standing and record of the company, and I invested the money I received in gilt-edged securities that in most cases managed to weather the depression, but not nearly so well as the A. C. Gilbert Company itself. I would have been much better off, financially, if I had kept all my eggs in that one basket I had made and knew so well. It did far better under stress than many other more famous and supposedly stronger baskets.

One interesting sidelight on this change in the company was the fact that Shields & Company insisted, when the deal was consummated, that I sign a contract with the company for five years at a salary of $50,000 per year. This was only natural because I was, to all intents and purposes, the creative engineer of the business as well as its administrative head, plus contributing significantly to the promotion ideas which put over our products. In the developmental work that went into our appliance line, for instance, I did a great deal of work.

193

I hold about a hundred and fifty patents, in fact, which have been an important asset of the company.

In connection with this sale that brought the public into the ownership of the business, it has been said and written that I have regretted it because I'm always at odds with the minority stockholders. That's not the case at all. My only regrets are that, despite the advice of financial experts, I would have been better off keeping all my holdings in the company. As far as stockholders are concerned, I get along with most of them very well. There has been only one point of difference, really, with a few of them. I have always believed in plowing a large share of the profits back into the business to expand and strengthen it. That is the way I built up the company from a barn to a huge factory. It is the most economical way to expand, provide more jobs, and satisfy more customers with more goods at less cost and of better quality. Some people, chiefly speculators, have said that I ought to pay large dividends and then borrow money from the banks for expansion. We naturally use the facilities of banks often and extensively, as any seasonal business must. But a business should grow and develop from its own resources. Furthermore, I hate like the devil to borrow money, even when I can pay it back soon. If there is a sensible way of avoiding it, I want to. It costs money, too, and reduces profits.

I've always made this company policy plain to stockholders and everyone who asks. I like dividends as much as the next stockholder, of course, but I have one interest beyond that of any stockholder, myself included, and that is the welfare of the company as a whole, and the people who work in it. If I ever forget that primary concern, then in time there will be neither profits nor dividends. People who agree with that policy can buy A. C. Gilbert stock and be happily welcomed as members of the family. I'm sure we will get along well together.

Fifteen

Maraldene

(As you drive north out of the center of New Haven along a street named Ridge Road, you enter a residential district in the suburb of North Haven with increasingly attractive houses. As the street climbs up to the long high ridge from which it takes its name, it is lined with tall trees, and well back from the road sit spacious homes with wide lawns and lovely gardens.)

(At a point where the land slopes down to the west, you come upon a long, low stone wall behind which a thick planting of evergreens and laurel almost obscures the large house on the side of the hill. If you turn into the driveway between two pillars, you see the house, built principally of rough-cut and uneven grey stones. It is a large house and would be imposing except for the fact that it sprawls comfortably along the hillside and, despite its size, seems to belong to its surroundings, as if it had

196

grown up out of the earth along with the trees and shrubbery around it.)

(It is a sound and attractive American version of a Tudor home, built for comfortable and luxurious, but not pretentious, living. Lead-paned casement windows are recessed in thick stone walls, and big fireplaces are found in many rooms. The living room is large enough to accommodate a good crowd but not so large as to make a couple feel lost. There is a beautiful library with bookshelves for walls, a stone terrace overlooking the gardens, a huge playroom in the basement, a wing with comfortable rooms for servants, and a separate garage with an apartment above. Upstairs there are a few touches not only of modernity but of A. C. Gilbert's brand of modernity, noticeable especially in the bathrooms, which have weighing scales flush with the floor, and towel racks with a little switch at one end for turning on a heater inside the rod. Thus towels are warmed slightly for use after the bath or shower.)

(There are Gilbertian touches in the several acres of grounds, too. One is the border of laurel all around the green lawns. Another is a nine-hole golf course ingeniously contrived from a total of nine tees and four greens. More startling, perhaps, is the waterfall, constructed of moss-covered coral and rock at a spot where the land dips sharply so that a rocky fall of fifteen feet looks completely natural. Nature did not provide a stream of water, however, so A.C. had to take care of that. Fifty feet below the waterfall there is a well, with a pump, and underground pipes lead from it to the top of the fall. When the pump is turned on—it can be done from the *house—water falls in a silvery stream, bouncing over the rocks in a fashion that nature itself would admire, to collect in a small pool at the bottom. From this point, it is pumped up to the top of the waterfall again. Thus the same water is used over and over again, and the well, serving only as a sort of primer, is not pumped dry. Spotlights, buried artfully among the rocks, illuminate the fall at night.)*

(The pump also supplies a full-size swimming pool closer to the house, next to one rather formal garden. But down in the woods behind the broad green lawn is water provided by nature, a small stream winding its way through the property. And here you will find the unmistakable Gilbert touch, for the stream has been dammed to form several small ponds, near one of which is a log cabin.)

We lived here at Maraldene for more than thirty years, and loved it. We got the name by combining the first syllables of Mary's name and mine, and adding "dene" which is old English for a house on the side of a hill. This was just farm country back in 1921 when I bought it, and people thought we were foolish to move way out of town. And now look at the neighborhood—completely built up with fine homes, one of the best residential neighborhoods in the country.

We and our dear friends, the F. O. Williamses, bought this property together, but then they decided not to build on it, and I bought their half. Originally it was between thirty-five and fifty acres here on the west side of Ridge Road, but now there are only four or five acres with the house. What I did with the rest of it, I'll tell you in a minute.

This first home was built on contract, but I became so interested that I watched every process of the building and learned a lot about it. Maraldene was built just the way we wanted it—an Elizabethan home that we wanted to make as bright and happy as that wonderful period, with its gay chintzes and shining brass and beautiful furniture. Naturally, we wanted to furnish it with Elizabethan pieces, too, and my business trips to London gave me the opportunity to do this. It all started when Mary wanted me to bring back an old clock for the hall, and at the American Club in London, where I stayed, I met a man who was buying old English furniture, and he helped me. Later I met Charles Duveen, brother of the famous Sir Joseph Duveen, whom I consider the greatest salesman in the world. His brother Charles was not far behind him, either. He took an interest in our place, helped us find many wonderful pieces of furniture for it, and in the end had a great deal to do with the interior decoration of it.

You don't collect a houseful of fine antique furniture in a hurry, of course, so we were busy buying, changing, exchanging, and trading Elizabethan furniture for many years, in the course of which we acquired many pieces that we have loved and loved to live with. And the search for the things we wanted was fascinating, too. Once when Mary went to England with me, we stayed at the Charles Duveens' home, a beautiful old Elizabethan place, and went on a trip with them looking at "museums."

These museums in England are really old homes containing many wonderful antiques. Some of the owners are actual dealers, but they all have many pieces that they do not want to sell at all, but just keep in their "museums." People can come and look, of course, but it is hard to buy any of these museum pieces except in very hard times, for the owners look upon them as money in the savings bank.

Once Mr. and Mrs. Duveen and Mary and I went on a trip and stopped at Shakespeare's home, Stratford on Avon, where there was a dealer Mr. Duveen wanted to see. We asked if there was a museum there, as we always did, and went to look at the collection of antiques in a fine old home. While we were there, Charles saw an old bed-warming pan with a brass handle. He had seen only one or two such pieces in his life, and knew exactly what estate this one had originally come from and its whole history.

Charles Duveen saw how much Mary and I loved this beautiful piece of brass, and he knew how well it would fit into our own home, hanging next to the big fireplace. So he told the owner a fine story, explaining about the fine Elizabethan home we had in America, and the excellent pieces we had collected so far, and how our place would be the perfect home for the rare brass warming pan. But the owner absolutely refused to sell.

We left the house quite disappointed, and when we got outside Mrs. Duveen said, "Charlie, I've never seen you fall down before when we wanted something as badly as we wanted that warming pan."

"I couldn't really do a good job," he said, "with you people around. You let me go back alone and I'll get it, all right."

Well, we drove down and parked the car in front of Shakespeare's old home, while Charles went back into the house. We waited about an hour and then we saw him walking down the street with that big brass warming pan over his shoulder and smiling happily. We all had a good time celebrating our acquisition of such a fine piece.

Just as the interior furnishing of Maraldene was something that took a number of years, so was landscaping and fixing the grounds. I built the swimming pool and the waterfall and laid out the golf course, built a house for the gardener, and a greenhouse. We laid out gardens and planted trees, and at this time I fell in love with laurel, the Connecticut state flower. It was while looking for laurel to transplant to the grounds at Maraldene that I ran onto the property that I later acquired to make the game preserve. I dammed the brook to make several ponds. I called them lakes, of course—the same kind of exaggeration or wishful thinking that makes me call our present home Mountain View, I suppose. Anyway, they were big enough for me to stock them with trout, and we had some good fishing there until the community really became built up.

Down in the woods near one of the ponds I built my first log cabin, a small affair made of cedar logs. It had a nice fireplace, and we furnished it with Indian things that made it very attractive. Four bunks were built into the cabin, and sometimes the children and I would spend the night there, having a wonderful time being pioneers out in the wilds.

Maraldene was a marvelous place for the children, and they all loved it. We had some awfully good times there together. No matter how busy I had been during the years of building up the business, when I worked days, nights, and weekends, I always managed to spend a little time with them every day, usually reading them stories when they went to bed. We always had dinner together, except when there were grown-up guests, and then I read to them. Actually, I told them the Brer Rabbit stories, rather than reading them, because I knew most of them by heart. My father had read them to me when I was little.

One Christmas when the children were still young I arranged a pretty spectacular stunt. They were having a Christmas party, with a lot of their friends in, and I hired an airplane and a parachute jumper from Hartford to fly down over our place. The jumper was dressed up as Santa Claus, with a big pack of presents on his back. The plane flew at about fifteen hundred feet over our back yard, and "Santa Claus" jumped. There wasn't much wind, so he was able to come down perfectly, just where he was supposed to. Then he passed out presents to all the kids.

Maraldene was quite an estate by the time I got through, but even before then I started selling land around the edges and building houses on some of the tracts.

This activity started when, shortly after we had moved into Maraldene, the owner of the big peach orchard across the street, on the east side of Ridge Road, telephoned me from Florida. Mr. Tiley had been involved in Florida real estate and was caught when the bubble burst there. He wanted to sell the old peach orchard, consisting of twenty-five to thirty acres. I was pinched a bit by the depression myself then and did not have a lot of ready cash, but I was tempted. For one thing, I wanted to do all I could to make sure that the neighborhood developed into one of fine houses. And I was confident that, even if it seemed way out in the country then, it would grow into a fine community. The city was growing that way and it was only a matter of time. So I offered Mr. Tiley $25,000 for the property and he accepted it at once.

I laid out the tract, got a bulldozer and put through a road or two, set up building lines and decided just what restrictions should be placed on homes built there to insure the high standard of the community. Then my brother and I found an underwriting syndicate to take the property off our hands. This was a group of successful young executives in New Haven anxious to find a good spot to build fine homes for themselves. They paid me exactly what I had paid for the property, and accepted all the restrictions I had placed upon it. It was a good buy for them, and it was good for the town of North Haven. It was good for me because it made certain that the homes around Maraldene would be first class.

But in a way I was a little disappointed. The building of my own home had aroused my interest in construction, and I wanted to do something in the field.

Therefore, when Mr. Tiley offered to sell me another piece of land, east of the peach orchard, I bought it. I called it the Old Orchard development and got to work. I laid out the entire tract for lots and homes, put through roads, doing much of the actual physical work myself. Each road had a parkway down the middle, with shrubs and trees planted, and I did everything I could to make it attractive.

There were two old farmhouses on the property which I remodeled and rebuilt as modern homes. I sold them both before they were even ready, and they are still fine homes today. That started me off, and from that day to this I have never really stopped my building operations a single day. From 1921 to the present I have been building houses, sometimes with a large crew of men, sometimes keeping only a small nucleus of three or four. Some of the houses were built under contract, but many of them I built myself, acting as my own contractor and often as my own architect.

For my first houses, and for the more pretentious houses I built later, I had as architect my old friend Bob Booth. We worked together well, and even when he did the full architectural job, many of my ideas were incorporated into the homes. I found out that in some way my imagination invested the houses with a quality that made people like them. There was always something a little different about them, and I was able to anticipate somewhat the trend of public desires as to housing.

The Old Orchard Road development was not made overnight, but extended over a period of several years. I found the work a diversion from my business, one that I enjoyed more than many men enjoy games for relaxation. I can't say that I have made a lot of money out of my real estate and housing ventures. I could have made a fortune, perhaps, if in each case I had kept aside some of the land for long-time investment. Some of the lots I sold on Old Orchard Road for $500 later sold for $5,000, for instance. But somebody had to start it, when nobody else wanted to begin such a project way out in the country, and I had to keep prices attractive. As time went on, I built more than a hundred fifty houses.

More satisfying by far than any profit was the pleasure I got from seeing people enjoy the neighborhoods I had developed, the houses I had built. I don't think I ever failed to sell a house before it was completed, and so far as I know I never had a dissatisfied customer. Oh, things went wrong, of course, but I always did something about them.

When the Old Orchard Road development was well under way, I realized that I could sell portions on the outside of the Maraldene property without detracting in any way from the beauty or usefulness of our own estate. So I started the Kent Place and Salem Road developments, which were obviously named by me—the first from my second log cabin at Kent, Connecticut, and the latter from the city where I was born. I put a great deal of thought into planning this development so that it would be accessible and secluded at the same time. Around the outside of the property I did a lot of planting, so that it was screened from the outside in a natural way. All roads inside the development were dead-end roads with big circles at the end to make turning easy.

It was a wonderful place to bring up children, and the families who lived there and still live there love their homes and their community. I never pass by it but that I feel a deep glow of satisfaction from the knowledge that I had a hand in creating this fine American residential neighborhood, in which countless families have lived fully and happily and where children have grown up in safety, with good places to play, and surrounded by natural beauty.

Sixteen

Dog's Life

(*Before A.C. goes home in the afternoon, after working
around the game preserve or inspecting a new house he
is building, he stops by his kennels near the farm to pick
up the two dogs that are his closest personal pets at this
time—Buster and Susie. He stops the car outside the
long, low building with its big playyard for the dogs,
and steps inside, to re-appear in a moment with two
prancing, jumping, smiling, tail-wagging animals. They
are both pointers, white with small brown or black spots,
sleek and muscular and clean. When greeting their
master, however, they seem to be bundles of tight
springs, bounding, twisting, leaping around him, then
scrambling into the car's back seat. Here Susie gets on
the left side, but Buster wants to get on that side, so he
pushes Susie out of the way. She tries to crawl over him,*

207

slips to the floor, clambers up on the seat again. And all the time two long, snakelike tails are wagging hard, mouths are open with tongues hanging out, and eyes are shining.)

(Then A.C. gets into the front seat, behind the wheel, and both dogs decide it will be more fun up there with him. They leap over the back of the seat, knocking each other over on the way, try to kiss A.C. in the excess of their affection and happiness. He orders both dogs into the back seat, and they comply immediately and eagerly, but sit down with signs of impatience, as if asking A.C. to hurry and start the car and go somewhere interesting.)

(When A.C. stays at home in the afternoon, Fred Toller brings Buster and Susie there about four o'clock. As they dash down the hall and into A.C.'s room, the same sort of scene is enacted except that here there is more room for cavorting. If A.C. is alone, the joyous reunion after a separation of eight or nine hours may last ten minutes. Even if A.C. is busy with a visitor, however, he takes time out for a warm greeting so the dogs won't be hurt. Then he tells them to drop, and Susie trots to a commodious basket, where she curls up, and Buster lets himself down on the floor. But both keep their eyes on A.C. for an indication that they may get up and play again. After an hour, they are calm enough to sit quietly beside A.C.'s chair and slip a head under his hand for a little quiet petting.)

(The surprising part of A.C.'s relations with his dogs is the combination of love and horseplay with strict obedience to his orders. He does not like badly trained

208

*dogs, but on the other hand he does not like dogs so over-
trained that they are frightened, timid, or inclined to
suppress their feelings of love and happiness. He obtains
the happy medium with his own dogs by insisting on
obedience to his orders while giving them all the affection they want and plenty of play.)*

I've been in love with dogs all my life. The first
dog I ever owned was a little cocker spaniel when I was
a boy in Salem. I can remember him as if I saw him
yesterday, because he was my constant companion for
many years. I don't think he was particularly well
trained, because I first became really interested in the
training and intelligence of dogs when I worked on the
farm at Hubbard and saw what wonderful work those
well-trained shepherd dogs did. My uncle gave me one
of them, and I took him home to Moscow with me.

When I went east to Yale, I naturally had to have
a dog, so I bought a bull terrier in honor of the college.
He was a good companion, warm and affectionate, and
I was very attached to him, but he wasn't really as smart
as many other dogs I've had.

One of the smartest was a circus dog. This was
some years after I was out of college, and I had gone to
Philadelphia to officiate in a track meet. While I was
there, I saw an advertisement in *Billboard* placed there
by a man with a circus-dog act. He could not take care of
his dogs any more, for some reason, and wanted to sell
them. I went out to see them and bought a very smart
little dog who could turn a beautiful somersault. I took
him back to New Haven and became quite attached to

him, but he missed his master and I could never quite get the feeling that he was truly my dog.

I really got into the dog business in a big way as a result of our starting a factory in Vienna. Once when I was there, the head of the plant, Hugo Klagsbrunn, took me to some dog shows and field trials featuring German Shepherd dogs, often called "police" dogs in this country. I was taken at once with their beauty and even more with their remarkable intelligence. Any dog that had earned the right to put the letters P.H. after his name—meaning Police Hound—could answer to one hundred separate commands!

German Shepherds were tremendously popular in this country after the first World War, and a great many were brought over here. Mr. Klagsbrunn brought me a fine dog named Vigo, the first Shepherd I owned. I became very attached to him and had him for many years. Once he was ill with distemper, and I nursed him personally until he had regained his health completely.

Vigo was a good dog, but he won no top honors when I showed him. Some of the finest dogs from Europe had been brought here and he faced very tough competition at the Westminster Kennel Club show in Madison Square Garden and other places. When I saw those other dogs, I decided that I wanted something even better than Vigo, not because I was particularly interested in collecting blue ribbons but because I wanted to own and get to know a truly great Shepherd dog.

That's when I built the Maraldene kennels and really went into business in a big way. They were fine kennels that I put up on the place, and I had two good men to run them—William Toller and his brother Fred, who had recently come to this country from Germany. Bill was a real professional trainer of dogs; they both understood dogs, won them over, and were kind to them.

One of the first dogs I bought after establishing the kennels was probably the greatest dog I ever owned —certainly the dog I admired and loved the most. He was called Alf, but his full name was Alf von Tollensetal, and he carried the coveted P.H. after his name. He had been trained in Germany by a famous woman trainer, but at the time I bought him was owned by an Englishman. I paid the first really big price I ever laid out for a dog—$2,500. In view of his fine training, and the fact that he had been champion of England and second in the World Von Stephanitz Award—the supreme honor among Shepherd dogs—that was not too high a price, by any means. And during the years I owned him, he earned that back many times over in stud fees.

I owned Alf for the rest of his life, and I find myself incapable of finding the words that will describe him adequately, that will tell how great was my affection for him. He was a great show dog, a great field-trial dog, and a wonderful companion as well. He used to sit by my chair every night while I worked. He was always on guard to protect me, but when people came in and I told him they were friends, he relaxed and treated them almost as if they were members of the family.

The whole family loved Alf more than any other dog we ever owned. He was a sharp dog in many ways, but absolutely dependable. A wonderful playmate for

the children, who were still small then, he would rough-
house with them for hours, having a glorious time, and
never caused the slightest worry or trouble no matter
what they did to him.

I remember one wonderful story about Alf and
the children. Mary went out to the Coast to visit her
family, and the children asked whom I was going to
sleep with while she was away. I answered, "Alf," without thinking much about it, then saw the looks of amaze-
ment and disbelief in their eyes. I felt pretty sure they
were going to check up on me. The next morning I was
awake before they were, and when I heard them tiptoe-
ing down the hall with the nurse, Ellen, I softly called to
Alf, who usually slept on the floor, and had him get into
bed and put his head on the pillow. Being a P.H., he
obeyed every command instantly, of course. I covered
him up, then quickly got into bed and closed my eyes,
muttering to Alf at the same time, "Tod!" I gave all commands in German, and I knew that when I told him to
play dead he would not move, no matter what happened.

I heard the door open softly and knew that three
heads were peeking into the room. There were little
gasps of astonishment and whispers to the effect that
yes, Dad really was sleeping with Alf!

The climax of this story really came a little later,
when the nurse took the children somewhere on the
street car. The kids were still full of the tale and immediately spread it to everyone on the street car, and the
whole car was convulsed with the story of how A. C.
Gilbert was sleeping with his dog Alf while his wife was
away.

212

Alf became champion of America, and came in second at the National Field Trial championship. He would have won but for one unfortunate incident. I was so busy that I could not go to the show myself, so two of my men took him. They neglected to feed him at the proper time, and when the show started Alf was terribly hungry. Now, one of the many requirements of a well-trained Shepherd dog is that he must not take food from a stranger, and one of the tests was to place a piece of liver near his nose and leave it there for five minutes. Well, Alf sniffed and sniffed at the delicious liver, and his mouth watered, and he looked at it hungrily. He knew that he should not touch it, and he would not have gone near it if he had had any food that day at all. But just before the five minutes were up, he reached out and grabbed it, bolting it down in a hurry. He had been first in every other trial, but that kept him from winning.

I remember one competition Alf entered against a bunch of bloodhounds. This was a stake trial, in which stakes are driven out in the field the night before, one for each dog in the competition. Then a different person walks from each stake out into the woods about a mile, leaving three articles at different places on the way. The next morning the dogs are brought to the stakes, and each dog is supposed to follow the trail of the person from his stake, bringing back the three items dropped and no others. Alf was always the first one back with his three objects, even against such specialists as bloodhounds. It was a great delight to watch him work.

I recall one sad incident in connection with Alf. The woman who had trained him wrote me a letter, after

I had owned Alf for several years, saying that she was coming to this country to act as judge in one of the big shows. Alf was too old by this time to show any more, and she knew it, but she asked if I might bring him to the Maraldene bench at the show so that she could see him. She had spent three hours a day for two and a half years with him, training him, and had never forgotten what a wonderful dog he was.

I brought Alf in to the show all right, and when the woman approached the bench and saw him, there was a wonderful light in her eyes. I knew just how she felt because I loved him so much, too. Then the terrible thing happened. As she approached him eagerly, Alf curled back his lips and snarled at her. She was amazed. She talked to him and tried to get him to remember her, but there was no friendliness in Alf until I told him she was a friend. I've never seen anyone quite so heartbroken as she was.

This incident proved to me what I have observed over the years, that the memories of most dogs are not nearly so long as many people think. It has been my experience that after six months with a new master who treats his pet well, a dog has just about forgotten the old master. Sometimes it takes longer, but dogs do forget, and rather quickly.

The most famous Shepherd I ever owned and undoubtedly the best known Shepherd dog in the world, was Asta von Kaltenweide, Sch. H., international champion of the world in 1922, 1923, and 1924. I made her American Grand Champion in 1926, and she won the coveted Von Stephanitz Award in the same year. Asta became the standard for all show dogs because she had a conformation better than any other, combining all the best features of the Shepherd in the most harmonious form. To this day, Shepherds are still judged by the standard set by Asta, as the ideal dog of the breed.

Asta was a wonderful pet, too. She wasn't a watchdog like Alf. Once, in fact, when my son Al came home from Andover Academy with some friends they arrived late at night when everyone in the house was asleep. They had to step over Asta to get to their rooms and she paid no attention at all.

Asta cost me more money than any dog I ever owned—$6,500, but her pups by Alf brought big prices, and she won many cash prizes in different shows, so that I got back considerably more than the purchase price. Later, a movie star offered me $12,000 for her, but I turned the offer down. When she died, I gave her body to the Peabody Museum at Yale, where she was mounted and still stands—the perfect Shepherd dog.

I had many other fine Shepherds at the Maraldene Kennels. There was Klodo von Boxberg, Sch. H. who had been champion of Germany and of Czechoslovakia. One of my favorites was Asta von Bodman, but she was a sharp dog devoted to one person only. The rest of the family didn't really appreciate her because she could not be depended on if friends came to the house when I was away. But she was a beautiful dog, and won four straight wins in four shows.

At one of these shows I had quite an experience. It was at the New England Specialty show in New Bedford and I took her there myself. I got permission from

215

the manager, because of her good training, to keep her in my hotel room with me. Well, when the show was over and we returned to the room, the dog lay down under the bed while I packed my bag. Then I called for a bellboy, who came into the room without knowing there was any dog around. I forgot about her training and told the boy to take the bag. He took it and turned around for the door—and Asta von Bodman was on him. She got him by the pants and ripped the seat right out of them before I could order her off. The poor bellboy was terrified, but luckily his skin was not even scratched. I bought him a new suit of clothes and gave him a little something, apologized and explained to the manager, and felt lucky to get out of the incident so easily.

There were many other well-known dogs that I raised and still others that I trained during the ten or twelve years I had the Maraldene Kennels. For two years I was president of the Shepherd Dog Club of America, and busy with dog shows all over the east. Why did I give up the kennels then? Well, there were several reasons. Some of my greatest dogs died, for one thing. And by that time the popularity of this breed had died down considerably in this country. Shepherd dogs were considered too sharp, possibly because many partially trained and badly trained dogs had been brought to this country at the height of their popularity. And styles change in dogs as in everything else.

I was fed up with the show business, for another thing. I found that people in this field were jealous and petty. I had expected that they would have a sporting attitude similar to that I had found in other sports, but there was not a drop of that spirit in the dog-show business in my time. I was happy to get away from it.

I might still have raised Shepherd dogs for my own enjoyment, however, had it not been for another interest that developed during the twenties. I went back to hunting again. One of my first hunting trips was with Fred Williams, who while he was alive was one of the finest marksmen in this country. He took me out to Missouri for some duck hunting and it was there I became acquainted with Spanish pointers, or rather American pointers.

That's when I bought my first pointers, and from that time on to the present that's the only kind of dog I've raised. I haven't shown any of these dogs, though I've had many fine ones, because I am not interested in that aspect of the business. I want my dogs for practical use, for hunting, and for companionship.

One of the fine hunting dogs I have now is Buddy, just about the most photogenic dog you've ever seen. He's a joy to watch, and I have many fine pictures of him. He has even been on the covers of magazines.

Many of the great guns who have shot at my game preserve comment more on the way my dogs work than on the fine shoot. They cover a field so methodically, "like a vacuum cleaner," as someone said.

One of my greatest loves, among all the dogs I've had, was a pointer named Lassie. She was with me almost everywhere I went, loved to go in the car with me, or hunting with me. She would ride quietly in the canoe with me when I went fishing, and would get just about as excited as I was when I caught a trout. I think Lassie knew me better than any person who ever lived. She even knew how my mind worked. Sometimes, when we'd be out hunting together, my mind would begin to wander to the business or other things, and Lassie knew it in a moment, through some kind of extra sense she had. And the moment she saw that my mind wasn't on my hunting, she'd take off for a run of her own, until I missed her and called her back to attention again.

Lassie and some of the other pointers I've owned have made my recent years very happy indeed. A dog is always glad to see you when you come home, no matter how tired or depressed you might be. You can scold your dog, and punish him, but he'll still come up and nuzzle close for a little affection. I don't know what my life would have been without dogs.

Before I leave the subject, however, I must tell about my St. Bernard. I had always wanted one of these magnificent animals. When I was a boy I had read about their heroic rescues of mountaineers lost in the snowy Alps, about their strength and intelligence, their faithfulness and gentleness with children. Although I'd had many different kinds of wonderful dogs, the long-buried desire for a St. Bernard came alive when I saw an ad for one in the paper, and I decided that my children should enjoy this great good fortune that I had missed. I bought the dog and brought him home to Maraldene.

He was a beautiful dog, all right, a mountain of strength and dignity, with every good quality of dogdom shining from his big eyes. He looked wonderful on the lawn at Maraldene, where there was plenty of room for him to roam and run and play with the children. He was as gentle as a lamb with them, and loved them from the first time he saw them. He loved them so much, in fact, that he showed his affection by rubbing against them, often knocking them down in the process, and nuzzling them lovingly. Every time he nuzzled, he left a smear of drool on their clothes, and he seemed particularly affectionate after they had dressed in their best outfits. Mary began to dislike the St. Bernard.

I was beginning to agree with her when we brought him in the house for the first time. It was like having a Shetland pony indoors, even in the big rooms at Maraldene, and the unerring aim of his tail made him more destructive than a cyclone. I could never figure out why he wagged his tail in friendly fashion just when his rear end was aimed at a table with a fine vase and other precious bric-a-brac. One sweep of that bushy bulldozer and the table was bare!

We built a house for the St. Bernard down near the garage. It looked almost as large as a summer cottage by the beach. At first he was lonesome and howled considerably, and his howl was one that could shake the rafters, but our neighbors were so far away that they were not bothered much. His loudest noise was made when he ate, and he ate tremendous quantities. No matter how much food we piled into his huge metal pan, he gobbled it up and then pushed the pan all over the place with his nose trying to get the last crumb. We had to stop feeding him near the garage, where the pan scraping over the concrete made a fearful clatter.

Such strength as this dog possessed should be put to use, I decided, so we got a little dogcart in which he could pull the children. He was patience itself as we harnessed him to it, and when he pulled the children happily around the yard in the pretty cart, I felt inclined to forget the unexpected drawbacks I had discovered in the beast. Passing cars stopped so people could admire the sight, and I beamed when I heard them exclaim about the beautiful St. Bernard.

Then on about the fourth cart trip, the dog's strength and high spirits got the better of his judgment, and he started racing. The kids squealed and he ran faster, until the cart tipped over and the children were thrown out. One of them was hurt pretty badly and was in bed several days. This just about finished the St. Bernard for us, but my old dream was dying hard, and I kept him until one night when I woke up with sounds of a terrible dog fight near the garage. I rushed down and found that one of my police dogs had got out, and the St. Bernard had gone after him. In separating them I was accidentally bitten in the leg. I never was sure which dog was guilty, but I preferred to blame the St. Bernard. I was laid up in the house for a week.

When I was back on my feet, I put an ad in the *New Haven Register* offering a wonderful St. Bernard for sale at a very reasonable price. That evening I received a phone call.

"I hope I have the right number," a man said in a thin, high-pitched voice. "Is this dog the beautiful St. Bernard I've seen in a yard out on Ridge Road?"

I said it was. The man explained that ever since he was a boy and had read stories about St. Bernards saving men in the Alps, he had wanted one, and his wife felt the same way. I knew I had my man, all right, and when he said he could not pay much for a fine dog like that I insisted that I would let him go very cheaply because I was concerned only with finding a good home for him. The deluded purchaser told me that he was ticket puncher at the entrance gate at the railroad station and did not make much money but would do almost anything to own a fine St. Bernard.

"Have you got a yard?" I asked.

"Yes, we've got a back yard. Why? Isn't the dog housebroken?"

"Frankly, I don't know," I said. "We don't keep him in the house. But he's kennel broken, I know that. And he shouldn't be kept in a house at all—he's too big. You'd have to keep him in the yard. And I've got a house for him that I'll throw in, too."

Well, we settled it then and there, although we didn't come to a decision about price. I wasn't worrying about that. I just wanted to get rid of the dog. So I called Joe, my kennel man, and we loaded house, feeding pan, and St. Bernard into a truck and drove to the address the man had given me. As we stopped in front of the house, I began to get worried, for it was one of a row of small identical houses, close together and with no yard that I could see.

The dog looked beautiful as we led him up to the door. We had brushed him till his coat gleamed and, most important, we had smeared his mouth and lips with alum to stop the drooling. The man opened the door and we stepped inside the little house. Immediately I gave the dog the one order he obeyed—"Drop!" He lay down obediently, and it was a good thing, for as I looked around the living room I saw that it was filled with tiny figures and vases and statuettes and such on end tables, coffee tables, and shelves.

The owner of the house was busy admiring the St. Bernard and calling to his wife who was upstairs. As she came down she gazed at the majestic creature, threw her arms around him, and sighed to her husband, "Oh, do you really think we can actually own a wonderful dog like that?" He nuzzled them lovingly as they petted him, and I was happy to see that the alum was still effective —not a trace of drool!

I looked out the back window and saw a small yard, wondering how much space would be left after we put the doghouse there. But that's where he would have to be, I told the people, for he was certainly too big to be kept indoors. They agreed, but wanted to settle the price. I could see they longed for that dog more than anything in the world, so I said fifty dollars would do— far less than the value of the animal. They looked at each other, hesitated, looked fondly at the dog, and then said they really couldn't afford it, though they realized it was a low price.

"Well, make it twenty-five dollars," I said. "What I'm most interested in is finding a good home for him, where he'll be loved."

"Oh, we'll love him, all right," they said happily, and the matter was settled. Joe and I put the house in the back yard. I gave the people the dog's feeding pan, but suggested that they place it inside a cardboard box so it wouldn't make so much noise. Then we left.

222

When I got home I warned the family not to answer any phone calls at all. The phone started ringing about half an hour after I arrived, and kept on ringing at regular intervals. I knew what it was about, so nobody took up the receiver. About six o'clock in the morning, however, it started again, and I knew I could not postpone the inevitable any longer. I answered the phone and heard the meek and harassed voice of the man who had bought the St. Bernard.

"Mr. Gilbert, will you *please* come and take this dog back?" the poor fellow pleaded. "I don't want my money back or anything—just take the dog."

"Why, what's the matter?" I asked, trying to seem surprised.

"Everything's the matter!" the man wailed. "The dog started howling the moment you left and kept at it for hours. The neighbors complained and complained, and finally they called the police. When the police came, we brought the dog inside the house, thinking that would keep him quiet. But he still howled, no matter what we did. He wandered all over the house and he wouldn't obey us when we told him to drop. Every time he walked past a table he knocked everything off it with his tail. He even knocked down lamps, shelves, and broke a leg off one of the end tables! And my God, Mr. Gilbert, I thought you said he was housebroken!"

"I didn't say that," I insisted. "I said I didn't know, but that he was kennel broken."

"Well, I can tell you—he isn't housebroken. And it's like having an elephant in the house—an elephant, I tell you, not a Shetland pony. My wife's gone to the hospital with a nervous breakdown, and I can't go to my job with this animal here, and the place is a wreck. Please come and take this dog away!"

There was only one thing to do—go and get the dog. When we got there we saw that the man hadn't exaggerated a bit. The living room was a wreck, with broken dishes and ornaments and even furniture on the floor, and it stank like a stable. There was no sign of the wife, although I doubted that she was in the hospital.

Joe and I took the dog and his house and pan back to Maraldene. Meanwhile, there was a dog show in Hartford, and I had Joe take the St. Bernard there. He won first prize and a big rosette as best in his class, and Joe put the rosette on his own lapel when he came back to New Haven by train. He got the dog from the baggage car and started to lead him out through the station. There, at the gate, was our friend whose house and perhaps marriage had almost been ruined. He saw Joe and the dog—and the rosette—from some distance, and as Joe approached he pointed to the rosette and said that we had won first prize of $1,000 in the Hartford Show.

Our little friend said, "I don't care whether he won $5,000. Don't bring him through this station! Get that dog away from here! Take him out through the freight station." The ticket puncher was obviously shaken up just by the sight of that beautiful St. Bernard.

I finally sold the dog to someone out of town and, although I waited fearfully for telephone calls for the next week, none came. Toll calls were too expensive, I guess. Anyway, I had managed to get rid of my prize-winning St. Bernard, the home-wrecker.

Seventeen

Back to the Outdoors

(Going west from the little town of Kent, Connecticut, the road heads up into the row of rolling mountains, part of the Berkshire range, that run along the boundary between New York and Connecticut. Houses and farms grow smaller and farther apart, as the hills rise up sharply on either side of the road and a stream beside it, and the country looks wooded and wild. A narrow road, not easily noticed, branches off to the left, marked by a small sign saying "Private Road—Preston Mountain Club." Turning and winding, the road climbs rather steeply, tunneling most of the way through thick woods and crossing and recrossing a brook that found this route down the mountain a few hundred years ago.)

(After passing two cabins in the woods, you turn across a narrow wooden bridge and pull up in front of

225

A. C. Gilbert's place, a long and low cabin of big chestnut logs, built against the side of the mountain. As you stop the motor of the car, you hear at once the sound of the rushing brook over which you have just crossed. Just above the little bridge, it falls about fifty feet in a series of leaps over rocks. Under the bridge it begins to quiet down as it moves into a rock-rimmed pool big enough for a short dip if not a swimming race, but usually too cold for any but rugged souls. Alongside the pool is a broad flagstone terrace from which doors lead into the living room of the cabin. The pool ends with another waterfall that makes a pleasant roar and sends up a fine misty spray.)

(The cabin itself is constructed of thick, long chestnut logs, with a roof of hand-made cedar shakes. As you step inside the thick front door, you see a stairway leading to two bedrooms on the second floor. Its steps are made of split logs and its railing of long chestnut poles. The post at the bottom took A.C. many hours in the woods to find, for it is the trunk of a tree, naturally curved so that it leads into the railing gracefully, while its roots seem to grow right into the floor. Farther along the hall there is a bedroom on the left, a large kitchen on the right. Straight ahead and down two steps you see the big living room, a beautiful room of perfect proportions.)

(In the center of the wall on your left is a big fireplace whose stones have been selected with an eye to beauty of texture, color, and shape. On either side of the fireplace, windowed doors lead to the terrace beside the pool, and another row of windows is cut into the opposite wall. At the far end of the room two bunks are

226

built into the wall, on either side of a door leading to a screened porch. Above the bunks and across the end of the room, which otherwise extends up to the roof, there is a balcony, and beyond it another bedroom, which is situated over the porch.)

(How do you get up there? By climbing a ladder against the bunk wall, and going through a trapdoor in the floor of the balcony. It is a room particularly prized by children, who inevitably prefer trapdoors and ladders to the more conventional stairway.)

(Mary Gilbert, who has no interest in hunting or fishing and is no fanatic about the outdoors, says, "I love the cabin at Kent as much as any place we've ever had. We've been coming here weekends and some vacations for more than twenty years, and I'm always ready to go again on a minute's notice. We've had some wonderful times here.")

Mary's right. We love this place and have from the very beginning. I built it back in 1930, and by that time I was beginning to return to my old love, the outdoors. I was going fishing and hunting again. I had started at Maraldene, of course, with the cabin there, fishing in the ponds I built, and hunting for quail in the thick woods below the house. Then I used to go over to the Connecticut River, near Essex, where I shot wild duck and rail.

In the last few years of the twenties I began searching for laurel to plant at Maraldene and found the tract of land that later became the Paradise Game Preserve. It was full of game, and I obtained permission from the various farmers who owned it to hunt there in season.

All this hunting was fairly close to home. The first trip of any length came in 1925, when Fred Williams, a lifelong friend of mine, took me out to Missouri for some quail shooting. That trip was all the more important because that's when I got my first pointer dogs.

Fred was president of the Preston Mountain Club, where my cabin near Kent is built. I joined the Club in 1929 and began to spend more and more time there whenever I had a chance. Right from the beginning I was getting my white-tail deer every year. The partridge shooting was and still is wonderful, and in those days the wild-duck shooting—mostly blacks—was fine. Later we began to stock the place with pheasants.

Fred Williams was a better shot than I was, one of the best in the country, but I had the advantage of him because of my wonderful pointer, Lassie, who knew me so well. She was so good because she worked *with* me and not just by herself. I could always tell when she was near birds, so I was ready to shoot before Fred knew what was going on. That's how I could hold my own with him. I hesitate to comment on the number of partridge we shot in those first years I belonged to the Club.

I had some great deer drives at the Club and some wonderful still-hunting, too. You can imagine what a wonderful diversion from business, what perfect relaxation it was to go up to the Club and hunt or fish and be with Ed Chase, who is head guide, a wonderful man to be with, a great hunter, a naturalist, and an optimist. Another important association I made at that time was with Jerry Gerard, another great outdoors man who loved the Preston Mountain Club, and with whom I have hunted and had good times for many years.

I started the game preserve in Hamden and built my cabin there, giving me another place to hunt even closer to home. But in the spring of 1933 I had the fever to go away on a real big-game hunting expedition, the sort of camping trip I used to take with my father up into the Cascade Mountains. At that time I met a man at the Preston Mountain Club who started me on the first big trip in so many years. He was Thierry Mallet, a great game hunter who had served his apprenticeship in the north country for the fur firm of Revillon Freres, of which he was then president. He has written some mighty interesting books, and became a great friend of mine.

Thierry Mallet introduced me to a guest he had brought to the Club, who told me he had just spent some time in New York with a Commander Pilcher of the British Navy, who had a wonderful camp up in British Columbia. It was hard to get to, he said, but if I wanted to have a real bear hunt, I should come to New York the next day and have lunch with him and the Commander.

I didn't waste any time getting to New York. I was told that the camp was simple to get into, that all the owner had to do was to wire his guide, who would meet me in Golden, and I would be in the camp the next day. It sounded too good to be true, and it was, for I was certainly sold a bill of goods. But I've been happy ever since that I fell for it. I made a rental agreement, and told the Commander to go ahead and make arrangements for me.

A few days later I was on my way, very excited. I landed in Golden where I was met by the guide as promised. This was the first time I met Arthur Nicol, with whom I have spent so many happy hours camping and hunting during the past twenty years. From Golden, we took a stagecoach and traveled into the early hours of the morning to reach a place called Fort Steele, where the pack train was supposed to be ready for us to start out. Arthur said he didn't know if we could get into the camp or not, as no one ever went in during the early spring, but he would do his best.

We had about ten horses, a horse wrangler, and a cook, besides Arthur and myself, when we started up to Wild Horse, a famous gold-mining settlement of the early days, not far from Kimberly, where the world's largest lead mine is today. We spent two days traveling, trying to get up over the snow pass into the valley where White Swan Lake was, the site of the camp. The country was beautiful, almost breath-taking, but the going was terrible, and I was not in particularly good shape. One of our packhorses fell off the side of the mountain and another horse was killed, but we still tried to keep going. Then the rest of the horses got completely mired down in the snow and we had to turn around and go back to Fort Steele to re-organize. There was only one good thing about this attempt—I had my movie camera along and got some thrilling shots of the accident when the horses fell.

Arthur Nicol decided to try another way in—the route I always used later—by way of Sheep Creek and

Summit Pass. We stopped at Canning's Ranch, right near Sheep Creek and on the edge of the Canadian Rockies, a stopping-off place for anyone trying to get into the mountains there. Mr. Canning seemed mighty surprised to see us, and asked if we were going to try to ford Sheep Creek above his place.

"Why? Don't you think we can make it?" Arthur Nicol asked.

"I doubt it," Canning said. "No one ever tries to take a pack train across the creek in the spring."

When we got to the ford I could understand, for the creek was a raging torrent. Arthur Nicol didn't hesitate a moment, but just plunged right in. I stayed behind last because I had my camera on the pommel of my saddle and wanted to get some pictures of the other horses struggling to get across the creek. The water came up higher and higher around them, and they started swimming, with the swift current carrying them downstream fast. I suddenly got panicky and decided I didn't want to try that creek all alone. It was better to be right in there with the rest of them. So I stopped taking pictures and plunged in.

The water came up around my legs and the horse floundered and pawed for a footing. I hung on to the pommel for dear life, and finally managed to get across all right, but everything was soaked. Some of the horses were swept a quarter of a mile downstream before they got a footing. We tried to re-organize, and found that everything was soaked through—our clothes, guns, dunnage, everything. But we started out just the same, going

231

up an old trail toward the pass. But here we ran into more trouble, for there were so many trees down that we couldn't make any progress.

We turned back and reached the Creek again, following it up as best we could. After a few hours, Arthur decided to make camp. He started a big fire, so that we could get the worst of the wetness out of some of our things, and put up a temporary lean-to. We weren't very comfortable, and I was so tired I wanted to sleep two days.

The next day we crossed over Summit Pass all right. The snow wasn't too deep here, but it was a long hard trip, and it was one more day before we reached White Swan Lake. That sight made the tough trip worth while—a clear blue lake in a kind of basin made by towering, snow-capped mountains. It was wild virgin country, full of beauty and full of game.

We were welcomed at the camp by Billy Stork, a trapper who took care of the place. He still traps there and looks after the cabin that I later built on White Swan Lake. He lived in a small log cabin which was fairly comfortable, but I liked it better when we moved into a tepee, which I had never used before but learned to like a great deal after my trips to British Columbia.

So much time had been wasted getting in to this place that was supposed to be only one day from Golden, that I had only about a week at the camp. There was no open season except for bear, so I didn't have much luck hunting. But I did a lot of photographing, and had a good time. On the way out, we decided to send the pack train back by the route we had used coming in, while Arthur

232

and I would try to make it on foot by way of the Wild Horse.

We put our packs on our backs, including our sleeping bags but no tent, took a gun and a few rounds of ammunition each, and started out. Arthur said that there ought to be a lot of bear around the place where the horse had been lost, and he certainly was right. There were plenty of porcupine, too, as I learned that night when we slept under a tree near the Wild Horse. I hardly got a wink of sleep because they were crawling over my sleeping bag all night—and I don't like porcupines. I must have killed at least five with my staff. Arthur never even woke up.

The next day we spent stalking around near the dead horse and finally cached ourselves, waiting for a big bear to walk into range. After a couple of hours, one of the biggest grizzlies I ever saw showed up, a very light-colored one and a trophy well worth getting. I am sorry to say that I flubbed this shot badly, and missed the bear which took off into the woods. So we got back to Fort Steele empty-handed, though by that time I wasn't worrying any more about my lack of game. I was wondering whether or not I would get there.

It was twenty-seven miles from the camp to Fort Steele, through the mountains, over tough trails, and with heavy packs. A few miles away, my leg muscles began to have spasms that hurt like the devil and crippled me so I could hardly walk. A mile from Fort Steele, Arthur left me and went on in to his place for a horse. When we finally reached his house, he got out some alcohol and rubbed me down, then put hot towels on my legs until they eased up enough for me to walk.

I had to go to the bank in Cranbrook, a few miles away, to cash a check so I could pay Arthur off. He drove me there in his car, but when we got in front of the bank, my legs had tightened up in spasms again and I couldn't get out of the car. Arthur went in and got the bank teller to come to the car, where he cashed my check for me. The teller laughed and made jokes about his bank's curb service, but it didn't seem very funny to me because I was suffering the tortures of hell.

Arthur gave me more hot-towel treatments so that I could get the train back to New Haven the next day. He told me later that he was sure that was the last he would ever see of me, after the terribly tough trip we had. It was, without doubt, the hardest trip I ever took, but later when I looked back on it, I wouldn't have missed it for anything in the world.

I liked the country so much, in fact, that I decided to go back again that fall to see how the place looked when it was open for shooting. First I got myself in good condition, starting weeks ahead of time to go on hikes in the hills north of New Haven.

It was a wonderful trip—everything that such a trip ought to be. Things went well, the hunting was good, and I got one of the greatest thrills that the outdoors has ever given me. This was the bugling of the elks which, to my mind, is one of the three most exciting natural phenomena I have heard or seen, the other two being the migration of the caribou and the return of the salmon to spawn in fresh-water streams where they were born.

From the camp at White Swan we made a day's pack trip to Elk Creek, and the place was alive with elk, right in the middle of the hunting season. Climbing up a pass with the pack train, I first heard the bugling of the male elk, as it echoed across the canyons, and the answering bugle from other elks on the mountains around. It made the chills run up and down my spine, and though I've heard it many times since, there has never been another experience like this first time.

On this trip I shot my first elk, and also got two Rocky Mountain goats and a fine sheep. There was an exciting story in connection with the bighorn sheep, which Teddy Roosevelt pointed out to me in 1908 as the greatest North American big-game trophy. One day I shot at a sheep and thought I hit him, but he took off and out of sight, so I concluded I must have missed. Then the next day we climbed up high, looking for sheep again—and when I say high I really mean it. Unless you've climbed the Canadian Rockies, you can't appreciate what a hard workout it is.

Well, we had climbed up to the skyline and, looking down about seven or eight hundred feet below us we saw a ram, apparently dead. I thought it might be the one I had shot at the day before, but the guide and the Indian horse wrangler, George Lum, both said it was an old fellow who had just lain down and died. I didn't feel too sure about it, so I leaned over the edge of the cliff and shot down at him. He jumped up like a flash—a long way from dead—and tucked his head under his body as he dashed along the side of the cliff. I took out after him, running along the edge of the cliff with everybody else hollering at me to stop because it was a thousand-foot drop straight down from where I was running. I didn't know what they were saying because I was too engrossed in getting my first bighorn sheep. It was an almost impossible shot, with the sheep way down below me and running for all he was worth, but I stopped, aimed, fired—and got him!

I'll never forget that as long as I live. It was one of the hardest shots I ever made, and I was mighty proud of myself. When we got the sheep, we found out that my first shot, while he was lying still, had gone through one of his horns. A couple of years later I was back at this spot and looked at the sheer cliff and the edge along which I had raced without thinking of anything but getting that sheep. And I knew then what a damn fool I had been.

Still, it was the high point of that trip, and one of the high points of all my hunting.

Eighteen

Paradise Gained

(*The cabin in A. C. Gilbert's game preserve in Hamden,
Connecticut, is essentially the same as that near Kent
but somewhat larger. The living room is half again as
big, with a beautiful stone fireplace at the far end instead
of one side. Above it, upstairs, there is a large bedroom
with a fireplace, in addition to three bedrooms and a
bath. A door from this large bedroom leads to a sort of
terrace on top of a screen porch, which looks over the
small lake, stocked with rainbow trout.*)

    (*The chief feature of the cabin in the game pre-
serve that distinguishes it from others A.C. has built is
the big addition beyond the living room—the big-game
trophy room. You know that it is something special the
first time you see it, even from twenty feet away in the
living room, for through the open door you can see a huge
brown bear lumbering toward you from one corner.*

More startling is the other Kodiak bear, standing ten feet high in another corner. Three huge bear rugs cover the floor, but there are more than bear in the room. Eight other species of the finest North American big game are represented here in magnificent heads, some of them prize-winning trophies. Elk, moose, Rocky Mountain Goat, Bighorn Sheep, Wapiti, White-tail deer, Mule deer, caribou—their heads line the walls and seem to peer steadily out of the big windows of the room or into the fireplace. Eighteen of them appear in the "Records of North American Big Game.")

(The walls of the big living room are decorated with far more trophies than the trophy room, but generally they are smaller and less spectacular, except for the mounted fish, the prize of which is a giant rainbow trout over the fireplace. A.C. is always careful to point out that he himself did not catch this one, which was hooked by a man fishing with him on the famous Newhalen River in Alaska. A.C.'s biggest was a few ounces lighter. On the wall among the fish are heads of coyotes, bobcats, squirrels, raccoons, woodchucks, rabbits, foxes, wolves, mountain lions, and other mammals.)

(Behind the cabin rises a laurel-covered hill. Across the pond is another hill covered with laurel. As you drive around the many miles of narrow roads through the game preserve you see banks of laurel here and there, or deep in the woods one bright blossoming bush in a spot where the sunlight pierces the foliage above. Finally you come to an entire laurel grove—several acres literally jammed with tall strong laurel bushes over 200 years old, glowing with white or pink in different shades.)

238

It was the laurel that first brought me here. I wanted laurel for my place on Ridge Road, and I wanted to find it in bloom so I could be sure of what I was getting, white or pink. August Dondi, a nurseryman, told me about this place and brought me out here. I fell in love with it at once, and in the twenties got permission from the several farmers who owned this area to do some hunting as well as take out laurel. I learned later, from one of the men in the State Agriculture department, that although this was not the largest stand of laurel in the state, it was one of the finest, with very old bushes, tall and lovely.

This area was called "Little Egypt" by most people in those days. I tried to find out once where the name came from, and went to see a man eighty years old who had lived around here all his life. His father told him it had been called Little Egypt as long as he could remember, but he had no idea where the name came from. Some of the old hunters around here still call it Little Egypt. I know that once it must have been an Indian hunting ground, because we found a lot of arrowheads around.

I finally decided I would like to buy the whole area, so I got August Dondi to obtain options on several of the farms making up the territory I wanted. I didn't let my name come into it until everything was lined up. Finally, in 1930 the property was transferred to me after a long search of all the titles involved, and I named it the Paradise Game Preserve.

The name Paradise came from Paradise Avenue, which runs along one side of it. Many years ago, a man built a home out here in the country and loved it so much that he called it Paradise. In time, the road leading up to his place came to be known as Paradise Avenue. I've loved the game preserve so much and got so much pleasure from it that it seemed a very fitting name to me.

I built the cabin in 1931, then set to work damming the stream to make the series of ponds and stocked them with brown trout, brook trout and rainbows. In time I learned that the rainbows stood the summer temperatures better than the others; they were more fun in fly fishing, too, because they break the water when they are hooked and put on a great show. For years I've stuck with rainbows. I also put in a system to help them through the hot weather in the lake near the cabin. A double pipe, one inside the other, runs from a cold artesian well close by, and a blower forces air through the inner pipe. This air is cooled by the water from the well, running outside the smaller pipe, and bubbles up through the lake at several different places. This cools the water a little bit and also serves to aerate it. On hot days, when we turn it on, you can see there are trout hanging around those spots especially.

I put up a fence around the area on the west side of Paradise Avenue, around 250 acres, in 1931 because hunters who had been coming here for a long time kept poaching on my land. When I got through, I found that a couple of deer had been fenced into the property, and this gave me the idea for my deer herd. I bought a few more white-tails from Virginia and put them in the preserve, and my entire herd of around a hundred grew from that nucleus.

The deer thrived, but not some other animals I brought in. Shortly after getting Paradise, I got some sheep thinking they might help clear up some of the underbrush. But in a few days they were all dead. They had eaten the laurel which is poisonous to all animals. The deer seem to know, and never touch it no matter how hungry they are. Years ago I tried to bring two elk into the preserve, but they began eating the apple trees and dogwoods. I couldn't stand that. But it is a wonderful place for deer and all kinds of birds, including the ducks and the pheasants we raise and the partridges that are here naturally.

Our dairy is one of the best, and has won prizes for its wonderful Jersey milk with which we supply the cafeteria at the plant. We raise chickens and turkeys, too, for the use of the cafeteria. Melville Roberts, who runs the dairy, first came with me to work in my greenhouse on Ridge Road, twenty-seven years ago. He's a fine dairy man, but he does a lot of other work around the place, too—clearing paths and roads with me, doing rock work on the dams and walls, and looking after the cabin.

Incidentally, I might mention one little byproduct of our dairy farm that shows how we try to tie everything in together. There are always lots of flies around a barn, you know, and we have these electric screens over all the windows, that electrocute a fly that tries to get through. Well, that's where we get the flies

241

for the slides that we supply with our microscope sets put out in the factory.

Building up a place like Paradise takes years, and I still work on it all the time. After the original purchase of the farms, I added a few pieces of property to round it out and had just over six-hundred acres when I was through, in two main parcels. All of it is fenced now, and we divide the deer herd between the two parcels. In time I built Paradise Park as a country club for co-workers at the plant, and later built our present home on the highest point in the preserve.

When I first came out here in the late twenties you couldn't get near the place by car. There were roads, but they were narrow, winding dirt roads that were just about impassable. I set to work right away trying to improve them, for I proposed a long-range program to develop this by-passed area into a fine semi-rural residential community, which it is fast becoming.

One of the first things that had to be done was to improve Paradise Avenue. I had the co-operation in this of Judge Rochford, First Selectman of the town of Hamden, and Mr. Wright, Town Engineer, as well as other officials. I gave to the town of Hamden a long stretch of land along Paradise Avenue so it could be widened from twenty to sixty feet and straightened out. Later, at my own expense, I built a mile and a quarter of hard surface road, Dunbar Hill Road, along which I put up my first houses in this area.

For me, Paradise has always remained first and foremost a game preserve, no matter what other activities I've undertaken in connection with it. Aside from the wonderful herd of deer, we've been raising mallard ducks and pheasants. As a head game-keeper I've had for more than twenty years Alfred James, an Englishman whose father and grandfather before him were game-keepers. Aside from looking after the deer and keeping out the dozens of pests and dangers such as foxes, snakes, turtles, and so on, Alfred's chief work is the careful raising of about two thousand pheasants and two thousand ducks each year.

The eggs are hatched out by hens, who look out for the birds when they are tiny. But we have quite a problem with the motherless ducks. They don't know how to fly, and we have to teach them. This is done by leading them from their regular pen up to a big pen at the top of the hill above their pond. Scattering feed along the way gets them there readily enough. Up near the big pen there is a long, wide ramp from the top of which you can see the duck pond down below. Well, one batch of ducklings at a time is let out of the upper pen right on to the ramp. They waddle up it and find themselves suddenly at the jumping-off place. They can't turn around and go back because more ducks are coming up behind them. Then they see home—their own duck pond—down below, and they want to get there somehow. Some of them take right off and fly down. Others hesitate a while, then leap and try their wings.

We lose about half the birds, both ducks and pheasants, that we start out with. Some die, some fly away over the fence, to the delight of other hunters in the neighborhood. But we put on wonderful shoots in the fall, with our fine pointers doing their beautiful work, and Alfred James and his assistants running things off smoothly. People who come here all love it and want to come back again.

Nineteen

Non-Participating Athlete

(*Quotation from Arthur Daley's column in the* New
York Times *of April 27, 1951: "Vaulting is easily the
most complicated event in track and field. It's as frus-
trating as golf and just as difficult to learn. The greatest
living expert on it is A. C. Gilbert of New Haven."*)

I studied pole vaulting thoroughly and scientifi-
cally, and I coached pole vaulters for many years. I had
been a pole vaulter myself. Since nobody else combined
these three things, I managed to accumulate more information about the sport than other people. Passing this
knowledge along to Yale vaulters for about thirty years
contributed, no doubt, to what sports writers love to
call the Yale dynasty in pole vaulting. Yale's record in
the sport is amazing, when you look at it, winning or

tying for first place thirty-two times in the Intercollegiates, out of seventy-three times the event was held.
I don't think there's another record like it in any sport.

It really started in 1915. Johnny Mack, Yale track
coach, had come to me in 1909 asking me to come out
and work with the pole vaulters. But I was so busy getting my business started that I didn't have a minute for
such things. Johnny had some good pole vaulters then,
with two of the four men who had won all places in the
1908 Intercollegiates. Charlie Campbell won the pole
vault in 1909 and Frank Nelson in 1910. They carried
on the technique we had developed at Yale while I
was there, and also passed it along to a young man who
was a freshman when Nelson was a senior. This was
Robert Gardner, who later became national golf champion.

Johnny Mack interviewed me a few times about
Gardner's work, but I can't take credit for this first man
to vault more than thirteen feet officially. I like to think
I contributed something to his success, anyway, and I
know I had a good deal to do with the later records set
by his nephew, Keith S. Brown.

In 1915 I began working regularly with the Yale
vaulters and have done so ever since, being a sort of
unofficial coach of that sport. Even when I was vaulting
myself, I had always studied the details of technique
very carefully with Johnny Mack and my teammates,
but now I set about doing a thorough job. I worked out
the basic principles of physics involved in pole vaulting,
and constructed a little machine that demonstrated those
principles accurately.

At the same time I began to take slow-motion movies of pole vaulting, the first ever made for a study of technique. I had a wonderful opportunity to get plenty of fine pictures, because I began officiating at track meets as pole-vault judge at the Intercollegiates and at the National Championships of the A.A.U. From that time to the present there have been only a few years when I was not chief judge of the pole vault.

I was thus able to observe every good pole vaulter in the country—and later in the Olympics the greatest vaulters of other countries—and was in a position to get such movies as no one had ever collected. I had hundreds of thousands of feet of film, in time, which I edited carefully to help me advise the Yale vaulters. Every spring the vaulters would come to my house, or to the cabin in the game preserve, for dinner and afterward the clinic on vaulting. I would demonstrate the physics machine, then show movies of good vaulting, or vaulting that showed certain specific faults in technique. In addition, I used to spend an hour and a half or two hours every other day out at the track during the training season.

For me this was a wonderful diversion from my business, and I enjoyed it tremendously, working with these young men and helping them improve in a sport I loved. I think I got just as big a kick out of helping develop a world's champion—and we turned out several at Yale—as I did out of becoming a world's champion myself. Some of these boys came to school just fair vaulters—a few really bad—and I watched them improve each year, adding six or eight inches or even a foot to their leaps from one season to the next. I don't mean to belittle the efforts of the boys themselves, for many of them were fine athletes, or of the coaches at Yale, who were excellent. But I know that my studies and my work had a lot to do with the good records set so consistently by Yale men. Nobody else devoted the time and study to the sport that I was able to, that's all.

From 1915 to the present I have been a member of the Track Advisory Committee at Yale, except during the years 1932 to 1940 when the University authorities took over more complete control of the athletic program and some advisory committees were dropped. For several years in the twenties I was chairman of this committee, which meant that I was also on the Yale Board of Athletic Control. Some of my pleasantest and most rewarding associations sprang from this work with other Yale men. I remember with particular warmth Charlie and Alex Coxe, two of the grandest men who ever lived. After their deaths, their family contributed the Coxe Memorial Cage at Yale Field in their honor.

One of the most important things I did in the twenties, in the field of sports, was the re-organization of the Yale-Harvard and Oxford-Cambridge Games, which had been allowed to lapse. I acted more or less as chairman of a committee to get them started again and played an important part in the so-called Swampscott agreement, which set up a kind of permanent organization for handling the games. Under this arrangement, we were to hold competitions every two years. Harvard and Yale would go to England, and two years later Oxford and Cambridge would come to America.

I made one suggestion that was probably the most significant contribution to this event. Previously, Yale and Harvard men stayed at some hotel when they went to England, generally in Brighton. The result was that the Americans did not meet many of the British athletes until the day of the competition. The same sort of thing happened when the Englishmen came here. I suggested that the visiting athletes should always be quartered as guests in the dormitories of the host university, so that these Americans and Englishmen could come to know each other well. I had learned from experience that one of the most rewarding and instructive things in life was meeting people, different kinds of people, and getting to know them, their feelings, their ideas, and their attitudes.

My proposal was welcomed at once and has been carried out ever since, much to the approval of everyone involved. I am sure that many firm friendships have been formed that might not have existed otherwise, and that a good deal of international understanding and goodwill have been promoted in this series of meets, which has been carried on every year except during the war. When English athletes have come to New Haven, we've always given a reception for them at Maraldene, and I'm looking forward to the next visit when I hope they will come to our new home, where I'm sure they will enjoy the deer.

In 1923 I became a member of the Graduate Advisory Committee of the Executive Committee of the IC 4A—the Intercollegiate Association of Amateur Athletes of America, working under the chairmanship of the

249

great Gustavus Town Kirby, who occupied that position for thirty-nine years. For the twelve years I served with this committee, Gus was its chairman, and it was an inspiration and a great privilege to work with him. I was also associated closely with him for many years in the A.A.U. and the American Olympics Committee. Gus was a member of the very first Olympics committee, when the modern games were started in 1896, and has been a member ever since, winding up as its honorary president. A really wonderful man, Gus has done as much for track athletics as any man living or dead.

("A.C. had plenty to do with helping the sport himself," Gus Kirby says. "He and I made quite a team, if I do say so, and we usually saw eye to eye on athletic affairs. He often supplied the idea and I put it into words for the book. He had the drive and the unfailing energy to put it across. Why, almost single-handed he put across the metric system with the IC 4A and the A.A.U., although I helped where I could. This is proved by the fact that they backslid later, when he was less active on their committees.)

("I have known and played and worked with him since he was an undergraduate at Yale, where he was champion or nearly champion of every sport in which he took part. But far more important than what A.C. did himself is what he did for others. He taught others how to do what he could do, and above all else, he had inspiration of character. He loves the game and wants to help and does help. He knows the rules and how to enforce them and how to suggest changes,

250

*if changes are necessary. He is determined; he is posi-
tive. He is well informed. As an Olympic official, Intercollegiate official, and Amateur Union official, he is
'tops,' able, calm, never riling competitors up but always
seeing that they performed according to rule.*)

(*"We lived together during several Olympic
Games, and I never saw anyone so devoted to his job.
There used to be quite a few parties and social affairs
connected with these events, and I always enjoyed a
good time, particularly if there were attractive women
about. But A.C. was never the least bit interested. He
was there to do a job and that's what he concentrated
on. He was always fun to be with, but he didn't go in
for the more frivolous things when there was business
at hand.*)

(*"There is no one like him, as an administrator,
as a competitor, as a sportsman, as a lover of the outdoors, and as a personal friend."*)

Yes, I was a member of the American Olympic
Committee from 1924 through 1948, and was on the
Executive Committee of the A.A.U. for several years,
member of its Board of Governors from 1929 to the
present time. In 1932, when I was chairman of the
A.A.U. Track and Field Committee, I was bold enough
to propose the adoption of the international, or metric,
system for track events. There were a great many reasons
for making such a change, I thought. For one thing, in
all field events, such as shot put, pole vault, and so on,
there would be no difference whatever. Heights and
distances could be measured and listed both in meters

and in yards, feet, and inches. The big change would come about in the running events, but here our runners were at a great disadvantage, under the English system, because they could not really establish world's records except at the Olympic Games every four years.

When you picked up a program at the Olympic Games and saw the listing of records in running events, you rarely saw an American's name, although some Americans were the fastest runners in the world, because the records printed were those in the metric system—100 meters, 200 meters, and so on. Except during Olympic years, American runners could not compare their achievements with those of most other nations, nor could they train properly for Olympic events.

There were a good many arguments and a great deal of sentiment against switching to the International Standard, chiefly from the old record holders, who did not like to see their events go out of existence. But my point was that very few people indeed remembered the actual records of any of these great athletes—they remembered their great achievements. I doubt that anyone can remember Charlie Paddock's time today, but everyone recalls that Paddock was the "fastest human" and a world's record holder, which is what counts.

I accumulated all the statistics I could, all the arguments I could muster, and started selling the idea of the International Standard, with the strong and effective support of Gus Kirby. And I must say I did one of the best selling jobs of my life, for both the IC 4A and the A.A.U. adopted the international or metric system in 1932. There was a battle the next year to go back to the English system, but we won out once more.

(*Arthur Daley, writing in the* New York Times: *"That the meter remains is due almost exclusively to the influence exerted by A. C. Gilbert of Yale, and Gustavus Town Kirby, one of the leading sports figures in the country."*)

Within a few years, however, when I was no longer so active in these organizations and could not continue to battle, the IC 4A went back to the English system. The A.A.U. stuck to it religiously until a couple of years ago when they decided to go back to yards and miles except during Olympic years. I think this was one of the biggest mistakes the A.A.U. ever made, because it is America's representative in international sports bodies and as such should have a world view.

There was one other campaign I put on in the A.A.U. and that was for the election of Avery Brundage as president. He is a grand person, a good friend, and I think has been one of the best and strongest influences for amateur athletics in the world. The whole world has recognized his great ability, for he has been head of the American Olympic committee and the International Federation.

I've wandered a bit from my pole-vault coaching at Yale, but I want to mention a few of the outstanding men we produced. One was Sabin W. Carr, the first man to go fourteen feet. He won the Intercollegiates three times and then the Olympics, and I must say he would never have won the Olympics if it hadn't been for his old friend, A. C. Gilbert. After finishing his last year at Yale, Sabin Carr had an unfortunate experience and sort of dropped from public view. But I located him, brought him to my home, and started getting him back into condition. He went to the Olympic tryouts, and just barely made the team. On the way over, however, he got in top condition and won. He was a real world's champion.

Keith S. Brown should have been the first man to vault fifteen feet. He tied twice and won the Intercollegiates once and was a truly fine vaulter. If he had trained for just one more year after school, I have always felt sure he would have won the Olympics and made fifteen feet, because he had been improving six inches each year. But he was ambitious and eager to get himself established in business, and I couldn't help admiring him for that.

Cornelius Warmerdam was not a Yale man, of course, but he was the first outsider to discover the fundamentals of what I call the Yale technique. Warmerdam worked it out for himself, with the aid of excellent coaches. He was a grand boy, a fine performer and a good competitor. He wrote a description of his vaulting technique not long ago, and it read almost exactly like a description Johnny Mack and I had written of the Yale technique twenty years before.

Some of the biggest moments in my life came in connection with the Olympic Games of 1928, 1932 and 1936. The 1928 games were held at Amsterdam, and the team lived on a boat that had been chartered for the purpose. General Douglas MacArthur was president of the American Olympic Association that year, with General William C. Rose—then Major Rose—as manager of the team under him. I was assistant manager working with General Rose and was also appointed Morale Officer under General MacArthur. On the boat, I lived in the stateroom next to that of General MacArthur. Consequently I got to know him quite well and admired him a great deal. He was a fine man, and I have never been able to understand the charges leveled against him that he was egotistical. If I saw any fault in his handling of the Olympic Games that year, it was that he kept himself too much in the background. If he had been conceited, he had plenty of opportunity to be in the public eye on important occasions, when he might have shone brilliantly.

I had charge of the entertainment on board the boat, and one of the stunts I worked out was a gambler's night. I had printed up fake thousand-dollar bills before leaving, and we gave them out for a Monte Carlo night on board. The person with the most fake money at the end of the evening got a prize. Everybody enjoyed it, because it was something different from the sort of entertainment they had had before, but the most interesting part of this was something that happened when we came into the harbor in Holland. The dock and shores were lined with people welcoming the American team, and the American athletes were craning their necks along the decks of the ship. Some of them began throwing some of their fake money overboard, and a few of the Hollanders, believing the wild tales about Americans who threw money around, actually dived into the water to pick up what looked like good bills to them.

The 1928 games were good training for me, because in 1932 and again in 1936 I was chairman of the Administration Committee of the American Olympic Association, which meant manager of the Olympic team, designated as *Chef de Mission* of the team. The 1932 games at Los Angeles were a great success, with a fine American team. The movie stars went all out to entertain the American athletes, so almost everybody had a wonderful time. The big stars and champions, of course, had invitations everywhere, so they were no problem. I'll never forget that great comedian, Will Rogers, who came to me and said, "Give me some names of the men and women who don't get invited everywhere. I'll see that they're entertained, and in fine style." And he certainly did.

There was a great deal of controversy before the Olympic Games in Berlin in 1936. Hitler was in power and there was a great deal of persecution of the Jews, so many organizations felt that America should not take part in the games. I was in favor of participation because I felt that it would put the Germans on their best behavior, and I didn't see why we should be prejudiced and act the way the Nazis acted.

I must say right now that the games were conducted as well as they have ever been, to my knowledge, and in the opinion of many Olympics officials. The German people were kind, considerate, and understanding. The German judges were scrupulously fair. The Olympic village was beautiful and comfortable.

256

It was a tremendous job to arrange for transportation and handling of between three and four hundred athletes, men and women, for a trip like this. There were many strong and conflicting personalities and interests, and it was my job not just to handle all the details but to keep everyone happy and in fine spirits. And there were half a dozen problems every day that had to be decided or handled in the most diplomatic fashion. For example, there was our landing in Hamburg, where the people went all out to give a great welcome to the American athletes. A women's organization put on a big buffet, and for this important occasion many of the ladies got out their fine old glassware. When the party was over, and the team was on its way to Berlin, I stayed around, as I usually did, to see that everything was wound up correctly and everything was all right. I inquired of the ladies and they told me that quite a few pieces of fine antique glassware had disappeared.

I told them how sorry I was and tried to explain that these Americans were not thieves. They were just exuberant young people who were in the habit of picking up anything loose as souvenirs. I said I would see what could be done. When I got to Berlin I called together the managers of all the different teams and explained what had happened, and they went to work. When the men understood the situation and realized that this was valuable stuff they had taken, they did just what I knew they would do—returned every single piece that had been taken. I had it packed up and sent back to the lovely ladies who had been so kind to our team.

Through these Olympic Games I met many wonderful people, both here and abroad. I also had many interesting experiences, among them a close view of Hitler on numerous occasions, and entertainments by Goebbels and other Nazi bigwigs, giving me a closeup of these strange phenomena that few Americans had.

In 1940 and again in 1948 I was asked to be *Chef de Mission* of the American team again, but in 1940 I was just getting over a serious illness and in 1948 I did not feel that I could tackle this ever-larger job in view of my other important activities. But I look back on those three Olympic years as great events, as satisfying as that of 1908 when I was a participant and a gold-medal winner instead of a manager.

Twenty

Boom but Not Bust

(Where Broadway crosses Fifth Avenue in New York stands a six-story building that attracts as many window shoppers as any in the city. It is the Gilbert Hall of Science, containing the New York offices, showrooms, and salesrooms of the company. The passing public knows only its fascinating displays on the ground floor, where Gilbert American Flyer trains—freights, passenger trains, and streamline diesels—race around an intricate maze of tracks with switches, sidings, water towers, stations, and numerous other structures, all situated among rolling hills, along flowing streams, or in the shade of miniature trees. This obvious Mecca for boys is also a strong magnet for people of all ages. Hardly a business man or lawyer or truck driver can pass the

259

window without stopping for a brief look, and many stay for a quarter of an hour, gazing at the layout they wish they'd had for their trains or hope to build for their sons.)

(Inside, there are more train displays, with stockyards that load cattle onto cars (one of A.C.'s inventions), with coal loaders and flatcars with automobiles that unload themselves at the touch of a button. There are moving models made from Erector, and displays of chemistry sets, microscope sets, and other Gilbert educational toys. In addition to these commercial, though entertaining shows, there are several pure-science displays with inviting buttons saying "Push me" that make sparks jump, metal rings leap through the air, and so on. Several hundred children a day push these buttons and watch the other sights, in addition to men of all ages and from all countries, for the Hall of Science seems to be a must on the sightseeing list of foreigners.)

(While advertising and promotion are at least half of the reason for the existence of the Hall of Science, very important functions go on in the rest of the building —service and repair division, advertising, export department, and above all sales to jobber and store buyers from all over the country. The displays made for such sales are far more spectacular than those open to the public on the ground floor. If they were open to the public, the A. C. Gilbert Company would get no work done in New York, for thousands would stream through daily. Special group visits can be arranged by schools and other organizations—and there are hundreds each year, enabling

*thousands of children to see the special displays. The
favorite is the big train display, eighty feet long with
miles of track, nine different lines connected by switches,
mountains, waterfalls, a lake, towns, crossings, sidings,
and every accessory dreamed up to date by A. C. Gilbert
and his engineers. The master control board can set nine
trains going at once, and buttons placed at spots around
the edges of the display can make every accessory work
for the benefit of a visiting buyer. Bob Schloss changes,
improves, repairs, and runs the big train display, under
the direction of Philip Connell, Sales Manager of the
American Flyer Division, who came with the company
when Gilbert bought American Flyer in 1938.)*

*(The third floor of the Hall of Science is almost
as fascinating for visiting groups of children and also
for even the blasé toy buyer, for here are displays of all
other Gilbert toys, featuring the father of them all,
Erector, with moving models of merry-go-rounds, ferris
wheels, parachute drops. Alfred Fletcher, magician and
son of a magician, makes new models and entertains
visitors with magic tricks.)*

*(The other floors contain displays of the motor-
driven appliance products, service and repair department, and many offices. The entire Hall of Science is
presided over by William D. Perry, who is also Sales
Manager of the company. He started with the Mysto
Manufacturing Company in 1916 as an office boy, went
to New Haven a year later to work in the shipping room,
and from there became a director of demonstrators in
the South, salesman in various divisions and territories,*

and manager of the New York office. When the Hall of
Science was opened, Perry was put in charge.)

You see one reason why I've always got such a
kick out of my business? Wouldn't it make anybody's
heart warm to see youngsters like Bill Perry come along
with the company as it grew, working hard, learning
more all the time, always loyal and devoted, taking over
bigger and bigger jobs and doing them well? He was the
obvious man to manage the Hall of Science when we
opened it in 1941, in kind of a lull between a hectic
decade of the worst of all depressions and a comeback
from it and another decade with the worst of all wars
and adjustment when it ended.

When the thirties started, nobody had any idea
what we were in for, of course. We had even arranged,
at the end of 1929, to purchase the Meccano Company
of America. This division of an English firm with world-
wide sales had always been hard competitors of Erector
but they really couldn't buck us and we finally took them
over. In the course of the next few years we used the
valuable Meccano name on several products.

The year 1930 was still good for us, and our sales
stayed up over the two-million mark, with profits of
$189,000. We began to feel the depression seriously the
next year, when sales dropped below two million for the
first time in quite a few years. We kept up our advertising, however, so profits were naturally down, to $74,000.
On May 1, 1931, we voted a 10 per cent salary cut for
executives, and I took mine along with the rest, despite
my contract with Shields & Company. I could not have

lived with myself if I'd taken advantage of that written contract when the others didn't have any. We voted a second 10 per cent cut in 1932, the first year of the depression we went in the red.

We were in that unfortunate color of ink only two years of the depression, 1932 and 1933, but even then our credit was never impaired, the banks never lost confidence in us, and we kept working as hard as we could. There were plenty of worries, but not about finances and credit, I'm happy to say. We were still alive and alert, even though discouraged at times. Some of my business associates have called me a pessimist, but I prefer the term realist. During bad times I expected troubles and wanted to be prepared for them. We got them and, I think, handled them pretty well. We fell behind in payment of our preference dividends in only one year, and then for only three periods, so that by 1939 we were all caught up again.

The depression brought personal difficulties, too, of course. The Mechanics Bank, of which I was a director, failed, and I wished that I had followed my father's advice of accepting no bank directorships without paying close attention to the bank's affairs. I had not done that, because the officers of the bank were alert, hardworking and honest men. A great many banks that were well run got caught in the whirlpool when runs started, but I was glad that in this instance I was not called upon to testify, because I would have been ashamed to admit that I knew so little about the affairs of a bank of which I was a director. I took a large personal loss in the bank's failure, because I had rather heavy deposits there. Al-

263

though I was not a large stockholder, I realized almost nothing on what stock I did hold.

By 1934 the company showed a small profit again, and in 1935 the profit climbed to better than $100,000. The next year, 1936, we struggled back up to the two-million-dollar mark in total sales and then continued to move ahead, although it was 1937 before we felt ourselves on an even keel again, and in a position to grow as I knew the company could and should grow. By 1939 we reached a figure of $2,847,000 and the next year went over the three-million mark. In 1941 we set a new record, with an increase in total sales of almost a million dollars, when our volume went to $4,335,000. Then we converted almost entirely to war work.

Figures don't mean much, really, when I think of the story of my business. I usually remember it in terms of people, and have to turn to record books for the figures. There were many important changes in personnel during the eleven or twelve years before the war. Charlie Hoyt, who had handled our advertising from the beginning, was killed in 1928 when thrown from a horse on Long Island. I missed him greatly and so did the company.

In 1936 one of those rewarding moments in a business history came with the election of Al Richmond as a director of the company. He had been one of the first employees of the Mysto Manufacturing Company, had worked loyally with me through good times and bad, and had held almost every position there was in the organization. The next year, another director and one of the best salesmen that ever lived, George Adams

Wood, died, and I realized that the company had been in business almost thirty years, a long time. You are bound to lose some close associates when you keep going that long.

A good many people wondered if I was going to pass out of the picture myself in 1939, when I came down with double pneumonia, dry pleurisy, and then empyema. I was in the New Haven Hospital for three months, most of that time with six nurses, and there was a long period of convalescence after that. It was a trying ordeal for everyone close to me, and not a period that I like to remember myself. I still have in my scrapbook a few of the pleasanter memories of that period. One was a letter accompanying a gift, sent by twenty-four executives, supervisors and foremen at the plant, people who had been particularly close to me. I was home from the hospital then, and they said they were glad and spoke of me as their "friend" rather than their boss. That speeded my convalescence considerably.

One of the letters that meant most to me during my long illness was a short one from Arthur Alling, who had been associated with me for so long. Since he was almost as reserved a person as I was in showing any emotion about things that meant most to him, it touched me deeply, restrained as it was.

(*"It was grand news to hear from Mary this morning that you are definitely improved. Keep up the good work. You and I were never strong on expressing our sentiments and affection for each other in words, but I think of you a great deal and miss you, and this is one*

THE MAN WHO LIVES IN PARADISE

*holiday I do not want to go by without telling you so.
I know you won't have as happy a Thanksgiving as usual,
but I hope you will be comfortable and optimistic. Don't
worry about business. It is shaping up satisfactorily and
better than we anticipated. Later when you are stronger
I will give you some good news in figures.")*

The tragic thing is that only a few months later
Arthur Alling died, in May, 1940. I have never gotten
over missing him, for he had come with me early in the
business and had for years been the associate closest to
me, the one on whom I depended the most. He had done
a tremendous job, for in all the years he was with me I
never once had to worry about finances. He handled all
that end of the business and did a remarkable job. In addition, he was for many years general manager, and knew
every part of the business from A to Z. Everyone who
came in contact with him liked him, and many is the time
I have wished he were still here.

A well-established business keeps going, it seems,
no matter who comes and who goes, and we kept going
during the thirties and through the forties despite all
difficulties. There were innumerable new products during the decade before the second World War, some significant and some of no more than passing importance.
We made many improvements and additions in our regular lines—fans, heating items, mixers, educational toys,
and put out several things that have since been dropped.
One product that might have been a clue to the future
was the addition of a locomotive to the Erector line in
1931. In that same year we put out a toy electric soda

fountain, which is in our line today, although not really a toy and now much improved. It is really a very complete home appliance, a drink mixer.

There was one household appliance during these years that swept us all off our feet and sort of hypnotized us, although it turned out to be just one of our most interesting failures. This was the Zol Coffee Maker. It really did make perfect coffee, but it was such a complicated operation that few housewives would even try it. Being toy and gadget people who like complicated operations that turn out well, we thought it was wonderful —blinded by our own particular interests. We even hired a jury of expert tasters to come up to New Haven and sample the product alongside coffee made by other methods, and they all pronounced it tops.

Zol had a glass bottom, like so many coffee makers of today, into which fitted a business run by an electric motor—making it a natural for our line of appliances. There was a perforated container inside into which paper filters were fitted. The coffee grounds went inside that, and another piece inside that. The whole thing fitted down into the water in the glass pot, with our motor and a special switch protruding at the top. You plugged it in, turned on the switch, and the motor whirled the container with the grounds. It automatically stopped in a moment, hot water seeped into grounds, then the motor started again and its centrifugal action whirled the water out again. And so on. You wound up with miraculous coffee, after a good deal of fiddling with the apparatus. Too much work, too complicated—that was the public's verdict, a correct one as usual.

In 1935 we brought out an educational toy that has been one of the most important in our line ever since —a microscope set.

By far the most important addition to our line came in 1938—the most important of any new product since the invention of Erector. This was not my own, but within a few years the A. C. Gilbert Company had made it so completely its own that you wouldn't recognize the original, and it has been one of the products that has enabled the company to grow to the size it has.

Late in 1937, W. O. Coleman was visiting me at my game preserve for a little shooting. He was a former president of the Toy Manufacturers Association, and the head of the American Flyer Corporation, manufacturers of toy electric trains. At the end of our hunt he suggested that it might be a good idea if the A. C. Gilbert Company should take over the American Flyer line. He said that his business had dropped to less than a million dollars a year, that he was making no profit, and felt that we could make something of it.

I was interested, of course. Who isn't interested in electric trains? But I knew it was a very big proposition, and I said that I was not prepared to undertake additional financing to swing such a deal, in addition to all the other work entailed. He asked $600,000 for the entire property, which was certainly tempting, but I turned it down.

I was driving Mr. Coleman to the station when he finally said that if it was financing that concerned me, he might consider a sale purely on a royalty basis—no cash down but a royalty on all merchandise sold for a certain period, up to a certain amount. Well, we turned right around at that point and went back to my house. I called several of my associates and we went into the matter thoroughly, finally arranging all details. Before going ahead with the concluding acts, however, we made a survey of the field and of the sales of American Flyer. What we learned was not too encouraging. The American Flyer line didn't have too good a reputation, and it was sold almost entirely on a price basis. To make anything of it would require lots of work, a great deal of creative endeavor, a big expenditure in advertising, and many headaches. But it would complement our toy line beautifully, and the terms were most favorable, so we finally went ahead.

As it turned out, it was one of the very best ventures I ever entered into. It has grown into a very big business, even if it did require all the hard work and thought we foresaw. It has already grown from less than a million to more than ten million dollars in volume, and we hope to keep climbing at the same rate.

American Flyer was made in Chicago, but it did not own its own factory there, as it leased the plant. Thus we were able to move everything to New Haven. We had to build a new wing on the plant, but we had been doing that at periodic intervals for a long time, and have kept it up ever since. If I were to try to enumerate the number of wings, extra floors, and so on we had built on the original Maxim Munitions plant, I'd get lost in the blueprints.

With the acquisition of American Flyer we also acquired some fine men who have played an important part in our business ever since. Among them was Guy Schumacher, who had been factory manager with the old firm, became superintendent of the American Flyer division at the time of the purchase, and has since 1944 been works manager of our entire factory. He was also elected a director of the A. C. Gilbert Company in 1945, and a vice-president in 1949. Obviously, in this good business deal we acquired much more than a line of electrical trains—men who have helped build the business.

I set our entire engineering department to work on redesigning and improving the American Flyer line at once. I knew that trains which were in scale were very important, and I wanted American Flyer to be a scale-train system, but that would take a few years. Meanwhile, we brought out the first H-O kits produced in America—locomotives, cars, and track to be assembled by the purchasers, all perfect replicas, in scale, of real trains.

Some of the big improvements in American Flyer appeared before the World War, but our long-range plan for the line was interrupted by that world-shaking disaster. That's why most of the American Flyer story comes after the war.

This period ends with our opening of the Gilbert Hall of Science in New York. For some years I had paid particular attention to this building at the northern end of Madison Square, and for some time it had been vacant. So, early in 1941 we took a five-year lease on it, at an annual rental of $15,000 a year. Herman Trisch took over the responsibility of making the necessary alterations in turning it into Gilbert Hall of Science. He put everything he had into this undertaking and was responsible for its great success. He redid the entire building and opened the Hall of Science, placing in charge Bill Perry, who among other things had contributed to the business his wonderful phrase for our educational toys—"career toys," the playthings that lead a boy to his eventual career.

It was a wonderful thing to drive up Broadway or Fifth Avenue and see the Gilbert Hall of Science, and I still get a thrill from seeing it there in such a prominent place. But the big moment was when we opened it officially with fifteen hundred boys as guests, and I dedicated it to the boys of America.

Twenty-one

Flares, Mines, and Booby Traps

(*A few miles east of New Haven, in the town of Branford, stand several one-story buildings constituting the
Branford plant of the A. C. Gilbert Company. Erected
during the war for the production of flares for the Army
and Navy, it is now devoted entirely to civilian production. It serves not only as the main warehouse of the
company but also as the center of several interesting
new processes, the kind that fascinate A.C. While these
new processes turn out a large volume of items or parts
for the Gilbert line of toys and appliances, they may
also be considered experimental in that research is continually going on to discover new products that might
be made or old products that might be made better by
these unusual methods. Gilbert has always managed to
combine production with research.*)

272

(*The most promising of these new processes at the Branford plant is that for making things out of sintered iron. Sintering means applying heat to a powdered metal so that it forms a solid, without enough heat to melt it. Powdered metal can thus be formed into various shapes in molds. These molded objects are then put into a special oven where there is heat at just the right temperature, and also the presence of the necessary mixture of gases. What comes out the other end of the oven is as hard as any metal you want. Certain gears for Erector sets used to be stamped out of sheet metal, then fitted to a brass axle. With wear, the fitting came loose, and moreover brass was pretty costly and often in short supply. The sintered iron gears never wear out, never come loose. A.C. and his engineers have already found dozens of uses for sintered iron and are working on more all the time.*)

(*In another new process, ordinary sawdust is mixed with certain resins, put in molds, compressed under heat, and comes out as the bases for microscopes or small fans. They look like some kind of plastic, but are considerably cheaper. You can't break them with a sledge-hammer or axe, and they take metallic paint and other finishes well.*)

(*A third process uses cold pressure on a combination of powdered materials for making the new Anchor Building Blocks. They have the necessary heaviness of real stone, without its abrasive qualities or susceptibility to breakage, and have been one of the main contributing factors to the successful revival of that oldest of all construction toys.*)

273

We had to build the plant here in Branford because state and city laws did not permit the manufacture of flares in the New Haven city limits. Although the flare work was the first sizable war work we did as a prime contractor, we had foreseen the possibility of our being drawn into the conflict as far back as 1940, and had surveyed the plant to determine what type of war work we could go into best. In 1940 we started at the main plant making some parts for the Browning Machine Gun, as a sub-contractor.

After Pearl Harbor, I offered the entire facilities of the plant to the government and switched almost our entire sales organization from civilian selling to contact work with the procurement divisions of the Army, Navy, Air Forces, and other branches of the government. One of the men transferred at this time was Kenneth P. Fallon, another old-timer who has risen to very important positions with the company. He had started with us in 1915, working with the Christmas demonstrations in the Boston area. In subsequent years he handled the same type of work in Philadelphia, New York, and other cities, then became a salesman, handling all of New England and increasing the territory year by year until he became eastern sales manager in 1935. With our entry into the war, I brought K.P. to New Haven to help, but soon sent him to Washington for the very important expediting and contact work there. There he became chairman of the O.P.A. Toy Industry Advisory Committee and a member of the War Production Board Toy Industry Advisory Committee.

Fallon's great qualities came to the fore in these

most difficult times, and in 1944 he became a vice-president of the company, two years later general merchandise sales manager. Meanwhile he had been elected a director of the Toy Manufacturers of the USA, of which he was later president for two years. It made me happy to know that an executive of the A. C. Gilbert Company was president of the association I had founded. K.P. is now general sales manager of the company and one of its directors.

With all of us putting all our thoughts and energies behind the war work, we were certain to do a good job. Our engineering department performed great feats, one of which came right at the beginning of the war. It was just after Pearl Harbor when we had a call from Curtiss Wright in Buffalo asking if we might be able to turn out in a hurry small electric motors for their famous P-40 fighter plane. The motors were needed to trim the tabs on wings and tail surfaces, small areas at the trailing edges which could be moved slightly to adjust balance of the plane. We put our chief engineer, M. H. Frisbie, on a plane for Buffalo, and he went over requirements with the Curtiss Wright engineers. Within seventy-two hours after his return to our plant we had designed a tiny motor to do the job, and he flew back to Buffalo where it received Curtiss Wright's okay after being put through rigorous tests. Within five weeks we were completely tooled up and in production. We made thousands of these little motors, and many like them later for Grumman, Vultee, and the famous Republic P-47 Thunderbolts. Incidentally, that little motor was later the basis of motors used in American Flyer locomotives.

We showed speed in getting started on flares for both the Army and Navy, too. Within four months of the time we were given the order, we had built the new buildings of the plant in Branford, bought the necessary machines, made tools and dies and trained workers so that we were in production. All during 1942 the flare production program gained momentum, and we turned out hundreds of thousands of them.

We were the first manufacturers instructed to make nylon parachutes, as all others were then using silk. We found that the nylon didn't hold up well, and started making our own tests, but under difficulties, since we had no airplanes or proper methods of testing. We learned a great deal, however, by releasing a parachute from the back of a truck going at high speed, which showed us where the weak spots were. We made changes at these spots, submitted them to the government, which accepted them as satisfactory after making their own tests. That's just a sample of the kind of improvising we did continually.

In 1942 we stopped making all Erector sets, trains, fans, and other products using critical metals. We had an inventory of parts that we wanted to use up by completing manufacturing of items for which they were made. They couldn't be used for anything else, and meanwhile, during our conversion to war work and making new tools and dies, we would be able to keep many workers busy who would otherwise have to be laid off. We went to Washington with this proposal but were turned down. Nobody benefited from this action; it did not save an ounce of critical material or any hours of labor that might otherwise have produced war goods. And we eventually had to write off about $600,000 worth of parts which deteriorated and were not usable during the war period.

The government encouraged us to continue making our chemistry sets, as they were aware of Professor Johnson's commendation of these for the part they had played in the development of America's chemical industry. So we continued these and other products using no critical materials, or very little. In 1942, therefore, our civilian business amounted to almost two and a half million dollars, with government war business totaling more than five million. During the rest of the war our civilian business was about a million dollars a year, while war work totaled ten million in 1943, twelve million in 1944, and dropped back to five million during the last year, 1945. We were able to make an orderly conversion so that our civilian business in 1946 came to better than six million.

During 1942, in addition to the flare program, we did a good deal of experimental work, in conjunction with the Army Engineers, on firing devices, which were soon to be our chief war work. We also produced range indicators for anti-aircraft guns, designed and developed by chief engineer Frisbie with the aid of our engineering department. They received special commendation from the government.

In 1943, the flare program began to diminish, as the government had plentiful supplies, but we were able to make another complete conversion of our facilities in order to produce firing devices. These were the actual trigger mechanisms for land mines, booby traps, and other such weapons of war, and here our creativeness and experience in making magic tricks came to help us. The first mechanism of this nature brought to us by the Army was an English device, which they found not very satisfactory. They asked us to see what we could do to improve it, so we put our engineers to work, collaborating with their engineers, and came up with something that was just right. From that time on we were in the firing-device business up to our necks, and during the war we produced 80 per cent to 90 per cent of all such mechanisms for all the allied forces. Our government depended on us almost entirely for such weapons.

I'm terribly proud of all our war work, and I think few companies can show the record we had in making these firing devices. By January 31, 1944, we had produced sixteen million of them without one single reject. In the year 1944 we made a total of twenty-six million firing devices, and we were never once behind schedule on any order.

(*Quote from a letter from Lt. Col. Ellsworth I. Davis, Chief, Demolitions Branch, Corps of Engineers, Fort Belvoir, Va.: "The quantity of devices furnished has been in accordance with our requirements, and the quality has been most satisfactory, as there have been no rejections." Further along in the same letter, recommending the award of the Army-Navy E, in speaking of the M 1 pressure and pull type firing devices: "In collaboration with the Engineer Board, they redesigned these two firing devices, in both appearance and mate-*

rials used, changing to zinc die cast alloy, saving many pounds of critical brass, and in addition to saving brass, also saved the amount of pounds necessary to construct these devices out of metal by many thousands of pounds. Special features were added such as additional safety features, which make them foolproof for soldiers setting them out. Also they have been engineered and designed to fire under water." The letter goes on to tell how the A. C. Gilbert Company completely redesigned another firing device, and "succeeded in greatly reducing the cost to the government on these devices." Then: "The entire resources of their engineering department and manufacturing facilities have been available for use by the Engineer Board, and they now are in the process of designing and engineering a number of other firing devices. Regardless of production obstacles, the A. C. Gilbert Company has kept a constant flow daily of firing devices. They have converted from a civilian type of factory to a war factory. The assembly of firing devices is accomplished by almost 100% female help. Production obstacles have been overcome and the best proof is that they have not been shut down a day since they started to make firing devices for the Engineer Board, whether the problem involved shortage of material or labor.")

There were many different kinds of firing devices, some of them very ingenious. There was the usual anti-personnel mine, buried in a field, which went off at a little pressure, sent a shell up about six feet in the air, where it exploded and fired shrapnel in all directions. There was a tiny device for slipping under doors, into desk drawers, under books, which detonated a charge when the weight over it was removed. We made booby traps that went off when a fine wire was tripped over or pulled, and then made another that fooled the enemy who found such a wire and cut it or detached it. Our device went off when pressure was either exerted or lessened. We made delayed fuses worked by corrosive acid and dropped behind enemy lines for use by saboteurs and partisans. And in the designing of all these devices, and many others, our men played a decisive role—principally Guy Schumacher, our works manager, V. E. Dowman, a master mechanic, W. J. Ziebell, a tool and model maker, and J. E. McLoughlin, a design engineer.

But everyone connected with the company had a lot to do with it. I met with the heads of different departments at seven thirty every morning to open bottlenecks, iron out difficulties, find ways of overcoming the myriad problems that arose. We made our own wooden and cardboard boxes, printed our own labels and instruction sheets, did our own painting, plating, and finishing, and handled shipments from a carload or trainload to a boxful. We changed our entire principle of manufacturing, for in our business of toys and ordinary household appliances we had never had to reach an accuracy calling for tolerances of more than .002. In our war work we increased that accuracy ten times, working with tolerances up to .0002, which meant that we made items so close to specifications that they came within one tenth of the diameter of a human hair of the measurement laid down for us.

Not many people had thought that a toy manufacturer could do such things, so we were particularly proud of our achievements. And the work we did received recognition, too, in four Army-Navy E awards. The first of these came in 1943, at which time we had something of a ceremony at the plant, with Judge Kenneth Wynne as Master of Ceremonies, Senator Francis Maloney as honored guest, and the representative of the Armed Forces none other than my old friend from the 1928 Olympics, General William C. Rose.

During the war we also received a visit from General William Knudsen, former president of General Motors who was then head of war production. He was scheduled to stay for an hour, but remained a good part of the day, asking if he couldn't come to my office and go over our whole program with me. He left our plant very pleased, very impressed. We came out of the war not badly off but not much better off financially than when we went into it, which is as it should be, I think. America had a big job to do, and we had to do our part. We did it well, as all government officials who dealt with us will testify.

(*A letter from Raymond P. Ackerman of Republic Aviation Corporation, congratulating A. C. Gilbert on winning the Army-Navy E: "I have always known you to be outstanding in your field, so much so that you have been known as the Ford of the electrical appliance and toy business. This spirit, originating with you, has made this conversion to the war effort a natural one and, no doubt, accounts for the high morale and resulting good work that you and all your employees are doing for all departments of the Army and Navy. 'Preparedness' is something you started personally a few decades back, by inspiring the youth of America with your Erector and Chemistry sets, and in my own sphere I have been amazed at the number of embryo engineers and chemists you have started on the road to success. The world of good you have done has not been publicized enough.")*

Yes, I am proud of our record in the war. We played a small but vital part in it, big for our kind of business. We worked hard and thought hard, all of us from top to bottom in the company. We could not have done the job in any other way.

Twenty-two

Fish, Bear, and a Volcano

(*In the basement of the Gilbert home in Hamden, there is a moving picture projection room just in front of the gymnasium. It is a comfortable spot in which to view some of the most remarkable nature pictures ever taken. A.C. does not look upon himself as more than a pretty good amateur photographer, so is always a little surprised when people compare his films with the fine nature pictures put out by Walt Disney. He ascribes their enthusiasm to the excitement and beauty of the subject matter. The fact remains that he has caught that excitement and beauty on film.*)

(*Each of his main pictures runs about forty minutes, being expertly edited from thousands of feet of film, by A.C. and Dick Landers, who started working with Mr. Gilbert as a boy and is now an important member of the Sales Department of the A. C. Gilbert Com-*

283

*pany. When A.C. shows his films before large groups,
he does his own narration. Every picture has been shown
to the company's workers in the big hall at the plant,
where movies are shown almost every lunch hour. Sometimes a battery of stereo viewers is set up here to show
colored pictures from one of A.C.'s trips, or photos taken
on such occasions as the annual outing.)*

*(Hunting movies are also shown, whenever a new
one is available, at the big dinner given by the A. C.
Gilbert Company for important toy buyers at the end of
the annual Toy Fair, with A.C. doing the running com-
mentary. Being an old radio master of ceremonies, he
handles the assignment well, and a packed banquet hall,
filled with celebrating visitors to the city, is completely
quiet for the running of the picture. The moving of
chairs, private conversations, and giggles subside when
the movie has run only a few moments, and this most
difficult of audiences sits absorbed for forty minutes.)*

*(Some of his pictures have been shown at dinners
of the Toy Manufacturers of the U.S.A. "They were wonderful," Horatio Clark, secretary of the association, says.
"Why, it has been more than ten years since I saw the
pictures about the fish and the bears, but I can still see
the marvelous shot of that big bear waddling along beside a stream, his belly so full of salmon that it almost
drags on the ground.")*

*(While most of A.C.'s movies are of his hunting
trips, he has made many reels of pole vaulting, and a
remarkable film about the Paradise Game Preserve,
taken over the period of a year to show it during the four
seasons, with shots of deer feeding and running, of*

*pheasant chicks just hatched, of ducks learning to fly
and coming in for a landing, of rainbow trout breaking
water, and of glowing laurel blossoms, pink and white.)*

During the war years I didn't take any real hunting trips, of course. I was too busy at the plant. I managed to get up to Kent for some weekends, and there
was always the game preserve, but no big trips such as
I had been taking in the thirties. After my two trips to
British Columbia in 1933, I had eight more wonderful
trips there before the war stopped me for a while. I had
bought the place and built a cabin, of course. And I took
five trips to Alaska between 1934 and 1942. The first of
these was to the Admiralty Islands with Pfeimister Proctor, the sculptor, and Mrs. Proctor. Another was to Southeastern Alaska with my old friend Campbell Church Jr.,
who knows Alaska in and out and for years had taken
parties there on his beautiful yacht. One of the best
Alaskan trips was to the Kenai Peninsula with Arthur
Nicol, my British Columbia guide, and Andy Simons,
who is undoubtedly the most famous guide in Alaska.
This was the trip on which I took pictures of the amazing
caribou migration, with thousands upon thousands of the
animals moving north—quite contrary to expectations—
for the winter.

I went to British Columbia every year through
the thirties, except for 1939 when there were two trips
to Alaska, one completely unexpected. I thought I had
diaries for several of these trips, but I can find only one,
after coming back from the Berlin Olympics in 1936. I
do have records of my wins in the big game competitions,

however. The 1934 trip must have been a particularly good one, for I won prizes for a white-tail deer, goat, and bighorn sheep. The next year in the National Championships, prizes were won by my mule deer, Rocky Mountain goat, and bighorn sheep. My elk and mule deer won prizes in 1936.

My old friend J. Watson Webb accompanied me to British Columbia in 1938 on a very successful trip which brought me prize mule deer, goat and a royal elk. One of the country's finest sportsmen and the greatest left-handed polo player who ever lived, Watson was a wonderful companion on a hunting trip, as was his wife, Electra, one of the country's best shots, a hard hunter, and founder of the famous Museum of Americana at the old Webb estate in Shelburne, Vermont. I have had some wonderful times with the Webbs in British Columbia, in Alaska, Nehasane, and at their shooting preserve at Robbins Island.

In 1939, Mr. and Mrs. Webb and I went to the Alaska Peninsula to hunt big brown bear, and it turned out to be one of the most exciting and spectacular of any trips I've taken to Alaska. Mary went along as far as Anchorage, where she stayed while we took off in a chartered plane of the Woodley Airways for Sand Lake. Andy Simons was with us. Another plane, with two guides, Guy Wadell and Max Shellabarger, and a cook, had gone on ahead to set up camp.

We ran into typical Alaska weather for May, windy and foggy, and had a tough trip with the pilot, Roy Holmes, having a hard time finding the spot where the river runs out of Sand Lake, the location of our camp.

For quite a while we flew only about two hundred feet above the ground and although it was rather nerve-wracking, we saw many reindeer, some caribou, bear and plenty of ducks.

Our camp was pretty miserable looking. The Alaska Peninsula is treeless, except for alders, so our tents had almost no protection. There was a wrecked airplane near by, and we learned that Woodley had flown in to this spot two years before with Andy Simons. A hurricane had come up so fast that the guy ropes wouldn't hold and the plane was blown out of the lake, crashing against the rocks. Woodley and Andy had to walk many miles back to civilization, a phenomenal trip.

Although the camp didn't look too comfortable, the scene around us was beautiful. The mountains were majestic, several of the active volcanoes actually smoking. The closest mountain to our camp was a supposedly extinct volcano, Mt. Veniaminof, about ten miles away. The snow was beautiful, pure white and shining. Although quite deep in places, it had a good hard surface so we could walk on it without snowshoes. We saw quite a number of caribou, but no bear at first. They were just coming out of hibernation, we knew, the time at which their coats are usually the best.

The day after our arrival we hiked twelve miles, went up to the end of Sand Lake, crossed a river in a rubber boat, and found a new valley. We saw caribou, wolverines, fox, ducks, snipe, swans, and a delightful sight of a mother bear with her three cubs sliding down a snowy hill just for the fun of it.

I might as well let my diary take over for some of the highlights of this trip.

(*May 16th. Windy, clear. Mrs. Webb killed first big brownie, over ten feet square. Fine fur, just out of its den, about five miles from camp. Beautiful day, but a hard wind. Andy and I walked 16 miles, got a fine picture of a big brownie coming right at us. Came within about fifty yards when Andy got his gun up and started hollering, so I dropped my camera and didn't take the very last part of his charge. If you ask me, I still think he was just inquisitive, but he was walking fast right at us. It was a great thrill to see this big bear right on top of us, and it ought to be a wonderful picture.*)

It was.

(*May 17th. Guy and Max brought out Electra's big brown bear trophy. Saw bears coming out of dens on top of mountains, and lots of tracks. Terrific wind to face coming down valley. Cold with snow and hail. Saw two brownies as we came into the valley, one near us on the flat. Passed them up—not big enough and too far to photograph.*)

(*May 18th. Hurricane hit us in the night. Kept most of us fighting to keep our tents. Stove pipes all down. We stayed in camp all day relocating our tents and built new wind breaks from the old Woodley wrecked plane. Fuel for the stoves hard to get.)*

(May 19th. Long trip up right creek. Got very close to a wolverine. Climbed up about 2,500 feet. Grand view of upper canyon, mountains gorgeous. Took a lot of footage. Left camp at 9 A.M., got back about 10:30 P.M. Longest day yet, tired out.)

(May 20th. Fine day, heavy winds. Travelled up Sand Lake Valley, about eight miles, crossed river in rubber boat, then to small lake. Spotted a sow with three cubs, playing together, —great sight. Also saw a big brown bear, but decided not to stalk as we wanted a bigger one. Then we saw a big bear high up, but working down through the deep snow, sometimes disappearing from sight completely, then showing up again. He looked like a really big bear, so we got pretty well cached and waited for him. Finally he came right down the valley, stopped and stood up, rubbing his back against the rocks. There was no question about it then—he was a big bear. Finally shot him at 90 yards. Could have waited longer as he was still coming but I think he felt something was wrong because he stood up on his hind legs when I first shot him. I shot him twice in the chest, then he lumbered down and was off like a shot. I thought I had missed him. He ran at least 100 yards through the alders, and when we followed we saw great masses of blood and knew I had hit him hard. Finally caught up with him

and he was dead. Size 10½ feet by 10 feet five inches.)

This was the bear that won the Clark trophy for the best North American Big Game shot that year.

(*May 21st. Hurricane winds. Mighty tough travelling on way back to get trophy. Guy helped Andy skin it out and they took turns carrying it on their packs—a terrific chore because even after it was dried out the skin weighed 121 pounds.*)

(*May 22. Bad day, terrible wind until 4 P.M. It is amazing—it will be perfectly clear and then five minutes later you will be in the center of a hurricane. We spent the day fixing up camp again and drying our clothes—everything drenched. Both Andy and Mrs. Webb down with colds.*)

(*May 23rd. Good day. Left camp at 9 A.M. and headed for South Bay. Great excitement. Mt. Veniaminof blew up! Impossible to describe this magnificent sight. It went up at least five thousand feet in the air. Ashes were falling on the snow all around us. Everything turned black near Mt. Veniaminof. Beautiful illumination on the way home and the grandest sunset I ever saw.*)

In spite of the erupting volcano only ten miles away, we kept on hunting, and I got another wonderful bear, but quite a few miles from camp. I was surprised to find that Andy was worried about the volcano and thought we ought to find some way of getting out of there. I didn't see how we could, because the plane was scheduled to come back and pick us up on May 29th. Andy and I made a kind of sled out of some duraluminum from the wrecked plane, which was a big help in carrying my second trophy the ten miles back to camp.

Everybody was somewhat nervous about the volcano, I think, but didn't talk much about it. One reason we didn't realize the seriousness of the situation was because the wind was blowing in such a way as to save our camp from the worst effects of the volcanic soot. But we could see all the mountains around, which had been so beautiful in their coats of white snow, covered with black ashes. There began to be signs that the bear were moving out of the country because of the volcano, and everyone was a little more worried. There was a great curtain of smoke going up at least ten thousand feet and we wondered if a plane could possibly get through. It did not arrive on the twenty-ninth, so the Webbs started off on a trip for a couple of days, as Watson and Electra wanted to get another bear.

The plane finally got through the smoke and landed on the 30th, and from the attitude of the pilot we realized that the outside world considered our situation more serious than we had ever dreamed of. He had instructions from the Government to bring Mr. and Mrs. Webb out at once, then come back and get the guides. But when the pilot learned they were gone, the only thing he could do was take the rest of us out with our trophies. We took off only twenty minutes after he landed, then flew through at least twenty miles of dense smoke. When we finally came out of it, there was the Bering Sea loaded with icebergs—a magnificent sight.

We landed at Iliamma Lake at ten P.M. and found a great many people waiting for the plane. I thought they wanted to see what kind of bear we had shot, but they wanted information about the volcano—the only thing on their minds. I realized then that we had been in a very serious situation. Then when I saw the newspapers I almost got scared. The smoke went up thirty thousand feet, the papers said, and the entire population of the village of Perryville, considerably farther from the volcano than we were, had been evacuated by cutters and fishing ships that rushed to their rescue.

The Webbs had a worse time of it after I left, but the plane eventually got back for them all right and everyone was safe. I did a lot of worrying until I heard they had landed in Anchorage. Meanwhile I took time to fish in the famous Newhalen River that flows into Iliamna Lake, where the largest rainbow trout in the world are to be found. In four and a half hours I caught twenty-one rainbows weighing from ten to fifteen pounds each.

Within a few weeks after our arrival back in New Haven, Cam Church telephoned from Seattle. He said that one of his charter parties had just fallen through and invited me to go on a camera hunt with him.

"I would love to go, Cam," I said, "but golly, I can't. I just got back from a trip to Alaska!"

292

At this point Mary picked up the phone and said to Cam, "He'll be there—don't you worry."

So on August 2nd I was on my way, flying to Prince Rupert, where I met Cam and went aboard his lovely yacht. For the trip we had two guides, Ralph Wooten and Ed Jahncke.

We sailed for Ketchikan, then to Petersburg, and finally to Gambia Bay in the Admiralty Islands. I'll let my diary pick up the story here.

(*August 7th. Ralph Wooten and I left boat for camera hunt in canoe, taking both cameras. We were delighted to see that the dog salmon had started their run up the creek, which was a great sight. This creek has very few rapids, but many shallow places, and I was intrigued to see the salmon, looking like outboard motor boats, propelling themselves up the shallow places, so many it looked as if you could walk across on their backs. We saw many bear tracks along the stream in meadow grasses. Tracks so fresh it made you think you could smell them. The remarkable thing about it is that we did not actually see any bear all day. Ralph was certain the bears were just investigating the stream and not actually fishing yet. Just inquisitive. He is under the impression that they go on the fish diet rather slowly.*)

(*We waded upstream, dragging the canoe, because it wasn't deep enough in many places to paddle. Salmon so thick they almost*

*knocked you down while wading, and made a
tremendous amount of noise. We finally picked
a very good place to take pictures, made a cache.
I set up my camera and spent several hours waiting for bears to show up.)*

They didn't show up, and I began to appreciate
the patience required of good nature photographers.
We saw eagles fishing for salmon, and many other animals, noticed humpbacked salmon among the dog
salmon going upstream. On August 10th we finally got
some good pictures, on Big Creek.

*(With Cam in front and me behind, and
Ed acting as gun bearer, we started up the creek.
We spotted one fine brownie coming down the
creek about 6 P.M. He kept coming toward us on
the same side we were on, and although he appeared to see us and was inquisitive, the wind
was perfect and he kept coming. He would have
come closer but Ed finally hollered at him as he
was within 75 feet. Both Cam and I were sorry
Ed stopped him so soon, but he insisted there
was no certainty he could drop a bear if he suddenly charged at a shorter distance.)*

*(After getting re-organized we again
started up the creek, and had not gone very far
before we spotted another big brownie coming
down on the opposite side, about 6:50 P.M. We
saw him 300 to 400 yards ahead and were able to
get the cameras set up in fine position for photo-*

graphing. He looked a long way off in the camera, but after I had run off my 100 feet of film, I looked up and it seemed as if he were right in front of me. At that moment, he stopped, took a good look at us, his mane up on his back. I wouldn't have been surprised to see him charge any minute. He was deciding what to do himself. I was sensitive of the fact that Ed stood just back of me with his sights on the brownie's head. He was a big bear. It was a thrilling sight to watch him, his stomach undoubtedly full of fish, swinging back and forth.)

In the following days, we got a few good pictures. Ed Jahncke suffered a very bad attack of lumbago and was laid up in my bunk where I gave him backrubs two or three times a day. We fished for salmon, and I shot a hair seal with just his head sticking out of the water— 127 yards away. The rest thought I had missed him, but I knew my bullet made no splash and was sure I had got him. We found his body when the tide went down, with a bullet through the head, and I was mighty pleased. On August 17th . . .

(Made cache on island at mouth of creek. Cam went up tall tree for outlook, and soon spotted two bear fishing. We then made stalk up creek and had a spectacular exhibition of a three-year-old brown bear feeding. Great sight. Sun came out and we were in perfect position for good pictures. I took Cam and bear together. We

were now camera-hunting without a guide. Cam carried a gun, but in his excitement taking pictures he left it on the beach. He doesn't worry about bear charging. Certainly a great sight and a wonderful thrill—one that I will always remember. One bear came within a hundred feet and saw me while I was changing reels. Bear raced up and down stream, fishing hard. We had lunch under a tree and saw a seal fishing right by us. We then moved up creek as tide came in. You could actually smell the bear. Dead salmon on banks every few yards. Bear now fishing at their best, but the wind is none too good for stalking. They cannot or do not see when intent on fishing, but they can smell if there is any kind of wind in their direction. We went upstream about three miles and saw signs of bear everywhere. I just couldn't believe there could be as many bear in a single locality.)

The next evening we moved the yacht up rather close to shore and watched from the deck.

(As the tide began going out at 5:30 bear began to appear. One sow with three cubs made a great parade along the beach toward righthand creek. On her way she ran across another bear that came out in front of her. He stood up and moved back to give her room and let her family pass. She was a very large sow, and her cubs were in wonderful condition. Another large bear ap-

peared to the right of the creek and headed up to fish. He reached the creek and began to fish immediately. Another bear appeared in the grass. Later on the sow with three cubs drove them all out. They scattered in all directions. Then the sow with the cubs put on one great exhibition, she fishing for all of them, they trying to help. She was a grand fisherman. Six bear were in sight for two and a half hours.)

Later we sailed for Anan Creek, the greatest black bear country on the American continent. We stopped at the camp of a famous Alaska character and an old friend of Cam's, 30–30 Jack, and he decided to go up the river with us, for the salmon were running at their best. We started up on August twenty-first, and this was not a creek but a real river full of waterfalls and rapids.

(What a day! What an experience! Different from anything I have ever had before. Anan Creek certainly lived up to its reputation. I counted up to ninety bears, and must have seen well over a hundred. And it didn't seem as if there was enough room in the river for the salmon. I have seen many salmon runs, but never one to equal this. These salmon run up the rivers and creeks to deposit their spawn, and seem possessed of an insane desire to get as far up into the small brooks as they possibly can. They pursue their mad course up over the boiling, foaming, raging rapids and abrupt perpendicular falls

297

where it would seem impossible for any living creature to go, absolutely regardless of their own safety or comfort. They travel in places where there is not enough water to cover their bodies, where they become easy prey to everything. At places we saw the salmon wedged in three deep. You can always hear a loud splashing and great commotion in the water. They are constantly thrashing the creek almost into suds in their efforts to get up to its head. After depositing their spawn, these poor creatures, already half dead from bruises and exhaustion, begin to drift down. You see salmon with their noses broken and torn off; others with their lower jaws torn away; some with sides, backs and bellies bruised and bleeding; others with their tails whipped and split into shreds; and still others with their entrails torn out by snags. In this sad plight they are beset at every turn in the river by their natural enemies —bears, cougar, mink, hawks, eagles, seals. The instinct of reproduction must indeed be an absorbing passion in these dumb creatures, when they will thus sacrifice life in the effort to deposit their ova where their offspring may best be brought into being.)

(Anan Creek is different from any stream we have ever been on. Most of the streams are easier for the salmon to navigate. Why they buck this one is beyond my understanding. One would have to see to appreciate this great movement of nature, which is really colossal, stupendous, un-

298

believable. No picture could ever do it justice. I personally took over 300 feet of film. At different times during the day we cameraed along the whole stream. We actually stayed until it got dark, long after it was possible to take pictures. The fascination of it gets you, holds you spellbound. Time flies by, the whole day seems like a few hours. You hate to leave, and you can't get back quickly enough the next morning. You feel as if you are missing something and wonder if you will ever see it again. The chills at times run up your spine, and you simply burn up film. This is camera-hunting in all its glory.)

(As soon as we got into the top part of the canyon where there is a series of waterfalls and cataracts, a great sight awaited us. There were several bear fishing when we arrived, and we no more than got our cameras in position when we saw a mother take her cubs up a tree and park them while she fished. Another later put two cubs up a tree, and others a single cub. The mothers all went up the trees with their cubs parking them on very high limbs of big pines. At one time there were fourteen bear in my view, among them some tremendously big black bear. One was so outstanding that Cam, 30–30 Jack, and I were all greatly impressed by it. I really believe that it was as big as some of the brown bear we had seen on Admiralty Island.)

(The bears began coming out in increased numbers at 10:15, and they were at their peak at

299

about 4:30. I made several interesting observa-
tions. One was that the bears are not friendly
with one another. If a smaller bear is feeding on
the creek and another bear comes down off the
side of the canyon, they size one another up, and
the smaller one beats it. We saw this happen re-
peatedly. When two bears of the same size meet,
they might put on a fight, although unfortunately
we did not witness any real, honest-to-goodness,
knock-down and drag-out fights. But even with
the loud noise of the stream and the battle of the
fish, we could hear them growl at each other
from the other side. There is one exception to
this—when a mother shows up with her cubs,
she apparently has the right of way. They all
make room for her in the stream.)

(Another observation—I found that the
mother cached only the yearlings in a tree. After
the second year she takes them fishing with her
—teaching them how to fish. I couldn't possibly
describe the many different antics they go
through. There is a great difference in their fish-
ing ability. Some are fine fishermen, rushing
down into the stream and getting their salmon
quickly and with great ease. Others fish for a long
time and cannot land one. Some appear to fish
just for the fun of it, and keep coming down for
more fish. There are many old logs in the river
and it is miraculous to see them get on these ter-
ribly slippery logs, with a raging current below
them, and not lose their footing, although one

bear we saw did slip from a log after grabbing a salmon in his mouth, and went down through the gorge—still hanging on to the salmon.)

(We started taking pictures from a cache, but when we found the bears were not disturbed, we got more bold and gradually went down to the very edge of the stream. First, Cam parked himself within about ten feet of the stream, while 30–30 Jack and I were high up to his left. All of a sudden a big black bear made a rush down to the canyon and actually brushed Cam's right shoulder. Cam never moved, then turned around and laughed at us. Jack got a great kick out of it. Personally, I wouldn't have had the nerve to sit there and let him go by as he did. He just rushed by, took a salmon from the stream, and went up the trail the other way. Cam was disappointed because we didn't get a picture of it. I was so busy wondering what was going to happen that I just couldn't operate. Then Cam insisted that I go down, because it seemed certain we were on the bear trail and the bear would go down. I finally consented, and kept my eye peeled for bears. Didn't have to wait long. We had agreed that I wasn't to move while Cam took pictures, but when I looked up and saw a good-sized bear looking at me, I couldn't stay there. I stood up and let him see me. Consequently no pictures were taken.)

(Then I went out on a big flat rock in the stream to take pictures from there. Bear came *within twenty feet. Some discovered me on the rock, although I lay very quiet and took pictures of bear from this position for two or three hours. I could see them up and down the stream, right among the mad rush of salmon. A really thrilling spectacle—salmon throwing water all around me, jumping on the edges of the rock where I lay, and the bear coming down from the opposite side of the canyon, fishing. I could see mother bears traveling across the stream, some on logs, some swimming, with the cubs following along behind. We finally got back to the yacht at 10:30 P.M.—clothes torn, tired, but happy.)*

We never expected to have another day like that, but the next one was just as good, and we got hundreds of feet of wonderful pictures. The bears went through more antics than you could possibly believe, and Cam and I laughed at times until the tears ran down our cheeks. One big bear almost ran over me, and Cam took pictures of me just twenty-three feet from a bear.

I waited for hours to get shots of the salmon jumping over the rocks, but bear always spoiled my luck because I couldn't take my eyes off of them long enough. Just as I'd get ready to take a good salmon picture a bear would show up alongside me. It was like a three-ring circus.

We finally left Anan Creek on August 23rd, and arrived at Vancouver on the twenty-fifth. I flew back home after one of the happiest and most exhilarating experiences of my whole life.

Twenty-three

Mountains and Glaciers

(*On the western slopes of the Canadian Rockies, in the southern part of British Columbia, lies White Swan Lake. Its cold blue waters, only a few miles across, occupy a basin inside a circle of jagged mountains, the lower reaches of which are heavily clothed in virgin forests. The upper parts, except the tall peaks, for about four months of the year are bare rock and sheer precipice. The rest of the time they and the whole country are covered with snow. There is no railroad, no automobile road, within many miles of Swan Lake. A few trails that follow the valleys, cross rushing streams, and climb steeply to passes between the peaks, are the only means of reaching the lake. Johnny Stork, a trapper who lives there, passes five or six months of every year without seeing another human being.*)

(*Although White Swan Lake is less than two hundred miles from Priest Lake, in northern Idaho, where A. C. Gilbert camped and hunted with his father as a boy, it is in a different world. Around White Swan Lake, in the heart of the Canadian Rockies, the mountains are far higher, the big game more varied and far more plentiful. Getting there is ten times as hard, and living there, even for a few weeks, much more rugged.*)

(*A.C. bought the camp at White Swan Lake and built a cabin there—his fourth—in 1937. Slightly smaller than his cabin at Kent, and with no modern facilities, it was nevertheless much more difficult to construct. The logs were there, and fine stones for the fireplace, but cement, glass for windows, hardware, and nails all had to be brought in on packhorses, fording the streams and climbing the passes.*)

(*The cabin is beautiful and comfortable, except for those who require running water, electric lights, and refrigerators. Really one huge room, with fireplace at one end and built-in bunks along two walls, it is lighter and brighter than the cabins at Kent and Paradise because it is made of pine logs instead of chestnut. The walls are decorated with a collection of big-game trophies that begins to rival the special room in the Paradise Game Preserve cabin.*)

It's a tough job getting a big head out to civilization by packhorse, so all but the real prize winners are left here. I like to look at them, and they make the cabin attractive. I love the place, not just to stay in, but because of the wonderful country we can reach with a half day or day's travel in any direction. You never saw any country like it, and there is usually plenty of game because it has been hunted so little—some parts never hunted at all before. Many of the lakes and passes and mountains have never been named and show no names on any maps. We have named a good many of them ourselves. There is Broken Jaw Basin where, on one of my earlier trips, I shot the jaw off a Rocky Mountain goat. Then there is Nicol Basin and Nicol Pass named for my guide, Arthur Nicol, and Kenneth Basin, named after Arthur's son who was a wonderful companion and guide on many trips with me. I thought as much of Kenneth as if he were one of the family. He lost his life the last day of the war leading a tank attack in Germany. Then there is Paradise Basin—you know where that name came from.

For a while I didn't think I would get out to British Columbia in 1940, and the doctors were very doubtful about the trip. I had been sick so long and so seriously that even by the end of the summer I wasn't very strong, and the drains had been out of my side only a little while. But I felt pretty good and was dying to get away into the real woods. My family felt a little better about the idea when they knew that Watson and Electra Webb would go along with me and would be there for the first few weeks. Electra was a competent nurse, and I took it easy for a while, staying in a good deal of the time when they went out hunting.

I was very upset, however, because I had hoped that the Webbs would see British Columbia at its best —they had heard me talk so much about it—but there was very little game. Although they didn't say anything, I knew they were disappointed, and only hoped that Mrs. Webb would appreciate, as time went on, her great achievement in getting a ram in the Canadian Rockies. It was a very pretty head, and they had some other nice trophies. Electra Webb is in my opinion the finest woman game hunter there is—unselfish and a good companion.

I stayed at White Swan Lake after the Webbs left and planned with Arthur and Kenneth some back-packing trips far back and high up in the mountains. We decided first to go up to Coyote Creek and make a lower base camp, then up higher for another camp. The trip would be mainly a camera hunt, and I would shoot only such game as might be really prize-winning trophies. We set a standard on the ram of not less than forty inches, a bigger elk than anything I had yet shot, a really good goat if we happened to encounter one, and any grizzly we might run into.

The others carried heavy packs and I took only a rather light one, but I still had to go slowly on the tough climbs. We went up to at least 11,000 feet, traveling along the skyline, which was really rough going. My diary of this trip will give an idea of what I saw.

> (*The mountains now have a tinge of snow*)—*it was October 7th*—(*and are beginning to look very beautiful. First we ran into a bunch of ewes and lambs—counted about twenty-one. Then we spotted our first ram, seven in all. They had seen us first and were walking up the side of*

the basin to the skyline, and went into that rough, rugged, tall country far beyond. We counted fifteen goats along the edge of the basin, and as we climbed the skyline into different ravines, we saw elk, three distinct herds totaling 31 in all. To get them we would have had to go up high and travel too far—and it was four o'clock. Before we got halfway to the end of the basin, we ran into a good billy goat close by, but in view of the amount of game in the basin it would have been foolish to shoot him. Took a picture of him, and stalked one herd of elk on the way home. Dropped off the skyline and got a good picture of a fine bull elk in the snow—ought to be a splendid picture. On the way home had a beautiful sunset. Back still sore from packing—a little worried about it.)

Each day I listed at the top of my diary entries the game seen during that day. On October 8th, for instance, there were 49 elk, 8 rams, 27 ewes, 2 goat, 1 eagle, and 4 mule deer. I had never seen as many elk in one spot, so it was an exciting time, one I shall never forget. We worked ourselves as close as we could to one big bull elk, with 18 cows.

(This is by far the most cows I have ever seen with one bull in my life, and he was some bull! I thought I might get an outstanding trophy, but when we put the telescope on him, Kenneth discovered that one of the prongs was

307

*broken on his left antler, up close to the main
beam. That ruled him out. What a tragedy. He
was a six-point bull, and the beam was the longest
I have ever seen. While we were studying this
bunch of elk, we heard one bugling right below
us—a five-point bull.)*

We also spotted eight ram from that place, but
some of the animals began to move off and we finally
sent Kenneth up above the timber in the end of the
basin to see if he could drive the elk down toward
us from the canyon, close enough for us to get pictures.

*(Ninety-nine times out of a hundred these
drives are failures, but this was one of the most
exciting experiences I've ever had. Arthur and I
dropped down to the bottom of the basin, where
there is a deep canyon, and saw a good elk trail
there. Arthur was to handle the camera and I
kept my gun in readiness in case a fine bull should
go by. In about an hour and a half Arthur hollered, "Here they come," and you could hear the
bugling of the bulls echo through the canyon. It
made the chills run up and down my spine! We
saw seven bulls, but outside of the one with the
broken prong, there wasn't a record head among
them. One went within fifty yards of me; Arthur
blew the bugle and he stopped right in front of
me. The darnedest freak I have ever seen—with*

308

dozens and dozens of points, but none of them made any rhyme or reason. I think Arthur was afraid I was going to shoot.)

(The other bulls kept trying to get their cows together and they got all mixed up, which accounted for all the bugling. They were challenging one another, and not all taking the same trail out of the canyon. The tremendous bull with the broken point went by us, too, and it made the tears run down my cheeks to let him go on by. When Kenneth joined us we all had a great talkfest and congratulated him on his fine job. He said he had a lot of fun getting the elk started out of the timber. Some refused to go, and he got right on top of the cows.)

The next day I was flat on my back in our trail camp. Arthur built a good fire and baked my back every hour, which eased it somewhat. Two days later I was able to go out again, saw a grizzly that I wanted to stalk but knew I couldn't under the circumstances. On October twelfth we climbed up to 11,000 feet. The skyline was jagged and we had to be careful, so decided thereafter to carry a rope. It was very cold and we could not lie still, spying, very long at a time. Two days later we saw 19 rams and 15 ewes, more than I had ever seen on all my previous trips to British Columbia put together. There were so many that we couldn't organize a stalk, strange as that sounds. So I got no prize head that day, although some fine pictures.

A few days later I finally got a grizzly in Paradise

Basin, and on our way back to the trail camp saw an amazing sight.

(Way up in the east end of Paradise Basin there is a salt lick, about halfway up a sheer, perpendicular mountainside. On it we saw a flock of goats. I have never seen goats go through such antics, make such climbs, in places that seemed so inaccessible, as they did to get to this salt lick. Innumerable trails led to this place from every direction. It would have been a long trip to stalk up close to it, but what a magnificent opportunity for pictures it would have been! If a person could only take pictures of the sights he sees through a telescope! We actually saw goats slip and catch themselves. The way they worked and climbed up the little faults in the rocks seemed impossible. Every minute we expected to see a goat fall off the mountain, but none ever did.)

On October 20th we had our biggest game day of the trip, seeing 8 mule deer (1 buck and 7 does), 62 goats in stalking range, 21 rams, and 26 elk.

(Crossed Tepee Basin, climbed the saddle and went along one side of Nicol Basin clear to the end, then climbed the next saddle into a country probably no one has ever been in, according to Arthur. Mountains on the map unnamed. Tremendous country—gorgeous beyond description.)

310

I got some wonderful pictures, but no trophies, for in spite of all that game, we didn't see one real record head. My back was feeling better, and I was regaining strength all the time, so we left our trail camp with packs for a two- or three-day trip. We saw a good deal of game during the day, then decided to make camp for the night.

(*It was getting late, and it was absolutely necessary to get some boughs for beds and get a fire going, so we climbed up high to the last tree line, where we saw some big trees in a sort of basin. As we walked into the basin, there, standing within 75 yards of us was a bull elk—five points on one side and six on the other. We saw another bull elk running. We had no idea there were elk in this particular basin. They went right up to the skyline and into the country far beyond. As we stood there, almost all the game of British Columbia, except the bear and mule deer, were right before our eyes—elk going up the rocky side of the mountain, the eight rams we had just passed still in view, and a few odd goat on the side hills. We made our beds under big trees, had a good fire and a good meal. The camp was cold, but it was comfortable in a sleeping bag, with a bubbling spring near by to lull me to sleep. Some people might call this a hardship, but with a nice eiderdown sleeping bag, a fire going, plenty to eat and lots of meat nearby, there is no hardship about this—and what a gorgeous country!*)

I finally got a good ram. On October 25th we were still out on our siwash camp when it turned cold and began to snow. We built windbreaks around the trees we were sleeping under and got ready for a blizzard. During our last night there we heard rams fighting, which meant the beginning of the rutting season. We could plainly hear them butting their horns together, something I had never heard before. And all night long we could hear rocks falling from the mountains, with an occasional great slide—probably caused by the sudden change in temperature. The next day it was snowing hard, and I knew Arthur was worried. A big bull elk walked right into our camp, a six-pointer with a big spread, but in the snow and wind I was shaking so that I could not study his points carefully. I hollered to Arthur, but he hardly looked, because he knew that shooting an elk at this stage was out of the question. We could never get the head out from this far camp in the storm. So I just stood and looked.

The blizzard ended and we made our way back to camp on Coyote Creek, then to Cranbrook. We got our clothes off for the first time in three weeks, had baths, and a rest. I felt strong and fit again.

The next year, 1941, I was back in British Columbia again. I was in top hunting form and saw more game and got more pictures than on any trip I ever took. During the first part of this trip, we took pack horses up to the Palisser River, north of Swan Lake, using Camp Levin as a base for other short trips. We were in the midst of lots of game from the very beginning, and had plenty of excitement.

(September 27th. Fisher Creek Camp. We rode 15 miles up the Palisser. Even with our good trackers we lost the trail twice. Best views of elk ever. Trees rutted everywhere, full of elk. They answered our bugles and came to our horses during the entire day. Looked through glasses at a number of bulls. Could have killed any number, but I wanted only an outstanding elk. Besides all the elk, which I could not keep count of, we saw 8 white-tail deer, 2 cow moose, 6 goat, and shot a number of fool hens. Saw tracks of grizzlies. Beautiful trees, magnificent mountains. Killed an eagle that had been hurt, after getting some awfully good pictures of it. A bull moose walked into our camp while we were away.)

A few days later . . .

(Weather—snow, sleet, cold. At times visibility good. On horses all day. Wet and nasty until we came out of the canyon, which was like coming into a new world. Great mountains on both sides. Great elk country. We must have seen forty today and heard bugling after bugling. Also killed half a dozen fool hens with a .22 automatic. Didn't leave the saddle all day. When we were going to make camp, spotted a grizzly and knocked him down twice, but he kept going. I hollered to Fred, the Indian, to join the bombardment, and he did, but I finally killed him on a slide a long way off.)

313

Then came another important day . . . .

(Weather unsettled in the morning, not good for photographing. Late in the afternoon we spotted a big bull elk way up on the mountain. We could see him clearly with the telescope and he looked like a fine head. It was a hard place to shoot—400 to 500 yards away. I decided to take a chance as he didn't answer our bugle and we couldn't call him to us. Missed the first shot, which startled him, so he began to climb and I shot him in the hip. Then he came down towards us and I finally got him just as he came into an opening where we were cached. A fine trophy. Spent the rest of the day skinning him out and getting him back to camp.)

Late in October we were up in the Nicol Basin country again, hunting and photographing. It was a tough trip, because the snow was deep, but it was wonderfully successful just the same. I never saw more game on any trip. One day, for instance, we counted 32 goat in stalking distance, 5 bull elk, 1 cow elk and one six-pointer that was pretty fair, 26 rams, 13 ewes, 1 lamb, 5 blue grouse. We did a lot of hard climbing to get up to the skyline for pictures. The snow was deep and climbing was hazardous, so we roped together at times, and my bamboo staff was a life-saver. I've always loved mountain-climbing and wished I could have done more of it.

Then the next day . . .

(Weather perfect, cold. Saw 20 rams to-day, 19 ewes, 2 mule deer, 3 elk, mountain lion tracks. Left camp at 8:30 and began to get into deep snow. Decided to climb anyway. Arthur was breaking through, a back-breaking job with the snow a foot and a half to two feet deep—straight up. We reached the saddle about 11 o'clock, saw one magnificent ram high up on a far peak. We started to work along the skyline and ran into 7 rams, all full circles—the most spectacular sight I've ever seen of a group of rams. We finally spotted again the big ram that we had seen a few hours earlier and started to stalk him. Banged into a big goat right in the path we were walking on, the first time in my life I ever saw goats and rams together in the same range. Finally made a good stalk for the ram I was after. Although it was a long shot, close to 300 yards, I killed him, and he dropped down the other side of the mountain. It was five o'clock, and Arthur said, "You beat it back to camp. No use of both of us staying out all night." I had difficulty finding the camp, and Arthur went down, skinned the ram out, wrapped himself up in the skin for the night, and got back to camp the next day.)

In 1942, in British Columbia, I saw more game than the year before. Today nobody really believes me

315

when I tell about it, because it seems to be a thing of the past. I killed one of my finest mule deer and a big grizzly.

It was a good thing I had a few trips that were so wonderful because for three years I could not go near British Columbia because of the war. I had another wonderful trip in 1946. I was tough and in perfect condition so we did a lot of real climbing. The next year I was back again, and won a prize in the National Championships for my Rocky Mountain goat.

In 1948 I had an operation, so there was no trip. Then came two trips to Alaska in 1949 and 1950 that I will never forget.

The first was another great trip with Cam Church on his yacht. We went back to Anan Creek and saw another wonderful salmon run, got more good pictures of it and the bear, and happened to be there at just the right time to see the legendary ghost of Anan Creek. Cam woke everybody up at 1:00 and told us to come on deck. I copied the description of the strange phenomenon from the captain's log.

> (*Mr. Church disturbs the peace and tranquility with the amazing revelation of the "Ghost of Anan," his first sight of it in thirty years. The highly touted ghost was first seen in this area by that sterling character, 30–30 Jack, many years ago. With mixed feelings and bated breath, nine witnesses observed the apparition, which was visible for approximately an eight-minute period, as two baleful, gleaming eyes seven-eighths of the distance up a heavily timbered*

316

*hill, where no habitation exists. When the moon
broke into the sky casting a soft eerie light over
the surrounding area, the "Ghost of Anan" completely vanished.)*

The captain was beside me on the rail watching
this weird spectacle, and I asked him what the gimmick
was. He said, "Honestly I don't know. It looks mighty
genuine. All I know is that when we anchored here tonight, Cam was very careful to see that we anchored
in an exact spot."

When it was all over we went down to Cam's
stateroom and after considerable fencing around I succeeded in getting him to tell me the inside facts of the
phenomenon. He said that just thirty years before, with
his father, he had anchored in the same place and had
seen the "Ghost of Anan" just as we saw it. The next
day he and his father went up the mountain and found
a fault in the mountain facing the spot where the yacht
was moored. The fault does not break the skyline, but
when the moon is exactly right its light shows through in
two places, giving the effect of a pair of eyes. Being a
navigator, he knew what time the moon would be in the
right position to shine through this crevice. That's one
thing I always like about Cam Church's trips—there's
something unusual and lots of fun.

On September 17th . . .

*(The big thrill of the day was a very very
light-brown bear sow with three cubs, all fishing
in a small pool. We made a beautiful stalk on ac-*

317

count of a log jam which enabled us to get up in back of them. I got up on top of the logs before the family discovered me. In fact, they didn't know I was there until I started to operate the camera about fifty feet from them. The mother was up ahead in the pool of water fishing for the cubs. They all heard the click of the camera, and stood up on their hind legs trying to spot me—a wonderful shot. Then she raced down, knocked them over to get them out of the way, and all the time my camera was operating. I took my full fifty feet of one of the most spectacular pictures I ever got.)

We had several days of hard rain, got some wonderful pictures of waterfalls in Red Cliff Bay, Baranof Island, visited the hot springs on that island, then headed for Glacier Bay for the grand climax of the trip. We saw big icebergs coming out of the bay as we approached, and took pictures of some big ones tipping over.

(Arrived at the head of Muir Glacier at 1:30 P.M. Entering this bay was a real thrill, one never to be forgotten. We got one ice-fall picture under the 300-foot face of Muir Glacier. We discovered that the enormous icebergs that we had seen as we went into Glacier Bay were coming out of another arm, and Cam commented on the fact that he had never seen so much ice in all his years in Alaska. We decided to go down to the

entrance to Cushing Glacier and see if we could get in. As soon as we got there it was evident that it was going to be a great job of navigation to work between those enormous icebergs, which were magnificently colored because of the pressure of the ice. The weather was bad, so Cam went up front and took on the responsibility of navigating the boat up the arm—a thrilling undertaking, and very dangerous. Icebergs were so close to the boat that we could reach out and touch them, although the light was so bad we could take no pictures. After about two hours, when we could see enormous icebergs even in the fog ahead of us, we decided to try to find a place where we might anchor in safety for the night. There was some risk, as the arm was so choked with ice that it didn't seem possible we could ever get through.)

(September 27th. It was a break of luck to have the sky clearing away. In my excitement and enthusiasm over all that took place today, I haven't room in my diary to describe this great experience, one of the greatest of my life. But I want to record here that it was a magnificent piece of navigation to work up through those immense icebergs. You couldn't believe it possible until you see it in pictures. You could actually reach over the side of the boat and touch the giant perpendicular sides of many of the big icebergs. The captain told me he would never be responsible for taking anybody else's boat into a

319

place like this and Cam had assumed all responsibility.)

(*Finally we got up where we could see Cushing Glacier, although we could not get right under the face of it because of the immense amount of ice that was coming off it with a thundering roar and a stirring of waves that tossed the boat around even a mile away. Several times we heard cracks as loud as the bolt of thunder after a nearby lightning flash, then saw the entire face of the glacier cave in, crumbling into gigantic icebergs as it crashed into the water below and sent up showers of spray higher than the glacier itself. And all the time the roar was so deafening that we had to shout to each other. There was an almost continual roaring sound, rising to hair-raising peaks as the entire face of the glacier broke off. There was still some fog, but the sky ahead was bright and beautiful so we got some wonderful pictures, simply burning up film— both Cam and I. We were running low on film, but we couldn't miss such shots as these.*)

The next day we maneuvered our way out of the arm and away from Glacier Bay. With my last few feet of film I took a picture of Cam that he didn't know anything about. When we were away from the ice, he came to the stern of the boat, relaxed and scratched his head, and I knew the picture would show how happy and relieved he was to get away from there without damage to the boat. The next morning we ran into a school of whales, with one sperm whale beside us blowing hard, but we had both run out of film and could not get a picture. I took a plane from Juneau for Seattle, but once there I canceled my plane reservation and took a single room reservation on the train. I wanted to sleep and relax for a couple of days. I was mighty tired but very happy.

The 1950 Alaska trip was entirely different. The primary purpose was to get a big Alaska brown bear for the Peabody Museum at Yale. Since it was for a museum, I obtained permission to hunt on Unimak Island, where the government customarily forbids all hunting. I planned, after getting that bear, to go back to unrestricted territory, around Hoodoo Lake on the Alaska Peninsula, and get one fine bear for myself.

I took one of Reeves' planes from Anchorage. My guide was my old friend, Andy Simons, and Alex Bolan came along to cook and help pack. Despite bad weather we flew to Cold Bay, where I had a plane chartered to fly us to Unimak Island. The diary can take over for a bit.

(We did a lot of reconnoitering because we wanted to establish our camp near the base of the volcanic mountains, but we found the lakes there frozen over tight, so we had to go down to Cape Lazaref on the Pacific Coast side. The pilot had never been there before and no one had ever camped there. He had to size up whether there was enough depth in the lake to land the plane. It was one of those calculated

risks, and I was a little nervous when we dropped into the lake, but he made a nice landing. I had hardly been in camp an hour when we saw a bear, and another that evening. It was quite a chore ferrying our camp equipment in a rubber boat in to the shore of the lake. We were not more than a quarter of a mile from the Pacific Coast, but could not see it because of the sand dunes between our camp and the lake. It was a pretty good camp, in the muskeg around the lake, which was about a mile wide. The pilot took off as soon as we landed our stuff, before bad weather set in. He would be back on Saturday, May 20th, and if we had got our Museum bear and the pictures I wanted, we would go out. Otherwise, we would stay a second week.)

I began to get the pictures on the morning of the second day, when the weather was clear and the mountains beautiful. Great volumes of smoke were pouring from Mt. Shishaldin, which looked close enough to touch in the transparent air. During the day we saw four bear and stalked one, but he was not really big enough for a museum specimen.

We had gone back to our camp about five o'clock, when the cook called out that he saw a big bear across the lake. We all looked, and he certainly was tremendous, a fine trophy, but Andy and I both decided there was no chance of getting near him before dark. Andy said he'd keep an eye on him, anyway, and that we might be able to stalk him in the morning. While we were eating dinner, the bear started walking down around the end of the lake. He seemed to be lumbering along slowly, but actually he was making very good time. Still, I couldn't believe that any bear was going to come to me instead of my going after him.

I went in the tent, but Andy kept watching him, and in a short while called to me to get my gun. He was obviously pretty excited. A big sand dune prevented me from seeing the bear, but I knew that he must be behind it.

I started running to get there, and ran up the side of the sand dune. And there he was—a real giant! I shot at him and Andy thought I had hit him, but I felt sure I had missed. I should have hit him, because he was so big, and only sixty yards away. But I was out of breath, whether from running or excitement I don't know. Anyway, the bear lit out fast, and I knew where he was headed—toward the lake. I ducked around the end of the sand dune to get another shot at him, and shot quite a few times. The bear still kept going, right into the water. I had to get him now or never. So I jammed my bamboo staff in the dirt and rested my gun on it. By that time all that showed above the water was the bear's head. I fired—and that shot got him.

The bear was about 100 yards out in the lake and we had the job of getting him ashore. Andy and the cook got the rubber boat and worked their way out to him, taking one end of a rope that I was holding on shore. They tied it around him, and then we started pulling him in. It began to get dark, and we all worked hard as the devil, eventually walking out in the icy water up to our shoulders to push and haul the big animal in. Once in a while we had to go back to the tents for hot coffee to get the chill out of us, then back into the water we'd go, finally rolling the bear over in the shallow water until we got him ashore. It was a magnificent museum specimen and among the record bears.

As my diary said . . .

(It's the only time I ever had the good luck to have a bear walk into my camp.)

With my bear taken on the second day, I could devote all the rest of my time to photographing. But on the third day hurricane winds—called williwas up there—swept down on us, with plenty of rain and cold. Two days later it cleared somewhat, and I got some fine pictures of a red fox that visited our camp. I'm sure he had never seen human beings before, which is not surprising because in all likelihood no hunters ever camped anywhere near there before we came along.

When the plane came we flew to Hoodoo Lake on the Alaskan Peninsula and made camp in one of the most beautiful spots I've ever seen, near a stream with a waterfall. I caught some fine Dolly Varden there, excellent eating fish, but gamier than anything I'd ever caught in southeastern Alaska. For days we took pictures, and saw lots of game, but no record-breakers. Finally, after being at Hoodoo Lake a week, I got my big brown bear, shot him at 125 yards, and he dropped on the spot. He was a fine bear and won a prize in the national competition that year.

In 1952 I went back to British Columbia, but not for shooting. I took along my good friend Ralph Morrill of the Peabody Museum, who wanted to collect small mammals from that area. Some wonderful photographs came out of this trip but no big game of importance. That same year I also took a delightful fishing trip to the Grand Cascapedia with Hal Eastman, fishing for Atlantic Salmon.

This reminds me that I've taken many smaller trips of this sort over the years. Several times I've gone to eastern Quebec, and I recall one trip in particular when Fred Williams and I stayed at L. K. Liggett's camp and fished for landlocked salmon. Fred and I also went quite a few times to Maynard's Camp on Moose River, Maine, for fishing. I've fished at Cape Ominee, Alaska, for King Salmon, and on the Russian River and many others up there, so many I can't remember them all. I've done deep-sea fishing off the Florida Keys and also at Cat Cay, the famous island resort owned by my lifelong friend, Louis R. Wasey.

I've hunted and fished over a good part of the North American continent and have loved every bit of it. One trip I planned several times and never managed to take was to Greenland, with Bob Bartlett, the famous Arctic captain. He was a close friend of mine and visited me many times in New Haven, and we were going to go to Greenland to hunt for muskox when the war intervened. Later, when we started making plans again, he took sick and died.

Twenty-four

Agent for Santa Claus

(*Gilbert American Flyer Trains are made in many different places throughout the A. C. Gilbert plant. An electric train involves the use of almost every division of this company with many different divisions. The hot and steaming die-casting department makes numerous parts, and in the least hot section of this wing, locomotive bodies are cast in a special, and quite expensive, high-impact styrene under heat and high pressure. Downstairs is the painting section, with fascinating machines in which toy railroad cars whirl, while fine nozzles spray paint at different angles to cover every spot evenly.*)

(*Busiest and most interesting spot connected with train manufacture, however, is the assembly line for locomotives—about half a block long, with workers ranged along both sides of this huge conveyor line.*

326

Frame and wheels, tiny electric motor and worm-gear drive, the cylinder that puffs smoke and makes the choo-choo noise, the little light bulb—each item is added as a locomotive makes its way down one side of the long conveyor. And at every step it is tested. Here you see the guts of a locomotive, which look like nothing you ever saw before, with wheels churning but getting nowhere because they are held up in a special rack. Later you see smoke puffing steadily although there is no smokestack, or even a body yet. Finally, you see the completed locomotive with its perfectly detailed black-iron or satin silver body, being subjected to the final inspection by a line of experts. As an inspector finishes his job on a locomotive, he sticks a piece of paper with his number on it in the engineer's cab, places the locomotive on a railroad track running along above the bench. There is current flowing in the track, so the locomotive chugs its way down the last ten or twelve feet unaided, turns off on to one of six dead-end spur tracks, and comes to a halt automatically. The switch behind it is automatically closed while it stands on the track, waiting for the wrapper who packages the locomotive. With six inspectors working, locomotive after locomotive moves under its own power down the last line of track, one every few seconds, sending out regular bursts of smoke, its headlight shining, and making such a realistic sound that if you closed your eyes you might think yourself in a railroad yard.)

American Flyer was the big thing with us after World War II ended, of course. We went back to making

Erector and other toys and all our appliances, and sales
were wonderful. Boys who hadn't been able to get Erector for three years bought plenty. Our sales in 1946 broke
peace-time records for the company by going over six
million.

We almost had to start from scratch with our
train line. We had begun to redesign the whole thing
when we bought it, had decided to make all our trains
true scale models, and had introduced a few new accessories. But the war really stopped us before we got very
far. In many ways, that was a lucky break, because in
1946 we could make every change we wanted without
worrying about a costly switch-over. Any other line of
trains that has been successful is seriously handicapped
in making basic changes because the new items may not
fit the millions of old train sets in use. That was no problem to us. American Flyer had sold poorly for a few
years before we bought it, and for several years none
had been sold at all. We could do whatever we wanted.

What we wanted above all was realism, so we
switched to two-rail track. Trains had always carried
the electric current through a third rail running down
the middle between the two tracks. But nobody ever
saw a real railroad like that. I knew from our years of
experience that children liked best those toys which
faithfully reproduced the real full-size products. So we
turned to two-rail track. Not only that, but we made
our track square on top, like real railroad track. It not
only looked better but gave better traction.

American Flyer and all other old electric trains
had made their locomotives and cars without a thought

of accurate reproduction. They were pretty tall and wide, and if cars had been proportionately long, they couldn't have turned a corner in any normal room. The sawed-off look of toy trains made them toys, not small reproductions of the real thing, which kids wanted. The growing popularity of HO Gauge kits, with two-rail track and accurate scale reproduction, proved our point. But HO was very small, too small for many boys six and seven years old to handle, too hard to put on the track. It was really for the adult hobbyist, and when we began putting out the first HO kits in this country, we sold them to hobbyists, not to young children.

We settled on something in between HO and O Gauges. Our trains had to be in scale, but not as small as HO trains. We selected a $\frac{3}{16}$-inch scale, meaning that every foot of a real locomotive or car is represented by $\frac{3}{16}$ of an inch on our locomotives and cars. We get the actual blueprints from the different railroads—New York Central, Pennsylvania, Santa Fe, and others—and reproduce their trains exactly, down to every detail. We even make sure that the colors on freight cars are exactly like the originals, and the style, color, and placing of any lettering. Not many people realize that it costs about $100,000 to design, engineer, and tool up before producing a new locomotive and tender.

We worked out a complete line of trains, of course—steam and diesel, freight and passenger, switch engines and special cars. Our engineering department has done a tremendous job, especially on Gilbert American Flyer and our appliances, under the direction of Director of Engineering Ray Smith and Chief Engineer

Marshall Frisbie. Another Smith, William R., who is invariably known as "Smitty," is our Creative Engineer. He is also known as "Screwball" Smith to some of his associates, and although he is quite a unique and colorful character, he is far from a screwball. An inventor of the old school, who likes to work alone and go about things his own way, he has turned out many of the attractive new features of Gilbert American Flyer, and can be counted on to produce many more. He works behind a locked door, has a great imagination and sense of humor, and enjoys himself most when tackling a really tough problem. Since I've been taking things a little easier and have slowed down somewhat in recent years, we had to have someone like Smitty around. That's why I snapped him up quickly when he came around with the idea for a talking railroad station, about the time we bought American Flyer.

We brought out the talking station, just before the war, under the too tricky name of A-koostikin, and then produced it after the war as one of our first startling accessories, calling it by its right name—talking station. It is a railroad station which, when properly hooked up to the track, causes an approaching train to slow down and stop. You then hear the sound of escaping steam, just as you do when a locomotive stops, and a train announcer's voice calling out the names of the next stops. Finally, with slowly increasing noises of a train pulling away, the train actually does pull away from the station.

Another attractive feature from 1941, put into all our new locomotives after the war, was the sound effect—"Choo-choo." As Gilbert American Flyer trains

330

roll along over the rails, you hear the rhythmic sounds made by all steam locomotives, produced by a small cylinder operating off the main drive shaft. It was simple to add smoke to this in 1945, since the cylinder could be used to puff the smoke out in regular bursts. It was not so easy to find the right substance for the smoke. It could not stain or smell bad or do any possible harm to cloth, paint, or skin. Smitty solved the problem with an oil contained in a small capsule, which now even smells quite pleasant, with a suggestion of pine woods.

Smitty tells the story of a frantic mother who telephoned the plant one day because the baby brother of a Gilbert American Flyer owner had swallowed one of our smoke pellets. We reassured her that there was no need to worry. "It might even be good for him," Smitty says. "The stuff is plain mineral oil."

We put out a complete line of accessories for the Gilbert American Flyer line—stations of different prices and sizes, semaphores and other signals, water towers, signs, bridges, tunnels, beacon-light towers, diners, newsstands and other products for making an attractive layout—and always we paid particular attention to realism, accurate reproduction, and correct scaling.

There were rather special accessories, too, such as an animated station, with people walking down a ramp to the trains, a baggage-loading platform, a loading crane for flatcars, a log loader, a coal loader, and a stockyard that would load cattle on to a special cattlecar by remote control buttons. This last was one of my own ideas, which I derived from a much earlier game we had put out, the Twenty Grand Racing Game. It used a solenoid cell which in vibrating made small figures move. The cattle-loader has been one of the prize attractions of the Gilbert American Flyer line, I'm happy to say.

We made different kinds of special cars for our trains, many of them operated by remote-control—a mail pick-up car, a baggage car which tossed out crates on to the platform, a boxcar of the same nature, a coal dump car, a log unloading car, an automobile unloading car, and so on. Also a wrecking crane car, a circus car, a track-cleaning car, and many others.

We improved our transformers and put out several of different sizes, some for dual control, handling two trains at once. On the larger transformers we devised a dead-man's control lever like that in real trains. Our diesel train whistle was an air-chime, a really accurate copy of the strange whistle on most diesels. In 1953 we put knuckle-couplers on all our trains. The older couplers had been efficient and easy, but knuckle-couplers carried out our desire to make everything on Gilbert American Flyer accurate copies of the real thing. Also in 1953 came Pul-Mor, which enabled the locomotives so equipped to pull a prodigious number of cars, even up a good grade—more than twice as many as before.

A great deal of creative work is being put into Gilbert American Flyer today, and important improvements will be coming up from year to year, aimed at making our trains always more realistic, and to make the handling and hook-up of the many remote-control accessories simpler. All this work goes on behind closed doors, for the field is highly competitive. I'm very proud

332

of the job we have done with American Flyer, and the big increase in sales of our trains shows that the job has been a good one. We have promoted the line vigorously, too. In 1950 we took to the television screens with our "Boys' Railroad Club."

We brought out other new toys in the years since the war, among them some fine pre-school toys made of wood, to which we were led by the continuing shortage of certain metals. Most spectacular of our new educational toys was the Gilbert Atomic Energy Laboratory. This was a top job, the result of much experimentation and hard work. We were unofficially encouraged by the government, who thought that our set would aid in public understanding of atomic energy and stress its constructive side. We had the great help of some of the country's best nuclear physicists and worked closely with M.I.T. in its development.

There was nothing phony about our Atomic Energy Laboratory. It was genuine, and it was also safe. We used radioactive materials in the set, but none that might conceivably prove dangerous. There was a Geiger-Mueller Counter. It was accurate; a carefully designed and manufactured instrument that could actually be used in prospecting for radioactive materials. The Atomic Energy Lab also contained a cloud chamber in which the paths of alpha particles traveling at 12,000 miles a second could be seen; a spinthariscope showing the results of radioactive disintegration on a fluorescent screen; an electroscope that measured the radioactivity of different substances.

It caused quite a sensation at the Toy Fair and

received a great deal of publicity. But there were difficulties. It had to be priced very high—$50.00—and even at that price we managed to lose a little money on every one sold. The Atomic Energy Lab was also the most thoroughly scientific toy we had ever produced, and only boys with a good deal of education could understand it. It was not suitable for the same age groups as our simpler chemistry and miscroscope sets, for instance, and you could not manufacture such a thing as a beginner's atomic energy lab. So we had to drop this wonderful new addition to our line of educational toys —and *toy* has never seem to me to be the right word to apply to such things. We adapted some of its features so that they could be added to our largest chemistry set —using the spinthariscope, some safe radioactive ore, and the atomic energy manual.

In the appliance field, we brought out Whirlbeater, the first of the small hand beaters which has been so widely imitated since. Then we made improvements on it, and extensive improvements in our line of fans, drills, and other appliances.

In 1948 we spent nearly $100,000 for an audit of the company and its executives by a leading firm of industrial engineers. We had become a big business, and knew that we had to be organized like a big business. One result of this was the creation of the post of executive vice-president, so that some of the duties I had handled for years could be taken over by another. Herman Trisch stepped into that crucial job. Another part of the survey that was particularly pleasing to me was the excellent report on my son Al, who had come with the company in 1946. These audits are, whenever they are worth their salt, brutally honest, and this one said that my son would be a better administrator than I was. Nothing could have made me happier.

Al had graduated with high honors from the Yale Engineering School in 1941, where he had been head of his class, Tau Beta Pi, and winner of his "Y" in swimming. I encouraged him then to join a big organization for a few years, because I thought that a son should start out working for someone other than his own father. For one thing, he is likely to learn some discipline and self-discipline that way, whereas his father might spoil him or he might take advantage of a family relationship if his first working experience came with his father's company. Aside from that, I knew that Al could get valuable experience with another firm, learn how other people did things, and broaden his whole point of view toward business and industry.

So, after his graduation, Al went to work for General Electric as a student engineer. At different G.E. plants he tested transformers, motors, and industrial equipment of various kinds; then during the war became a design engineer for Naval Ordnance Equipment. The experience was valuable, and he did a good job. After the war ended, he came with the A. C. Gilbert Company in January, 1946, as assistant to the president. Later in the year he was elected a director, and in 1947 became secretary. As he turned more and more to the handling of financial matters, Al was made financial vice-president in 1951. Later that year, upon the retirement of C. W. Tansley, who had been treasurer and controller since my brother F. W. left the business, Al became treasurer.

Right from the beginning, Al was a very valuable addition to the company—and to me as head of the company. Entirely aside from our personal relationship, I valued him for his advice and help, and for the load he took off my back far sooner than I had expected. The wonderful part of it was that he did his job quietly and without throwing his weight around as the son of the president. The proof of this is his popularity not only with the other executives, but with the rank and file of our co-workers in the plant. He knows far more people by their first names than I do, and they feel at ease with him, knowing that he is a friend of theirs. I have been increasingly impressed with the job he has done, no matter what he was called upon to perform. And he has done things that were absolutely essential in these changing times—studying and learning about new factory and business methods that seem too complicated and abstruse for me. Looking at it even from an objective point of view and forgetting as much as possible that he is my son, I know that it is fortunate indeed that the A. C. Gilbert Company has Al Gilbert there in these days and for the future. What has pleased me particularly is the wonderful teamwork between Al and Herman Trisch, who get along fine and handle between them the big burden of the running of the business.

(In recent years A.C. has been advised to reduce his business activity and serve primarily as a kind of inspirational spirit around the plant. But this role is not

quite fitting to a man of such energy. He has finally agreed to go home after a big half-day, most of the time, but still insists on coming to the factory one evening a week to see and talk to the people on the night shift. During his mornings at work, he is not helped greatly toward an acceptance of retirement, for executives burst into his office repeatedly for advice and decisions that, in their opinion, only he can make. And in a brief tour of the plant, he will see and take note of at least three matters that need tending to—that no one else has noticed. What bothers him most, perhaps, is a worry that in a big business with busy executives the personal, individual touch will be lost. A.C. insists that each of his approximately 3,000 co-workers is a human being with likes, dislikes, hopes, fears, and dreams—and these should be, must be, taken into account. Some of his associates think he is too lenient in personnel problems, as he undoubtedly is with customer problems. For many years he answered with a personal note every letter from the ultimate consumer. When these passed the 200,000-a-year mark, he had to turn over some to other people although he insisted that any serious complaint, and most letters from boys, be given directly to him. He is too inclined to send a new locomotive to someone with a grievance about the one he bought, with no questions asked; or to give an extra batch of Erector parts to a boy who has written in a suggestion.)

(Recently, on Christmas Eve, he received a personal telephone call from a man in New Orleans who had ordered a special set of Gilbert American Flyer

337

trains for his boy for Christmas. The dealer didn't have it and ordered it from the jobber, but it had not arrived. The man said his son would be heartbroken if he didn't have the trains Christmas day. A.C. went into action, roused his sales department, learned the name of the jobber, got his home phone and called him, persuaded him to open his place and see that the customer received his set in time. On top of this, he sent the customer a check for the cost of the long-distance call. Many people think this is rather ridiculous for a 70-year-old man of considerable wealth, whose company does about $20,000,000 worth of business yearly. But if there is one thing A.C. cannot stand, it is an unhappy or unsatisfied customer. He is not purely idealistic about this; he gives a cannily practical reason for such actions. That man in New Orleans, for example, will tell his story of personal attention from A. C. Gilbert, the story will spread and result in the sale of more Gilbert American Flyer trains in New Orleans than a big advertising campaign. Some of the old-timers have become imbued with the same attitude; Herman Trisch has been known to leave a Christmas Eve party to go to the plant to get a train or Erector set for a previously unknown customer who waited till the last minute and found the stores out of what he wanted.)

In 1946 we opened a Gilbert Hall of Science at 1610 K Street in Washington, D.C., with Oliver A. Quayle, Jr., as owner-manager. There was a big opening with speech-making and much publicity, and several hundred boys a day visit it. Another Gilbert Hall of

Science was opened in Miami, under the ownership of Leroy Jahn, one of my old salesmen and a lifelong friend whose company I have enjoyed greatly over the years. He is one of the old-time magicians who has made good, and does an excellent job. In October, 1953, we opened a Gilbert Hall of Science in the Congress Hotel in Chicago.

We had hardly made our reconversion to civilian production when the Korean situation called part of our plant and staff back to defense work. We took on some tough jobs—one motor project that was particularly complicated, and a difficult fuse assignment.

Since the war the business has kept growing at a good rate. In 1948 we reached eleven million, and the next year came close to fourteen million. 1950 showed a slight setback, when there was considerable difficulty getting certain metals and other raw materials, and we dropped to twelve and a half million. The next year we were on the way up again, despite continuing difficulties, to fourteen and a half million. In 1952 we passed eighteen million, and in 1953 came close to twenty million. With costs and taxes as high as they are, we couldn't maintain the same percentage of profit we showed in the old days, of course. We have to keep increasing our volume of business to earn the same profits we did a couple of decades ago, when we were a fourth as big, but that is true of most business. Sometimes it's discouraging, but profit is not the only reason for running a business. I have never been much concerned about money for its own sake. Dollars are just a way of keeping score. To me business is a game, and I'm not the kind of man who can stand still and be satisfied. I've got to keep building and improving. If any project of mine became completely finished, I'd lose interest in it right away and turn to something else that needed hard work to develop it.

Twenty-five

Co-workers

(*The Recreation Hall at the Gilbert plant is a big place, capable of holding about six hundred people. At one end is a stage, a full-size movie screen, and the microphones of a public-address system. At the other end is a cafeteria, and behind that a dining room with plain tables and chairs. The hall is filled with rows of wide-armed chairs where most of the people who eat at the plant have their lunch. Some bring their own food, but many hundreds each day buy the excellent lunches, served at very low prices and below cost, prepared by the company cafeteria. Rich milk, excellent chickens, eggs, turkeys, and some vegetables come from Paradise Farm, which in recent years has been leased by the company for a modest sum to supply the cafeteria with these items. A pasteurization plant is in the factory, and the*

341

company has won prizes and citations for the quality of its milk and the cleanliness of its dairy and pasteurizing plant.)

(Three days a week first-run movies are shown in the Recreation Hall during lunch hour. Each movie is divided into three parts so that a complete feature may be seen in one week. Those who do not want to see the movies eat in the rear dining room, where checkers and gin-rummy games of several years' standing go on after lunch. There is no separate dining room for executives, as A.C. disapproves of any social distinction between management and wage-earners, and encourages their getting together on an equal footing.)

(The Recreation Hall is used for many other purposes—for the party given every Christmas for children of co-workers in the plant, for large meetings of foremen and other groups. Most important of these meetings is the annual wage conference, usually held in November or December, whose primary purpose is to enable the co-workers to check up on management regarding its promise to pay prevailing wages or better in the New Haven area. Reports are also made on the condition and prospects of the company and developments that may affect everyone connected with it. This is just one part of a program initiated by A.C. when the first person came to work for him more than forty years ago—to keep his people honestly and thoroughly informed.)

(The wage conference is a big job for management, for it involves seeing face to face every co-worker in the plant, requiring four or five sessions even in the big hall. A great deal of work goes into the preparation of the conference, to make certain that it goes smoothly, that all facts are presented clearly, and that every important point is covered. A.C. himself always opens each session with a few words of welcome, of explanation for new co-workers, and of brief news about the points to be taken up. In the 1951 conference, for example, A.C. scotched a rumor that had been running through the plant to the effect that there would be a serious layoff. Most of the facts of the conference, however, are presented by other executives, whom A.C. calls upon one after the other, with brief interpretative comments. Someone answers all questions that have been placed in a box before the conference—signed and unsigned queries alike. The bulk of the conference's time is taken up with the wage survey. Four other manufacturing plants in the New Haven area, chosen because they are the largest employing the same kind of workers as Gilbert's and use the same system in classifying workers in ten labor grades, have been surveyed as to wages paid. Charts are shown on the screen comparing wages in each plant with those at Gilbert's, and each chart is thoroughly explained.)

(This big part of the conference is usually presented by Ken Burrell, Personnel Director, an earnest and friendly man who came with the company in 1945 and has become so thoroughly imbued with A.C.'s ideas about handling people that he is as ardent an advocate of this business philosophy as A.C. himself. His sincerity and his conviction are obvious to all co-workers who hear him, and he is so approachable that people feel free

343

to talk to him about any employment problem. This quality is one that A.C. insists on in every executive, supervisor, and foreman, one that he exemplifies himself more than any other person in the management of the company, no matter how big it grows. Half of the co-workers call him "A.C." and obviously feel at home with him. They don't jump to attention and try to look very busy when he walks into the room, but go on with what they are doing, after a greeting, even if that is talking about yesterday's ball game with the man at the next machine.)

(The figures comparing wages are convincing because they are simple and clear. There is no finagling about them, no effort to confuse or deceive. A man sitting at the wage conference knows his labor grade and his own pay rate. He sees that comparable workers at plants A., B., C., and D., get so many dollars and cents. He knows the figures are correct; they could be checked up on too easily for one thing, but aside from that he knows that A.C. does not hold the wage conference to smooth troubled waters or put something over—a point not often understood by union organizers and some other business executives who visit the plant by the score to see how A.C. does it. They are looking for tricks, and A.C. uses none except in magic performances. He is naively honest, a trait so rare that few people recognize it for what it is at first.)

(If the comparative figures show that Gilbert's is not paying prevailing wages, Ken Burrell outlines the pay increases that will bring them up to the level and fulfill the Gilbert promise. In 1952, for instance, a 5 per

cent increase was announced at the conference, al-
though it was subject to Wage Stabilization Board ap-
proval, which came through.)

(A.C.'s son Al usually makes a report at the wage
conference, when Ken Burrell has finished, on the finan-
cial position of the company and the business outlook,
citing actual figures on volume of business, net profits,
etc. He also makes announcements about changes in
group life insurance, vacations, and other benefits.)

(Herb Pearce, factory superintendent, then re-
ports on production problems, safety measures, defense
contracts, and so on. Herb is a young man who has come
up through the ranks; he knows his job, the people in the
plant, and the language they speak. He gives them facts,
and they listen. This is true of the entire conference, for
it is designed to give information, not appeal to the emo-
tions. There are no inspirational speeches, no waving of
the company flag.)

You do not build a business like this just with
good ideas and inventions, hard work, fine machines,
and money. You build it with people, the right people—
not just the executives and managers but everybody up
and down the line. The most important single factor in
the success of our business has been what people put
into it, and the most important contribution I've made
is a certain philosophy of business conduct, chiefly
in the human relations involved in running a business.

I didn't start out with a philosophy, with a book
of Creeds and Policies such as we have now. These are

formulations that came later, the putting into words of the things I did naturally and almost instinctively as the business and I grew up together. Certain basic concepts were at the bottom of everything, of course; the ideas that I grew up with, that I learned from my father, that I derived from my athletic activities. They governed everything I did. Some people let the pressure of business and the desire for profit push them away from their own principles. But I made my business and my search for profit conform to my principles. If I couldn't succeed by those principles, I wanted no part of it.

Some of these principles are the good, old-fashioned ideals that everybody praises and too few practice, and they sound pretty naive in this cynical day —honesty, hard work, high quality, fair dealing. They are still sound, even if they seem corny to the sophisticated. Beyond these, there are a few special ideas that have meant a lot to me. I've always had a lot of fun out of my business, no matter how hard the work was. I wanted everybody connected with it to enjoy it, too. They couldn't get the kick out of it that I did, perhaps, because the man who creates and nourishes something of his own can get greater pleasure from it than anyone else. Still, people in my business should receive pleasure and satisfaction from their work and associations here. Their jobs should not be mere drudgery borne for the sake of earning a living. I wanted Gilbert's to be a place where people liked to work, a friendly place where even the most routine job, the dirtiest and poorest paid job, gave some satisfaction other than wages.

There are dozens of factors that make Gilbert's

346

a place where people like to work, and the large number of co-workers who have stayed here a long time proves that it must be. There are about four hundred of them now who have been with us ten years or more, and about a hundred who have been here twenty-five years or more. That's quite a record for a company only forty-four years old.

The main reason people stay here, I think, is that we treat every person not as a number, a cog in a machine, but as a human being, an individual different from the next fellow, with likes and dislikes, problems, special capabilities and faults, hopes, hobbies, and needs. A company cannot be doctor, preacher, lawyer and family confidant, but it can recognize that people need them, can supply at least a small measure of the human qualities that give meaning to a person's life. People spend a large part of their lives at work, and that part must be as pleasant and rewarding as possible.

(*From* "The Gilbert Welcome," *a handbook for new co-workers, written by A.C. in 1917:* "Brick and mortar and machines are the least important parts of a manufacturing plant. These things are after all simply so much merchandise which anyone can buy if he has the money. There is another element which is the real heart of the plant and that is the 'man-power' element. And when you hear people talk about a great institution, whether it is a great manufacturing plant or college or institution of any sort, you may be sure it is great because of the men connected with it and not because of its big buildings or immense wealth.")

347

In the early days of the business I used to go out at the lunch period and play ball with the men. I had a horizontal bar set up behind the plant, where I used to work out regularly with them. It has been many years since I could do that, but there has been a sports program at Gilbert's since 1912. An athletic association is open to all co-workers, is run by the members themselves, who finance their activities from the sale of candy, cigarettes, and soft drinks in the plant, so there are no dues.

There are the movies and dancing in the Recreation Hall at lunch time, the cafeteria itself serving good food at low cost, the Christmas party, a wonderful annual picnic, an annual dinner for everyone with the company ten years or more. Our recreation director will also help along spur-of-the-moment activities of groups or individuals, arranging dancing in the Recreation Hall, theater parties, vacation tours, getting television or radio show tickets, and so on. We started mid-morning and mid-afternoon rest periods as early as 1916, when few plants in the country had thought of such things, and we make a rule that people must not work during these periods. I know myself that there's nothing like a short break, a little talk, a cup of coffee, a cigarette, to send you back to your work with renewed vigor. Incidentally, our cafeteria is prepared with coffee to be taken to various departments during the morning rest period. In 1932, having installed a public address system throughout the plant, we began playing music at rest periods. I think we were the first plant in the country to do such a thing, though I can't be sure. The people in the plant like it, there's no doubt about that.

All these things contribute to making Gilbert's a pleasant place. Beyond this and other such activities, we train our foremen and supervisors to be pleasant and understanding people. They have to be, or we are handicapped badly. With a factory the size of ours, I can't possibly have personal contact with very many of the people in it, nor can anyone in top management. We've got to rely on our foremen and supervisors, who *are* management in day-to-day relations with all co-workers. They've got to know their jobs, of course, but beyond that they must be experts in getting along with people. They have to like people a great deal. They have to be good listeners, so the people under them will air their grievances instead of bottling them up and griping about them to the others at the next benches. I have long insisted that a plant can stand or fall on the quality of its foremen.

We have a printed foreman's creed that everyone in the plant knows about, and every foreman has pledged himself to live up to it. Whenever a foreman falls down, a co-worker can point out that he has failed to live up to the creed, and it is the most serious charge that can be leveled against a man. The creed is far more than fine-sounding words; it is a must in daily behavior. We give lots of authority to our foremen, for I believe in decentralizing a big plant as much as possible, but we expect a great deal from them. There is one definite limit to a foreman's authority in his department, however.

349

He cannot fire any co-worker from the employ of the company. He can move him around within the department or ask to have him transferred to another department, or recommend dismissal with all reasons given, but he cannot discharge on his own authority. In this way, we eliminate the possibility of unfairness resulting from an unfortunate clash of personalities. Personalities *do* clash, and we must face the fact. But we don't have to let anybody suffer loss of income because of that fact.

We have had some wonderful foremen in our plant, and have a fine group today. I'll cite just two examples in Bessie Cloux, who has been with the company thirty-seven years, and Dwight Bradley, with thirty-six years of service. They are not just foremen, they are the friends of the people in their departments, and everyone knows it. They represent management, yes, and explain to the workers under them the policies and problems of management. But they also represent the people in their departments, explaining their problems to management. They will fight for their people when they believe them to be right, without a bit of kowtowing to management. They'll stick their necks out for their people over and over again. They gain the loyalty of all co-workers in their departments, and thus the company gains that loyalty. A good foreman cannot be just a stooge for management, nor can he be merely a spokesman for wage-earners no matter what they say. He must serve in a dual role, and that is not easy. A good foreman is as highly prized as anyone in our company.

Foremen and supervisors play a most important role in another basic principle on which the Gilbert business has been built—teamwork. There's nothing wrong with the principle just because it sounds trite and worn out. But you've got to make the principle live rather than give it only lip service. Everybody in our plant is the member of a team with a single goal—more production, high quality, safety, security, better working conditions, better earnings. I don't want to have the biggest business, but I want the best run business, and you get that only by having everyone pull together. You get them to pull together not just by having cheerleaders, inspirational talks, and exhortations. You've got to show clearly and plainly to each individual person in the plant that it is definitely and concretely to his personal advantage to work with everybody else as part of a team.

You cannot show him that without telling him what is going on, and that brings up one of the most important tasks of management in our plant—keeping people informed. A person must know more than the fact that, as right guard, he is between the center and the right tackle; he must know how many yards from the goal the whole team is, and the condition of the field, the strength and nature of the opposition. The co-workers in the Gilbert plant are told not only about their own jobs, their own departments, but the condition of the entire business, the business outlook for the industry, and the country. We try to do this job in many different ways. We have, like most companies, a magazine, *Gilbert News*. We have bulletin boards in every department with all important events posted. Most unusual, I think, is the financial scoreboard, also in each department, showing the volume of production this year to date, costs, earnings, and so on. Many of these points are also covered and amplified at the annual wage conference, and almost daily by foremen and supervisors in their regular contacts with co-workers. One of the most important methods, however, is the public-address system throughout the plant, over which various members of top management speak when the occasion warrants. I often give a little talk just before Christmas, not just to wish everyone a happy holiday but to give a few facts and answers about questions that might be in the air. I usually talk just before vacation time, and several other times during the year. On other occasions, Al may speak, or Herb Pearce, or Guy Schumacher, or Ken Burrell, depending upon the subject to be covered. Not only do we give information that everyone ought to have, but we answer all questions that are dropped into the question box. Some of the serious beefs spreading fast through the plant come to our attention this way, and we usually find that they are the result of a lack of information. When we give full information, our people understand what is going on. The facts are not always bright and cheerful, by any means, but people don't complain too much when they know exactly where they stand, and that steps are being taken vigorously to correct unfortunate situations.

Now, I realize that we can make the plant as pleasant as possible and we can keep people fully informed, and none of that will make much difference if they don't earn a good living. They've got to receive good wages, as good as those of any of their friends in other plants doing the same kind of work. That's why we made our promise years ago to pay prevailing wages or better, and we do just that and always will. This is much more complicated than it sounds, because we have so many different kinds of operations in our plant that figuring out fair and sensible systems of pay is a business in itself. We have day workers, hour workers, job workers, piece workers, incentive workers, two shifts getting bonus pay, time and a half over forty hours, double time on Sundays, pay rates while a job is getting started as opposed to when it is running, apprentice workers, learners, and a score of other complications. We have studied the problems from every angle, called in many experts, and finally selected a system of Elemental Time Value that seems fairest to all concerned. This business has become so complicated, in fact, that I begin to feel lost in it, and let Al and others handle the details. I insist only that we make our system as fair as possible, that we explain it fully, that we correct all inequities that appear, that we listen sympathetically to all grievances, and pay prevailing wages or better. I think we have a good system, and we work continually to improve it.

In addition to wages, we have seven paid holidays a year, vacations that increase in length with length of service, even after six months with the company. We give pensions to those who retire after long service, and we pay every bit of it. We have life insurance and Blue Cross Health and Accident insurance, of which we pay half the cost. And we've given Christmas presents of cash every year, depending on our financial condition.

In other words, we do just about everything we can to make people feel secure. Women can get leave of absence on account of pregnancy. We pay generous rewards for new ideas, and have received some wonderful ones over the years. Seniority rights are observed strictly, and promotions are made from the ranks whenever possible. On this last policy there can be no question in anybody's mind, for he just has to look around the plant and see how many of the top positions are held by people who came up from the ranks.

The company has won prizes for its safety record. It has one of the best first-aid rooms in the country—as a doctor I saw to that. And we have a doctor in attendance, as well as a registered nurse. That doctor is also there to give advice to any co-worker in the plant. This means not treatment for regular illness of himself or family not connected with work, but advice as to seeing a doctor, going to a hospital or clinic, and so on. We also have a lawyer who will give co-workers similar advice regarding legal matters. The company has a credit union, and a Goodwill Committee to which co-workers and management alike make contributions, and from which co-workers in serious need can obtain loans or help. We have a company store at which all co-workers can buy Gilbert products at a discount.

We were one of the first plants in the country to put out a handbook to welcome new employees and give them essential information. Ken Burrell has recently prepared a new one which is a book in itself because it tells fully and in detail every single thing the co-worker needs to know, including all the systems and classifications concerning wages. It also explains our grievance procedure which is, I think, one of the best. If a co-worker has a grievance, he takes it up first with his foreman and must get an answer within eight hours. If he gets no answer, or if it is not satisfactory to him, he can go to the Personnel Director and take it up with him. Ken Burrell must then make a decision as quickly as possible, and if that is unsatisfactory, the man goes to Guy Schumacher, the works manager, and then to me. And don't believe I don't get them, and see them, too. My door is open and everybody knows it, and it will be as long as I'm around. The men on this grievance ladder below me know how I feel about things, and that I lean over backward to favor the co-worker when he has any kind of point in his favor. They share my point of view, and so grievances don't get far without being attended to in our plant.

I want to say a word about the term *co-worker*. It is rather commonly used now, but not when I started it back in the early days of the company. Words don't mean too much, I realize, unless actions back them up, but they are symbols for an attitude. I didn't like the term *employees* or just plain *workers* because they carried no suggestion of teamwork, or of my attitude toward the people working *with* me, not just *for* me. *Co-worker* suggests co-operation, and that is what I have always striven for. For note this—I am a co-worker too. Some writers have tried to say that anybody in our plant is a co-worker who is not a union member. This is just not the case. Everybody working in our plant is a co-worker, and some of them have belonged to unions for many years. No one has ever suffered one whit in our plant for joining a union, because he is a free man and can do that if he wants without my saying anything about it or doing anything about it.

I am not a union hater, as I have frequently been called. I think unions play an effective role in many industries, and many big executives in other lines of enterprise have told me they could not operate efficiently without unions. I just think I can do a better job for the co-workers in my plant than a paid union organizer or representative who may not work in our plant or even know a great deal about it. So far the people in the plant have agreed with me, and have not seen how a union could obtain benefits for them that they do not have anyway. And I am willing to stand on the record, now and in the future. When a union can make our co-workers happier and better off, then it deserves to represent them, and undoubtedly will. So long as our management does the job right, we won't worry too much about the problem, but will go on trying to make Gilbert's a place where people like to work.

Twenty-six

Trouble in Paradise

(In the hills and woods about a mile below A. C. Gilbert's home lies Paradise Park, a section of the original game preserve which A.C. developed as a country club for the co-workers at his plant and their families. The fact that it is not operating according to his dream makes for one of the greatest disappointments he has suffered in his life, for it is more completely his own personal creation than any project he has undertaken.)

(As you drive in the main gate of the Paradise Park Country Club, you pass a small caretaker's house and a huge parking lot for several hundred cars. A bank of trees cuts it off from the main recreational area, of which the outstanding feature is a pair of small lakes, fed by two streams. Beyond these is a large athletic field, used chiefly for softball games. Partway up a

357

sloping hill west of the pond is an open pavilion for
dancing, and nearby are neat buildings for refreshment,
bathhouses, first aid, etc. There are swings for children,
fireplaces, trails through the woods. One of the lakes
has in it a few rowboats and canoes, which can move
up one of the streams feeding into it, cross through a
short canal built by A.C. to the other brook going to the
lake, and thus make a circle through thick woods to the
starting point. The lower lake has a raft and diving
boards, and a fine sandy beach. The sand for this beach
illustrates effectively A.C.'s ability to make each of many
diverse operations help the next one, for the sand came
in part from excavations made when a new wing was
added to the factory and in part from the basement for
a house A.C. was building in a new development on the
other side of the game preserve, on Dunbar Hills Road.)

(Some distance away from the lakes, in a safe
spot, is a rifle range, with an earth embankment serving
as the backstop. And a short distance to the east, the top
of a small hill has been chopped off and leveled by bull-
dozers to make three excellent tennis courts. Paradise
Park is obviously a lovely spot in which several thousand
people can have a wonderful time.)

Paradise Park was intended to be one of the
special benefits that made Gilbert's a place where people
liked to work, a source of pleasure for co-workers and
their families such as no one in any plant around New
Haven, and few factories anywhere, could possibly
boast of. Here I was with about six hundred acres of
land in a beautiful spot near New Haven; there were

a farm and a preserve for the deer and fowl, but it was easy to find a few acres that could be made into a country club for the people in the business.

I had a wonderful time just finding the right spot, aside from developing it. And the place was so thickly overgrown that it was not a simple task figuring out where the park should be developed. I had walked through the whole six hundred acres so many times, from top to bottom and from one side to the other, that I knew every inch of it. And I could picture how it could be when cleared and fixed. That takes a good deal of imagination when you are climbing on your hands and knees through growth so thick you cannot get through it any other way, and you cannot see the sky, let alone the next hill. But I figured out that the swampy area around the meandering brooks, where they came together, could make a lake and maybe two, that this hillside above them would make a fine spot for the pavilion and main buildings. When the work was done I was pretty surprised myself to find out that it had turned out just about the way I had pictured it.

I did a great deal of the work myself, with two men from the game preserve helping when they could. I spent Saturdays and Sundays cutting underbrush and trees, clearing roads so that trucks and bulldozers could reach the essential spots. And even the bulldozer I supervised a good deal of the time, deepening the two ponds and broadening them, pushing the debris into a depression to make a flat athletic field. Over about two years I worked on the place, calling in other laborers only when I had to have them. I don't know if I ever put quite so much of myself into a job, so much initiative and creativeness and plain sweat and labor. But it was enjoyable and thoroughly satisfying. And I think you'll have to admit, when you look at it, that I found the right spot for a recreation area.

We opened the Paradise Park Country Club in the summer of 1947 with the annual picnic for Gilbert co-workers. Our picnics had always been happy occasions, with a lot of thought and planning going into them to make them outstanding, but this was something special, of course. At this picnic the people of the plant were enjoying and christening their own country club, and they had a wonderful time. About fifteen hundred people were there, swimming, playing ball, dancing, eating, hiking, boating, and having a glorious picnic. It was written up with full-page spread in the *New Haven Register*, with many pictures. And when I saw how happy everyone was, I got as big a thrill as I ever had.

For a year the co-workers at Gilbert's enjoyed their country club, and then trouble came. The officials of the town of Hamden decided suddenly that I was violating a zoning ordinance by conducting a commercial enterprise in a district that had been designated as Residential A. Since the nearest residential district was my own Dunbar Hills development a mile away, and I could see nothing the slightest bit commercial in building this park and turning it over to my co-workers at no profit to myself or the company, I fought the decision. I carried it clear to the Supreme Court of Connecticut and lost. The Hamden zoning ordinance exempted from Residential A, among other things, "a community house or club," so I thought and my lawyers agreed that we were permitted to establish a club. The Supreme Court in effect changed the wording of the ordinance, by ruling that the intent of the law was to exempt "a community house and club," so the only club allowed would be a community club. It was a terrible disappointment to me, because I had put so much into it, with this one goal in mind, that I could not imagine anyone's objecting to it. I think it was an outstanding job, and probably my greatest contribution to the community.

I retained ownership of the land, of course, but the park itself had to be turned over to a community association, which was formed for the purpose, made up of residents of the surrounding areas, most of whom were living in my own development. The association is a good one, alive and active, and the members derive a great deal of pleasure from the park. But it is not what I hoped for when I spent those many hours working so hard. Only one thing was salvaged. The company was granted the right to hold its annual picnic there. We've done that every year since, and they have been wonderful outings, but for the rest of the time, the park is not used or enjoyed as fully as it should be. I still make many improvements there each year, and keep the place as attractive as possible. Thousands of people have gained great pleasure from it, as there is nothing like it anywhere near New Haven. I hope more can enjoy it in the future.

Another outgrowth of the game-preserve property was my most recent big housing development, which I have called Laurel Hills, but is more popularly known as the Dunbar Hills project. A few years after I had started developing the game preserve, I saw the possibility of doing the same sort of thing that I had done on Ridge Road when I first moved there. This was way out in the country, without normal facilities, just as the Ridge Road area had been. It was an even lovelier spot, the choicest location anywhere near New Haven, under the shadow of West Rock, amid rolling hills, and with a view in places of the far-off sound. There were no sewers, gas, paved roads, or water, but that had not stopped me before. It need not stop me now.

Before I could make a development for homes, there had to be more roads. I selected a high ridge at the western side of the game preserve as an ideal spot, and proceeded to build at my own expense a road sixty feet wide and a mile and a quarter long, now called Dunbar Hills Road because it connected with a road of that name. I did a great deal of this work personally, too, and directed every step with my own men. I rented a steam shovel, bulldozers, and other equipment, and fortunately I found a big gravel mound right near the beginning of the road. We cleared the strip of land of trees and undergrowth and started bulldozing, Archie at one end and Melville at the other. We laid logs as a base across swamp areas, put gravel down, and made a fine blacktop road, which was then given to the town of Hamden.

With this completed I could start to build houses. I laid out the entire project myself, designed and built many of the houses here with my own crew of men, and the help of Robbin Spencer, my head builder, whose association I have enjoyed for many years. It has been a lot of fun working with him. I'd outline plans in the evening and submit them to him the next day, and we would go over them together, ironing out all difficulties. By this time I had had a good deal of experience and knew what people loved, what they wanted in a house. This development was different from that at Ridge Road in that houses were not so large or elaborate, for times had changed. But they were bright and attractive and comfortable, and I have found that people who live in them love them, just as they love the country and the community that is fast growing up around them. A fine school has been built in the Dunbar Hills area, and the town is growing in that direction.

Each lot with a house backs up against the game preserve, so the people who live in these houses actually have the whole game preserve for their back yards, with its beautiful banks of laurel, thick woods, wandering deer, streams, and ponds. I don't think there is a person living there who does not love it, and the greatest enjoyment I get out of this work is to go around and visit a family after it has moved into one of my houses, to see them enjoying it and to make sure that everything is all right. It is much the same sort of enjoyment and satisfaction that I've had from my business, in which I know that I've made thousands of boys and girls happy with toys I invented and made.

I've built my own home here, too, of course. Mountain View, or as Mary would have it, Hilltop, is built at the northern end of the game preserve, on the highest spot anywhere around. I was so insistent on finding the highest spot, in fact, that I spent many days with Melville trying to locate it. We tied red rags in the top of tall trees and then went off a few miles in different directions and looked with telescopes until we could see them. The rag marking the highest spot, still fluttering from a tree outside the house, finally rotted and fell down only this past year.

When we found the right spot, I could hardly walk through it, so thickly was it grown up. Then I found the huge natural growth of laurel which now surrounds the clearing around the house, and I knew that it would grow and bloom when it was cleared enough for sunlight to reach it. First I built a small hunting lodge up on top of the hill, a one-room affair that I used to enjoy on weekends. Then when all our children were married and had homes of their own, Mary and I decided that it was silly to go on living in Maraldene. We built a house around my old hunting lodge, which is now my own room here. I laid out the floor plan with the help of my old friend, the architect, Bob Booth. Although it is not an Elizabethan house, as Maraldene was, we planned it to take our prize pieces of Elizabethan furniture and I think they fit in here beautifully.

We've been here a few years now and are very happy. It is a simple house but a comfortable one, just right for us. And no home near New Haven has a more beautiful setting. We like it so much that it didn't even bother us to know that Maraldene was sold recently.

Twenty-seven

It's Still Exciting

(*Darkness comes down slowly as A.C. sits in his room, looking out the big window and talking. Long Island Sound disappears, then distant New Haven, and the rolling hills near by. A last light clings for a while to the white house on the hilltop and the clearing around it, from which the deer have begun to wander away into the deep woods. A.C. turns on a light and looks at the three red beacons on radio towers a few miles to the south, at the occasional sweep of automobile headlights on the Wilbur Cross Parkway, and at the few faint beams from houses and buildings far below and far away. Except for these, the world outside the house is black.*)

(*Suddenly something emerges from this darkness, just outside the window on A.C.'s left. It is the head of a young buck with a graceful spread of antlers. Al-*

365

most imperceptibly he moves closer to the window, staring in at these strange creatures who usually stare at him. He stops about five feet from the window, his head cocked slightly on one side, his eyes wide with eager curiosity. There he stands, soaking up the scene inside the lighted room, until A.C. moves his head slightly for a better look. The buck wheels and bounds away with a toss of his white tail. A.C. laughs quietly.)

If I'd kept absolutely quiet he would have come up and stuck his head in the window. Most curious animals I ever saw, white-tail deer. Some hunters know about this trait and use it. If you're walking through the woods and start up some deer unexpectedly, they'll go dashing away and you'll have no chance of stalking them. But if you stand still, some of them are quite likely to come back just out of curiosity, to get a better look at this strange new creature who startled them and then made no more noise.

Anyway, life can never be dull when there are animals around. I've been studying white-tail deer closely for more than twenty years now, and I knew them pretty well from hunting and camping in the woods before that. And I still learn new things about them every year. I'd like to write a book about the white-tail some time.

I had an operation in the summer of 1953 that prevented a trip to Alaska, but I expect to be there again before too long, and at my camp in British Columbia. The really tough mountain climbing, stalking for goat, may be too much for me, and I'd better not plan on spending a night under a tree soaked to the skin. But there's still plenty to do. I suppose that I'll do more camera hunting than shooting, as time goes on, as I have in recent years. That's just as exciting and rewarding, and more people get pleasure from the pictures I bring back than from my trophies.

In addition to camera hunting trips I expect to take, there's always the Preston Mountain Club at Kent and my Game Preserve for good hunting, fishing, friends, and work. You never finish a job like developing Paradise. We've been building a new stone wall, and there are a couple of more trails I want to cut through. Some roads need fixing, and a few beautiful stands of laurel must have trees cut away so the bushes will get the sunlight. I expect to do a lot of this work myself. I don't try running the bulldozer any more, and last winter I got hit by the branches of falling trees twice. Maybe my reflexes aren't so quick, so I'll have to be a little more careful. Sometimes I think it is less wearing to work than watch, however. When I was getting over that last operation I was watching some of my men work on the stone wall, and it almost hurt me not to be able to go over and pick up stones and fit them into place. I was more worn out from watching than if I'd done it myself.

I plan to keep on building houses around the edges of the Game Preserve. The Dunbar Hills development is really just getting started, and it's going to be one of the loveliest residential communities anywhere around New Haven. I expect to have two houses under construction, with my own crew of men, for quite a few years to come.

As for business, there was some talk about my retiring at seventy, but nobody really believed it. I don't think I'm the indispensable man, but I get a big kick out of the business and I think I still have a lot to contribute to it. Creative ideas and inventions don't come to me as often as they used to. I suppose I'm sort of like an athlete who has gone stale. But I have some ideas, and I can encourage others and give them help. Smitty finally licked that problem about a new——no, I'd better not mention that because it isn't on the market yet, but it is a wonderful thing for the Gilbert American Flyer line. And Ray Smith tells me that within two years the engineering department will have completed work on improvements that will revolutionize toy railroading. I want to be right in the middle of that, and I want to be there when we put these new things on the market and promote them. I'm willing to let Al worry about new cost-accounting systems, time studies, and finances, and run the business, but I'm going to have plenty to do and say about engineering, new inventions and products, promotion and advertising, packaging, and co-worker relations for many years to come, I hope. I'm not going to be an inactive chairman of the board after Al becomes president of the company.

It's a good thing we bought American Flyer, not just because of the wonderful business we've done with it, but because it gave me so much stimulation. It was a challenge, an almost dead project that required new ideas, hard work, ingenuity. It was something to build and develop almost from scratch, and that's what appeals to me more than anything else. When a project is completed, I'm likely to lose interest and turn to another challenge. Gilbert American Flyer is a big field for my creativeness and initiative, and that's what holds me.

As long as I'm alive I'll enjoy and worry about the business. I *am* a worrier, I admit, which seems a strange characteristic for someone who has so much fun. The difference lies, I think, in the fact that I don't worry much about myself personally. I worry when the company owes a lot of money to the banks. I worry when I think business is falling off for lack of materials, because I don't want to lay off any of our co-workers even for a short period. I worry about the responsibilities I feel toward other people. Perhaps that helps me to fulfill those responsibilities, so I can then proceed to have a good time. Anyway, I never have expected a life that was all fun and no trouble—and half the fun is in overcoming the trouble. Perhaps anyone who gets as much pleasure out of life as I do must worry harder as well as play harder. I expect to go right on doing both.

In the course of this book, I haven't said much about my family, a personal side of my life that I consider private and not particularly interesting to anyone outside of the family. Anyway, I'm willing to tell stories about myself, but I hesitate so far as others are concerned. Al, of course, is associated with me in business, but I know him, too, as a son, a husband, and a father. He and his wife, Jean, have four children. My oldest daughter, Charlotte, married Bob Chase, and they have three children. Lucretia had two boys by her first husband, and now a daughter by her second husband, George Rowbottom. So Mary and I have ten grandchildren to remind us of the days when our own three children were growing up, and to keep things lively. But they turned out to be more than that. They have become a real toy clinic for the A. C. Gilbert Company. They can all be counted on to make life more exciting for me as the years roll by.

Family, business, hunting and fishing, building houses, the outdoors, my dogs, some athletic officiating, the birds and deer and other animals on the game preserve, and all kinds of activities with a host of good friends—these will keep me busy and give me a full life. I have no time to spend with regrets even if I had any. I would have enjoyed being a mountain climber or an explorer. I might have handled my business better if I'd learned engineering. I know I would have gone much farther if I had concentrated on one or two activities instead of spreading myself in so many directions, but I doubt that I would have had half as much fun. These "might-have-beens" are few and feeble, and I never worry about them.

Now that this story is off my chest, I can stop looking backward and return to my lifelong habit of looking ahead and enjoying the present. I'm looking forward to new developments in business, to the blooming of the laurel in June, to hunting with Buster, to fly-casting for rainbows in the lake at Paradise or in Alaska, to the many wonderful weekends Mary and I will spend in the cabin at Kent, to a pack-trip over Summit Pass to White Swan Lake, to another trip on Cam Church's beautiful boat, to the movies I've been taking of the animals on the game preserve. But more than all these,

I anticipate with eagerness the unexpected invention that we'll add to the Gilbert line, the trips I haven't even contemplated yet, the new friends I'm going to make, the fresh ventures I shall no doubt plunge into.

Yes, I'm still living in Paradise.

Notable Events in the Life of A. C. GILBERT

Date	Event	Chapter Reference
1901	World's Record, 40 pull-ups on horizontal bar, Pacific University, Forest Grove, Ore.	5
1902–03	Captain, Pacific University Track Team	5
1902	World's Record, Running Long Dive, 15′ 9″, at Oregon Agricultural College, Corvallis, Ore.	5
1903	Northwest Wrestling Championship, 135 lbs.	5
1904	Northwest Record, Pole Vault, 11′ 7¾″	5
1904	Intercollegiate Wrestling Championship, 135 lbs.	6
1905	Winner, Heaton Testimonial Award as All-Around Champion, Yale University	6
1906	World's Record, Pole Vault, 12′ 3″, Irish-American Athletic Club Games, Celtic Park, N.Y.	7
1908	World's Record, Pole Vault, 12′ 7¾″, Olympic Tryouts, Philadelphia, Pa.	7
1908	Olympic Championship, Pole Vault, London, England	8
1909	Founded Mysto Manufacturing Company, Westville, Conn.	9

NOTABLE EVENTS

1909   Unofficial World's Record, Pole Vault,
        13′ 2″, Westville, Conn.   10
1913   Erector first introduced, Toy Fair, New
        York City   10
1915 to present—"Unofficial" coach, Pole Vault,
        Yale University   19
1915–32 and 1940 to present—Member, Track Ad-
        visory Committee, Yale University   19
1915   Polar Cub Fans introduced   11
1916   First successful use of enameled wire
        for motors   11
1916   Mysto Manufacturing Co. becomes The
        A. C. Gilbert Co.   11
1916   Founder and First President, Toy
        Manufacturers of the U.S.A.   12
1920–22 Member, Yale Board of Athletic Con-
        trol   19
1923–35 Member, Graduate Advisory Com-
        mittee of the Executive Committee,
        IC-4A   19
1924–48 Member, American Olympics Com-
        mittee   19
        1928—Assistant manager, American
              Olympic Team, Amsterdam
              Games
        1932—Manager, chef de mission,
              American Olympic Team, Los
              Angeles Games
        1936—Manager, chef de mission,
              American Olympic Team, Ber-
              lin Games

373

1926   Winner, Von Stephanitz World Prize for Shepherd Dogs, with Asta von Kaltenweide   16

1929 to present—Member, Board of Governors, Amateur Athletic Union   19

    1930–35—Member, Track & Field Committee

    1934–36—Member, Executive Committee

    1927 to present—Chief Judge, Pole Vault, all Indoor Championships

1929 to present—Member, Preston Mountain Club; President 1933–34, 1941–46   17

1930   Paradise Game Preserve established   18

1935   Cabin built at White Swan Lake, British Columbia   17

1938 to present—Member, Boone and Crockett Club; first chairman, National Big-Game Competition; member, Records Committee   17

1938   American Flyer purchased   20

1941   Gilbert Hall of Science dedicated, New York   20

1943–45   The A. C. Gilbert Company wins four Army-Navy "E" Awards   21